FIGHTING
BACK

FIGHTING BACK

ROCKY BLEIER
with
TERRY O'NEIL

STEIN AND DAY/*Publishers*/New York

First published in 1975
Copyright © 1975 by Rocky Bleier and Terry O'Neil
All rights reserved
Designed by Ed Kaplin
Printed in the United States of America
Stein and Day/*Publishers*/Scarborough House,
Briarcliff Manor, N.Y. 10510

Library of Congress Cataloging in Publication Data

Bleier, Rocky.
    Fighting back.

    1. Bleier, Rocky.   2. Football.
I. O'Neil, Terry, joint author.   II. Title.
GV939.B57A33   796.33′2′0924[B]   75-12865
ISBN 0-8128-1845-8

For the soldiers of Company C 4/31
196th Light Infantry Brigade
of the U.S. Army . . .

For the men of the Pittsburgh Steelers
football organization . . .

And, especially, for our parents.

ACKNOWLEDGMENTS

In the actual preparation of the manuscript, several people made large contributions: Joe Browne of the NFL; Joe Gordon of the Steelers; Lynn Gunn-Smith of the Pentagon news bureau; Bob Goodrich of ABC Sports, who allowed his New York apartment to be turned into a writer's den during winter weekends; Terry's sister, Kathy, our first reviewer, who proofread and critiqued each page as it came out of the typewriter; and Rocky's family and friends, who cooperated so fully in assembling the story.

On another level, we must thank Les Zittrain, Rocky's attorney–player representative, who supplied guidance and support from the very outset of this project; his wife, Ruth, a lady as erudite as she is charming, who devised our title; Jacques de Spoelberch, the finest Belgian-American righthander ever to pitch in the Philadelphia Phillies' farm system, and not a bad literary agent, either; Howard Katz of Trans World International, who steered us to Jacques; Michaela Hamilton, our editor, who improved the work considerably; and our publishers, Patricia Day and Sol Stein.

Rocky Bleier
Terry O'Neil
May 1975

Contents

1] *Super Sunday*   11

2] *Appleton*   17

3] *Notre Dame*   32

4] *Pittsburgh*   50

5] *Drafted Again*   67

6] *Vietnam*   79

7] *August 20, 1969*   94

8] *Rehabilitation*   112

9] *Coming Back*   129

10] *Steelers '71–'73*   148

11] *Super '74*   169

12] *New Orleans*   188

13] *The Game*   211

Index   220

FIGHTING BACK

1] *Super Sunday*

It's January 12, 1975. The Steelers and Vikings are playing the Super Bowl today.

I mean, *I'm* playing the Super Bowl today. I can't get used to the idea.

I'm prowling a small, dingy locker room in Tulane Stadium. Adrenaline is gushing through me in jet streams. I can't remember ever being so charged for a football game.

It's 11:30 A.M. Kickoff is 2:00. None of the other players has arrived yet. I came early by taxicab. I always like to take my time—dress slowly, have my ankles taped, get a rubdown, organize my thoughts. Besides, I've waited years for this day. I'm going to savor it as long as I can.

An equipment attendant walks by and says, "How you feelin', Rock?"

He doesn't wait for an answer. He's only making conversation. He doesn't realize what he's just asked. *How am I feeling?* I can't tell him. I'm feeling everything—scared, happy, anxious, fulfilled, tentative, exhilarated, wary, eager.

I say, "Fine," and he nods over his shoulder.

Clothes hooks are tacked to the wall, all around this drab room. Above one of them is a piece of adhesive tape, marked with a black felt-tip pen, "20 Bleier." I sit in front of it on a long wooden bench, and run through our plays one more time.

"On counter-fifteen trap, my key is to influence Marshall, the right end. If he closes hard, I block him. But if he plays it normally, I fake like I'm going to hit him, then slip past and get the linebacker, Hilgenberg. That leaves Marshall for Mullins, the backside guard. If Hilgenberg blitzes and gets penetration . . ."

I do that for all our plays—about thirty runs and thirty passes. I know them, of course. I rehearsed them this morning before the team meal. And last night while I lay in bed. And four days last week, and four days the week before . . . Still, it reassures me to think through them one more time.

For any situation that arises on the field, I want to have an experience to draw upon, even if it's only a mental experience. Unfortunately, most of my experience as a pro running back *is* mental. This is my first season as a starter. In the four seasons prior to '74, I carried the ball exactly four times.

I call this thought process "Zen Football." I guess it's rather incongruous that an Irish Catholic should be using the meditation aspect of Buddhism. But I find it soothes my nerves to imagine every contingency, and program myself with the proper reaction.

My concentration is broken when the other players arrive. They seem more tense than ever before. Some are pensively smoking cigarettes, some reading the game program, others talking quietly. All week, we've been loose and relaxed at practice. Now the room falls nearly silent for long periods . . . until Glen Edwards, at the top of his voice, lets out a hideous shriek.

"What the hell is this?" he screams. We all laugh at our anxiety, but we do not escape it.

As we take the field for pregame warm-ups, our tension suddenly seems an asset. We burn off the nervous energy with a few quick drills. That excess gone, we're left enthusiastic, explosive, tightly wound. It feels good.

By contrast, the Vikings seem almost listless. I notice Wally Hilgenberg, my former roommate with the Steelers, and Ed Marinaro, another friend. They shuffle onto the field, waving to me, and go through their calisthenics aimlessly. This is Minnesota's third Super Bowl. They haven't won yet. They've heard whispers about being "losers." They're an old team. They know this could be their last chance. You'd think they might seem desperate. But no. Perhaps they've lost the zest for this game that we're discovering in our first trip. We're young, and too impetuous to wait for the next time. I think we've got an emotional edge on the Vikings.

Certainly, the crowd is with us. As I pan the stadium, I'm amazed to see so many black-and-gold-tassel caps with our Steeler logo on the front. It looks and sounds like a home game for us. The collective effort of 80,997 voices washes over me like twenty-foot surf. I can recall playing only one game at such volume—Notre Dame versus Michigan State in 1966.

New Orleans is cold and raw this day. The temperature is 46

degrees, but the wind is whipping and swirling at 17 miles an hour. The artificial turf is wet in several spots from three days of rain during the week. It's cloudy and threatening again today.

After testing the field, some players change to a new shoe made in Canada—one with pliable rubber "brush spikes" covering the sole. The normal turf shoe has blunt, quarter-inch spikes fixed stationary around the perimeter of the sole. Uncertain footing is a terror, especially in the defensive secondary where one slip often equates to six points. Cornerbacks and safeties live in fear of that "big mistake."

Tony Parisi, our equipment manager, says to me, "Rock, if you want them, we have the Canadian shoe in your sizes."

I decline, sticking with the turf shoe. But I catch Tony's careful emphasis on the word "sizes." I'll be the only guy on the field today wearing a 10½ left and a 10 right. Several years ago, a hand grenade blew one-half shoe size out of my right foot.

It was August 20, 1969. I was an infantryman in the U.S. Army, thirteen thousand miles from home, stationed in Southeast Asia. Crossing a rice paddy, my platoon ran into a North Vietnamese ambush. Small-arms fire pierced my left thigh. A couple hours later, after the enemy chased us into the woods, I saw a live grenade come rolling toward me. I started to jump . . . it exploded. I had shrapnel blown up both legs, and several shattered bones in my right foot.

We were near to being overrun, or burned in a forest fire, when reinforcements finally came. All twenty-five of us were either killed or wounded. Another platoon half-dragged, half-carried me out of that hell. One guy, God bless him, carried me over his shoulder, fireman-style, for five hundred yards. In the confusion and darkness, I never found out his name. But the strength and courage in his marvelous face will always be with me.

In a hospital several days later, I told the doctor I was a professional football player. I told him to give it to me straight. What did he think were my chances of playing again?

He didn't even want to talk about football. He wanted to talk about walking normally again.

For seven months, there were crutches, and canes, and operations, and leg casts, and physical therapy. When the medical people had done all they could, I put on sweat clothes and went out to see if I was still an athlete. I ran only a quarter of a mile before collapsing onto the grass. I lay there panting and crying, thinking the doctor might have been right. But I would not concede.

I stood up, wiped away the tears with my sleeve, and ran some more. Then I went to the gym to lift weights. And I did not stop running and lifting, running and lifting, running and lifting . . . until . . . well, I still haven't stopped.

For two years, while I was something less than a football player, I stuck around through an incredible combination of circumstances and the benevolence of Arthur J. Rooney Sr., the Steelers' owner. By 1972, I was capable again. Slowly, agonizingly, I progressed. And now, today, I'm ready to strap on my hat for the biggest football game in the world.

This is the game that will make my odyssey complete. Seventy-five million people will be watching—more people than have seen any sporting event, moon shot, assassination, impeachment, or coronation. The largest audience in American television history will see whether I've really come all the way back. A check for $15,000 and a world championship ring are waiting, if I win.

And yet, I already have more than the Super Bowl can give me. I have an experience. A singular, highly personal experience.

I have the memory of those first, horrifying weeks, when nothing seemed to work. Not physical manipulation. Not electric-shock treatment. I braced on the examination table, holding back tears. Shots of pain launched up through my leg . . . but the toes held fast, immovable. The therapists nearly gave up.

I have the memory of an alarm clock stirring me up at 5:30 A.M. It was dark and cold outside. My body was still sore from yesterday, and the day before, and the day before that. Something inside me said, "Later. You can do that workout later. This afternoon or tonight. Go back to bed."

I have the memory of resisting those temptations on a thousand painful mornings; of seeing a thousand different sunrises while I ran myself to the brink of exhaustion; of finishing a workout, my skin tingly with perspiration, my legs wobbling unsteadily, my head feeling light and faint, my lungs gulping and gasping. I have the memory of endless afternoons in colorless weight rooms, lifting a million tons of iron; of sprinting workouts at night, sometimes under a streetlight after darkness.

Ultimately, I did it all for myself. I did it so I couldn't ask myself, ten years later, "What if I'd rehabilitated? What if I'd gotten into super condition? Could I have made the team?"

Through the whole ordeal, I was at peace with myself. My fulfillment—strangely, almost masochistically—was in the workouts, in the sweat, in the ache, in conquering the 5:30 A.M. temptations. I was content merely to try, even if I never played another minute of professional football.

This is not to say I never dreamed. As any little boy knows, goals are the stuff of dreams. And I did not deny myself that pleasure. Through all the agony, I allowed myself a picture, a moment of epiphany.

A moment something like this one. Chuck Noll, our head coach, is writing on a blackboard. The first play he writes is "92 tackle-trap." That's one of my plays. I'm going to carry the ball on the first scrimmage play of Super Bowl IX. A shiver runs through me.

"These are our first two running plays, our first possession pass, and our first short-yardage play," Noll says, pointing to the board. "All right, you know what we're here for. We've worked hard all year. This is our opportunity. We can beat these guys. Now let's go out and do a job."

A burst of excitement fills the room. There is slapping and patting, exhortations to "have a good game." We file out of the locker room.

Our runway to the field is blocked by the crowd. As we stand waiting, I am pressed in tightly, dwarfed by my teammates. Differing shoe sizes are not my only distinction among these men. I will be the smallest player on the field today. The official roster lists me as 5-feet-11. But don't believe it.

I'll probably be one of the blindest guys on the field, too. I'm nearsighted, 20/100, but I can't wear glasses when I play. And contact lenses bother me too much. I just have to concentrate extra hard while those long passes come into focus.

I'm also the only guy who knows how big his check is going to be this week. My government check, that is. Whether we win this game or not, I'm going to get my regular $123 because the Army and the Veterans Administration rate me 40 percent disabled. I'll be the only guy on the field with a hole in his left thigh and three toes on his right foot that have no feeling and very little movement. Tonight, when I'm really tired, I'll probably be the only guy who limps a little bit.

As the crowd clears and we move to the head of the runway, I feel a stark, unmistakable contrast with the athletes on either side of me. To my left is Terry Bradshaw, quarterback, 6-feet-3, 230 pounds. He was the No. 1 player chosen in the NFL draft of 1970. To my right is Franco Harris, fullback, 6-feet-2, 235 pounds. He was the thirteenth player chosen in the NFL draft of 1972. I'm standing between them . . . 5-feet-9½, 210 pounds. In 1968, I was the 417th college player to be drafted.

But the introduction of starting lineups makes us equal. "And finally, the Pittsburgh Steelers' backfield," the public-address announcer says, triggering a roar. "At quarterback, number twelve from Louisiana Tech, Terry Bradshaw. At fullback, number thirty-two from

Penn State, Franco Harris. And at halfback, number twenty from Notre Dame, Rocky Bleier."

We jog across the field together. Terry and Franco seem composed. I'm effervescing. At the sideline, the other forty-four players assemble to greet us. I jump into the air, screaming and clenching my fists. I'm ready to play . . . except for one more thing.

In college, I made final preparation for each game at the Grotto of Our Lady on the Notre Dame campus. In the pros, I do it just before kickoff, during the playing of the National Anthem. So I begin the Super Bowl like any other game:

> Well, Lord, here we are again. Another Sunday with the breeze blowing, the flags flying, and all these people ready to enjoy themselves. Thanks for giving me another opportunity to be here.
>
> You know what I'm going to ask for. Please give us the strength to play the kind of ball we're capable of playing . . . good, hard-nosed, heads-up football with no mistakes. Help our guys to realize the importance of this game, and give it a hundred and ten percent. Don't allow us to let down. Make sure we suck up our guts when we need a big effort.
>
> Also, please give the Vikings this same ability to play. I'm not asking for us to win this game, or lose it. Just give us the fortitude to get through. Help us to know our assignments, so we don't screw up. Give us a game without too many fumbles or interceptions or mental errors. Let both teams play their best, and we'll take our chances.
>
> One more thing, Lord. Please allow me to play the way I'm capable of playing. Let me have a good game, so I don't embarrass what I stand for—my religion, my school, my family, or myself. You've given me the grace to be out here. Now give me a little more so I can do a good job. Thanks, Lord.

Have you ever heard so many clichés in one sixty-second prayer? It's a wonder He still listens to me.

2] *Appleton*

In the long ago, before there were Super Bowls and other modern inventions, there was Appleton, Wisconsin. Let me take you back. I think you might like it.

In 1673, Joliet and Marquette explored the Fox River of eastern Wisconsin on their way to discover the Mississippi. At the southern end of the Fox Valley, they noted a wide, fertile clearing in the woods.

One hundred sixty years later, an Englishman, Samuel Appleton, came upon that same clearing, and gave it his name. At the time, there was only one other settlement in the area—Green Bay at the northern end of the valley. Then, as now, the Fox provided industry for those two, and several other cities that grew up along its banks . . . Neenah, Menasha, Little Chute, Kaukauna, Wrightstown, and De Pere.

My history teachers used to say it all began with huge logs bobbing at the surface of the blue water. They were floated downstream to simple sawmills and gristmills along the river bank. In 1854, Appleton had its first paper mill, a three-man operation. Today, the immediate area has twelve paper mills, including Kimberly-Clark's world headquarters in Neenah.

There are about sixty thousand neighbors in Appleton these days. They are largely German and Dutch, perhaps fourth-generation Americans whose immigrant forefathers wore similar blue-collared shirts and carried similar lunch pails to similar mills in nineteenth-century Appleton. They are likely to be Roman Catholic; if not, probably Lutheran. Few feel the need for a college education. They might belong to the Elks or the American Legion. They're accustomed to an average January temperature of 15 degrees, and a wind-chill factor of plus-two. They have strong backs from shoveling the forty-seven inches of snow that fall each winter.

My hometown is mostly quiet and friendly. It's a workingman's town, watered by workingman's bars. Bars where a guy can get a shot and a beer at eight o'clock in the morning, before work, and several more shots and beers after work. Bars where he can take his family for Friday or Saturday night dinner at reasonable prices. Bars like Bob Bleier's.

That's my father. He'd worked during the war as a printer for Kimberly-Clark. But on the day before his wedding, he decided to get into a "people business" and be his own boss. So he quit his job.

As you can imagine, the news of his unemployment, coming as it did on the eve of their marriage, was something of a surprise to the young and beautiful Ellen Grandpre. That's my mother.

But she took it with equanimity, as she would take every other surprise in the next thirty years. Thus it was that on July 1, 1945, a young man of twenty-five named Bob Bleier took his bride of two and a half months into a bar on the corner of Lawrence and Walnut streets, and announced, "Well, honey, this is it."

My mother really must have loved him, because a woman of her intelligence would normally have turned and walked out. The place was so old, it actually had a stable attached. And on the side, it still had hitching posts and troughs for horses to drink water and eat oats, while their riders were drinking whiskey and eating grubsteak inside. For this, he had borrowed $1,000 and agreed to the outrageous rent of $100 a month.

But my parents were steeped in that old Puritan ethic of thriftiness and hard work. They took in roomers on the second floor, and I'm told they always had a full house at $3 a week. That money and their 50-percent share of the jukebox (nickel a tune, six for a quarter) paid the rent. They saved all profits from the bar, which, in the first three years, came to $12,000. So in 1948, they borrowed another $4,000 and bought the place. Bob Bleier's Bar was finally Bob Bleier's bar.

You can't imagine how hard they worked. My dad would be up as early as 6:30 A.M. to open at 8:00. He'd spend the day bartending, greeting the patrons and bringing up stock from the storeroom . . . until he closed the place at 1:00 A.M., or 2:00 during Daylight Saving Time. My mother, meanwhile, was the accountant-bookkeeper-roomkeeper. She paid all the bills and ordered all the supplies. She also cleaned and changed the linen in those seven rooms upstairs. And as an added bonus, they both were required to carry roomers up the steps, late at night, when they'd had too much to drink at the bar. Which was all too frequently.

This was before my time, but they say the worst one was a fellow named John Rizzi, an immigrant from Eastern Europe. He ate a lot of

Dad surveys his domain from behind the bar.

fresh garlic and onions, his self-prescribed cure for high blood pressure . . . and he kept them in his room. When my parents had to carry him to bed, it was real penance, because the vapors emanating from his room would knock you down.

We had some other interesting roomers. There was Butch Hansen, who had only one tooth in his mouth out of the thirty-two he was issued. There was "Mousy" Krause, who every day, winter or summer, wore the same outfit—a dirty undershirt, a dirty plaid shirt, a dirty red kerchief around his neck, dirty work pants, and a pair of old, scuffed boots. There was "Hammerhead" . . . nobody knew his real name. He worked for the city. And there was one other roomer, who shall be nameless for the sake of his family. He was our honest-to-goodness, living, breathing, belching alcoholic. I guess every inn should have one.

That was the cast of characters until I arrived onstage. And if it hadn't been for those roomers, I might not have gotten my nickname.

Our living quarters were in the back section of the ground floor, just off the dining room. We had a very small living room, minikitchen, and even smaller bedroom for Mom, Dad, and me when I was first born. In my first few weeks, Dad would bring some of his customers back to the bedroom to take a peek at his son. This might be eight o'clock in the morning and I'd still be asleep, lying there kind of robust, kind of roly-poly, as my dad describes it now.

"Son of a bitch looks like a little rock," my dad would whisper proudly.

Then, about five o'clock in the afternoon, these same people would return to the bar for another couple boilermakers, and they'd ask my dad, "Hey, Bob, how was your kid today? You know, that little rock."

So I was "Rocky" before I ever departed the crib. And it stuck like epoxy. I've had friends—close friends—at Notre Dame, in the Army, and with the Steelers, who never knew I was baptized Robert Patrick Bleier.

"Rocky" is a helluva nickname for a guy who tries to play football for a living. And I owe it all to those roomers. If not for them, I might have been stuck upstairs in a second-floor bedroom like most babies. Then nobody would have peeked in and been inspired to such a graphic description of my chubby little body.

As the family grew, we phased out the roomers and took over the second floor for living quarters. After me came Patty. She was the fastidious one, always well-scrubbed, properly mannered, and very demanding that things be just so. She once spent an entire day sitting on the back steps, refusing to go to school, because the bow on the back of her dress didn't feel right. That attitude persisted until high school, when she discovered sculpture. She's been messy and dirty, up to her elbows in clay, ever since.

Patty met her husband, Paul Rechner, in the sixth grade. People who hear that story usually sigh and say how romantic it is. But for me, Paul had a different dimension. As a third-grader, he helped a group of us fifth-graders to win our first recreation league championship. A mere third-grader, mind you. Paul was always a good athlete, and our careers traveled parallel tracks. He played running back and captained the football team at Lawrence University in Appleton. Now, he and Patty live in Elgin, Illinois, with their two sons. Paul teaches high school social science there.

Next in the family is Dan. He's our artist. He graduated in fine arts from Dayton University and the Dayton Institute. Last spring, he got his master's degree from Pratt Institute in Brooklyn, New York. In many ways, Dan and I are opposites. He's about 5-feet-7, 135 pounds . . . small enough, in fact, that I thought New York might devour him when he moved there. But he loved the city, and found lots of artists who shared his passion. His specialties are pottery and graphics. Soon, he'll accept one of several job offers to teach ceramics. Yet Dan is a true artist. If there were no worldly considerations to contend with, he'd pursue art for art's sake.

The youngest is Pam. She's in San Francisco now, working as a nurse's aide and going to the City College of San Francisco. In typical form, two years ago, she packed her Volkswagen one day and announced that, at the advanced age of twenty, it was about time she saw California. She drove the whole route in two days, and arrived in the Bay Area not knowing a soul.

Pam was the achiever in school—always the best student in her dance and acrobatics classes, the best cheerleader, the best cornet player in the band. She learned to play the guitar without lessons. She's the only one in the family who can sing on key. She's always had an angelic face, an alluring figure, and more boyfriends than any five girls I know.

If I was the straight arrow, this lady was the free spirit. I remember the day of her high school graduation. She was wearing a low-cut dress without a bra, which was the new fashion rage. Now Pam is very well endowed, and she looked sensational in that dress. But the Bleier grandparents were coming, and my parents asked her to wear a different outfit. Pam refused, and there was no argument. She wore the dress without a bra.

That little episode tells you something about everybody involved.

The Bleier grandparents: staunch, conservative, Irish-German, Roman Catholic, Midwestern, unalterably opposed to the new fashion rage. Pam: not given to changing her mind, especially for an excuse she considered more flimsy than her dress. Our parents: two understanding people who respect both the grandparents' traditional views and the children's rights as individuals.

So far as I can remember, my father had only one rule in the house: Each child had to take lessons on a musical instrument long enough to see if he enjoyed it. Most of us did, except for Dan. He came stomping into the house one day, hurled his saxophone into the closet, and screamed, "I'm never going to play that thing again."

That was it. There was no scene with Mom and Dad. Nobody even responded to his tantrum. And I think the message was not lost on Dan. Several years later, on our parents' silver wedding anniversary, Dan gave the simplest and most eloquent toast: "I want to thank Mom and Dad for letting us be whoever we wanted to be."

In 1957, Bob Bleier's Bar began serving dinners—rib eye, tenderloin, and New York strip steak on Wednesday; perch, lobster, shrimp, and haddock on Friday; roast and fried chicken and barbecued spareribs on Saturday; combination plates on Sunday, Family Night. In addition, there was a fish luncheon on Friday afternoon.

Serving that sort of menu demanded extensive preparation. My mother, for instance, would spend an entire afternoon breading fish or cleaning chicken and cutting it into portions. My father spent all day Thursday barbecuing 120 pounds of ribs. He'd spend another day, each week, changing the grease and cleaning exhaust fans. Another day, he'd wash all the windows. Another day, he'd go to the produce market.

With Dad working so many hours, Mom came to rely on me for a soft shoulder. We'd have a long talk every evening while we washed dishes, and she'd tell me about the rising cost of everything from bourbon to beer nuts.

The results of all their hard work were in plain view, though, standing out there at the door . . . twenty or thirty people some nights, waiting for a table. At Bob Bleier's Bar, you took a number—just like at the bakery—and hoped it wouldn't be more than a half hour.

The food was great, and the prices were better. When they sold the place in 1973, they were still offering an eight-ounce tenderloin steak for $2.95, a New York strip for $3.95, a rib eye for $3.25, roast or fried chicken for $1.95, rib dinner for $3.25, and their Friday fish luncheon for $1.60. A twelve-ounce draft beer was only 20 cents, a highball 50 cents, a boilermaker (shot and beer) 60 cents, and a cocktail 75 cents.

The Bleier children, Christmas 1955 and Christmas 1968.

In the twenty-eight years my parents operated their bar, it was closed for precisely two weeks and two days. And every day, my father either opened or closed the place, sometimes both.

The two-day closing came in 1957, when they knocked out a wall to begin remodeling. But they reopened before the job was complete. For the next several weeks, the workmen did their business around the patrons. And vice versa.

The two-week closing came in 1970 for a trip to Florida, the first vacation Mom and Dad *ever* had together. Except for that excursion, they stayed open and worked hard, just like their customers. Even after my parents got over the hump, their bar didn't lose the earthy appeal that had made it a success.

They kept the ten-foot windows, the old wooden bar with etched-in scrollwork, the foot railing, the brass spittoons, and the huge overhead fans. I often think about my father's place as I visit these big-city bars which try so desperately for a little nostalgia, or a century-old feeling in their contrived decor. If Bob Bleier's Bar had been moved intact to New York, it would have been considered an antique, or maybe a museum. And Dad might have needed the riot squad to control his crowd.

Eventually, what he needed was a little peace and quiet. After working seven days a week for twenty-eight years, he and Mom took a rest. They traveled the West for several months, and when it was over, they were ready to start again . . . Mom at a seafood wholesaler in town, Dad at a men's clothing store.

They have lots of fond memories of the bar business, but they're happier and more relaxed now, living on the other side of town in an apartment which has nothing under it but another apartment. It took some courage to leave a successful livelihood and change life-styles as they did. But I imagine they did it one night after reading their own place mats. Dad had them emblazoned with the Bleier coat of arms, under which he added the inscription: "Prayer-Work-Thought-Decisions." That was their creed for living and for raising their children.

They did a pretty good job, if I do say so myself. Now that we've all moved away, I especially enjoy visiting them in Appleton . . . and observing them. Mom still has a lot of the mannerisms of the young lady who came from the farm in Marshall, Minnesota. Her voice and conversation have a charming quality that is almost little-girlish. She explodes with laughter at everybody's jokes, no matter how bad they may be. And when she's laughing, which is nearly always, it seems to enhance those Irish-French good looks. Her face seems designed to have the lips curled up and the dimples showing. She's just one of those "sunshine people."

Dad is very masculine-looking. He's also rather quiet, which might ordinarily make for a forbidding appearance. But Dad has this warm, gentle, knowing smile. He comes in the door and stands there a second, saying nothing, looking very much like the family bread-winner, home from another tough day. Then he smiles down at you, and the smile says, "Hi, son."

My dad still has all his hair—more than I have, in fact—which is now a mixture of russet and gray. His eyes are still a crisp brown behind wire-rimmed glasses. He dresses nattily, as a clothing salesman should. And his frame is still trim and athletic-looking, the better to model his product.

Several of his friends have told me what a fine athlete Dad was. He never told me, himself. That's not his style. But when it came time for me to play—as long ago as I can remember—he was supportive and encouraging. Which brings us to tales of triumph and tragedy on the athletic fields of Appleton.

It all began at that very interesting corner of Lawrence and Walnut streets. On one corner was our bar-apartment. Across the street was the Adlerbrau Brewery, where our own local Appleton beer was made. Another corner was the site of the St. Francis Catholic Bookstore. The fourth corner was the home of the Weisgerbers, who owned Adlerbrau and had a son named Dickie, my first important playmate.

Dickie was important because I could score a lot of touchdowns on him. His father was a big, strapping guy who wanted Dickie to be an athlete, so he bought him all the equipment—helmet, shoulder pads, jersey.

I had none of the gear, but I was fairly big for a first- or second-grader, and how I loved to score. Some days I'd have as many as fifty touchdowns before Dickie gave up. My greatest games were played right there on Weisgerbers' lawn. After that, it was all downhill.

Quickly, in fact. In fifth grade at St. Joseph School (half a block from our apartment), we played just one game, my first experience with organized football. The seventh- and eighth-graders killed us, 19–0. I caught one pass as a wide receiver, played linebacker like a sieve, and twisted my ankle.

Sixth grade was a disaster. St. Joe's cut out the football program. Then, as I was turning to basketball, I was diagnosed to have Osgood-Schlatter's disease, commonly known as the "growing disease." I was already 5-feet-6, 140 pounds, and my bones were growing much more rapidly than the muscles, ligaments, and cartilage. Our family physician, Dr. Arthur Taylor, told me I couldn't play any sports for three years. He warned me that exertion might tear cartilage and ligaments completely away from the bone, leaving me crippled for life.

I didn't know if that would be better or worse than having my heart ripped out. No football, no basketball, no baseball in the summer, no running of any kind. Worst of all for my ego, the doctor said even one-on-one games with Dickie Weisgerber were too much of a strain. That's how I *knew* it was serious.

But it only lasted one year. In seventh grade, I began playing basketball again without telling my parents. I was getting away with it quite craftily until one afternoon when a teammate's father walked into the bar.

"Hey, Bob, you going to watch Rock play basketball tonight?" he asked.

My dad just laughed.

"Well, are you going, Bob?"

"Rocky can't play basketball," Dad said. "He's got Osgood-Schlatter's disease."

"Well, if he does," the man said, "then all those kids should have it."

We were pretty fair that year, with Paul Rechner, Paul Schreiter, Joe Bowers, John Besh, and some other talent. But the next season, eighth grade, was our year. We beat everybody—St. Mary's, our arch-rival about four blocks away, St. Margaret-Mary of Neenah, Sacred Heart, and St. Therese. We won the Fox Valley Conference and all the tournaments with yours truly at center, scoring about twelve points a game with his one and only shot, a very unimaginative layup-hook.

Football returned to St. Joe's in eighth grade, and we had a good season, highlighted by a big victory over Wilson Junior High, the public school. Joe Bowers played halfback, Jim Pagle was the fullback, and I played quarterback in our first year after converting from the single-wing to T-formation. I threw the option pass quite adeptly . . . it traveled end over end, giving my wide receiver, Paul Schreiter, the option to catch it at either point. He actually made me look very good with his receiving, and I felt it was about time. Paul grew up two doors away from me. By coincidence, he also lived over a bar, owned and operated by *his* father. Paul was bigger than me in our growing years, and he possessed a proclivity for beating me up. Now that he was catching my passes, however, I wasn't so mad about it.

After St. Joe's, I enrolled at Xavier High School, which had been built on the outskirts of town just two years previous. It was coinstitutional, which, for those of you who never suffered through it, means the boys' classes were taught in one wing of the building by Christian Brothers, and the girls' classes in the other wing by the Franciscan

Sisters. We saw each other only at lunch. And even then, you had to be awfully quick, or awfully discreet, to talk to a girl. The good Sisters were always watching.

I say, without reservation, Xavier was probably one of the five best high schools in the country. The staff was young, energetic, and mostly brilliant. Brother Peter, our principal, was a super administrator. Father Al Lison, our counselor and good family friend, was sympathetic and contemporary. "Dutch" Schultz directed a band that won the "Best High School Band in America" award for three consecutive years, in spite of a mediocre trumpet player named Rocky Bleier. But nothing at Xavier was as good as the athletic department, for two reasons. First, we had a marvelous pool of talent, coming from eight Catholic grade schools and from some of the public schools. (We could be very ecumenical about a good non-Catholic ball player.) Second, we had Gene "Torchy" Clark.

"Torchy" . . . as in red-haired fiery-tempered. He was our football coach, basketball coach, and athletic director. How good was he? Well, let me put it this way: Torchy coached eight years at Xavier. His combined basketball-football record was 241–22–1. He won fifteen out of a possible sixteen Fox Valley Catholic Conference titles.

More important for me, he brought out and developed the competitiveness I would need later in college and the pros. Torchy likes to say I always had that intensity. He says he noticed it the first time he saw me, in a seventh-grade basketball game. We were leading by seven points with four seconds remaining, but I was still flailing my arms and jumping around like the game was up for grabs. That's the way I always played.

But I recall Torchy's boys playing even more fanatically. When I was at St. Joe's, he coached St. Mary's into a frenzy. They were the first grade-school team I ever saw that pressed—zone press, man-to-man press, half-court press—nonstop pressure the whole game. After the shock of playing St. Mary's had worn off, I thought, "Gee, I'd like to play for Torchy."

Freshman year, I got my chance. He had been hired by Xavier, and brought his pressure defense along. I pressed like a madman for him. In return, Torchy started me with the varsity.

That year, we had only three grades at Xavier—the original class was now in its junior year—so we weren't yet eligible for the conference championship and playoffs. In my sophomore year, though, we got it going and finished third in the state.

Junior year, we tore through everybody, went 25–0, and won the state title. Senior year, we got to the state championship game again by winning twenty-four in a row. So we'd won forty-nine straight, the longest winning streak in Wisconsin scholastic history. The guys in my class who had played freshman ball, then jayvees, then two years of varsity had never lost a game. They were 82–0 for their high school careers. They needed only one more victory for a perfect record. Our cry rang through Milwaukee Arena: "A-P-P again . . . L-E-T-O-N." We were playing in front of eight thousand people against Marinette Central Catholic, a team we'd beaten twice before that season. A second consecutive state title was waiting for us.

Except we lost. By six points. Marinette played a slowdown game, and we couldn't seem to make them run with us.

More than any other emotion, I felt relief that the season was over and the pressure of the streak had ended. As captain of the team, I accepted the second-place trophy, carried it back to the bench, and handed it to Torchy. He wouldn't take it. He said to me, "No, you guys keep it. You won it."

How he hungered for victory. If we played badly, he'd kick the bleachers with his heel, and make the Brothers cringe with a "Goddam it." He'd actually swear in front of girls and parents! One night during the streak, we fell behind by ten points at halftime. He came into the locker room to find us deathly silent. "I have only one thing to say to you guys," he raged. "You're a bunch of chickenshit motherfuckers." And he stormed out. Needless to say, that got our attention, and we came back in the second half, led by Bill Timmers, for a great victory.

Torchy was also a great tactician. Against Marquette High of Milwaukee, our press had them rattled. He noticed they were substituting their best dribbler, and called time-out. He told me to press this boy especially hard, because if we forced turnovers from him, we could break their whole team. Sure enough, Marquette inbounded to their star dribbler. As I hounded him, I could see the panic in his eyes. It was the first time I'd seen that sort of fear in an opponent. He bounced the ball off his knee, I stole it for an easy hoop, and we crushed them . . . just as Torchy said.

In football, we never saw his true ire, because we never lost a game. We had three 9–0 seasons and one state championship (junior year), which was decided by a poll of sportswriters and broadcasters around Wisconsin.

In my sophomore season, the big game, as usual, was against Premontre High of Green Bay. They had been the perennial conference champions. But now, in our first year, we were a threat.

We played in Green Bay, and they held a slim lead in the fourth quarter when Tom Timmers, Bill's brother, intercepted a pass at the

Premontre 35-yard line. A few plays later, I took a quick pitch at right halfback and started circling the end. One tackler missed. Another shoved me almost out of bounds. My left foot was just inside the sideline; my right foot was dangling precariously in the air across the sideline. But I regained my balance, and took it in for a twenty-three-yard touchdown, the winning score. Incidentally, a classic picture of that tightrope act currently rests in the Xavier trophy case, along with—how's this for pretentious?—the left shoe I wore that night, now bronzed.

That first Premontre game was a capstone for the newfound confidence of a young football program. On that basis, it was probably the most important game I played in high school. It was not, however, a better game than our senior-year battle with Premontre, also in Green Bay. I carried the ball thirty times and was hit by everybody in town, except Ray Nitschke. But, eventually, I punched over the only touchdown in a 7–3 win. After that game, Ted Fritsch, the Premontre coach, told Torchy, "Coach, you're lucky you have Bleier. My linebacker hit him so hard on the play before his touchdown, he knocked himself out."

Ted was always a nice man and a very good coach. He was an All-Pro center for the Packers, and his son, Ted Jr., is now a center for the Atlanta Falcons. Every time I see Ted Sr. at a banquet, he points at me and says, "There's the reason I had to quit coaching."

Those thirty carries were my all-time high for a single game. Usually, it was more like twelve or fourteen. One game, I recall carrying six times and scoring four touchdowns. (It was kind of like playing Dickie Weisgerber again.) That's how well our line performed. Most games, I was on the sidelines by halftime, watching the reserves finish the job. A Wisconsin high school publication, in fact, questioned my stamina because I rarely played a full game.

I did play enough, though, to realize the goals I'd set as a sophomore. In my first game, I scored two touchdowns and intercepted two passes. So I figured I should do that in every game . . . and, averaged out, I did. I scored at least one touchdown in every game I played. I gained more than one thousand yards in each of my last two seasons, which came out to the obscene average of 12.4 yards per cary. I made all-conference as a defensive back and linebacker. On offense, I was an all-state running back for three years, and I even made a few All-America teams, one of which got my picture onto a national magazine cover. Under the other pictures were printed things like: "Fred Carr, Phoenix Union HS, Phoenix, Ariz." "Warren McVea, Brackenridge HS, San Antonio, Tex." "Gary Beban, Sequoia HS, Redwood City, Cal."

I didn't know it then, but I was in some pretty fast company.

The twenty-three-yard "bronze shoe run" against Premontre (*Photos Appleton Post Crescent*)

3] Notre Dame

If you're familiar with some of those wild, dicey tales of illegal college recruiting practices, I'm afraid you'll be a little disappointed in the story of how I got to Notre Dame.

I wasn't one of the "blue-chippers," as recruiters call them. I received about twenty letters of interest, mainly from Wisconsin state schools, the Big Ten, and a few independents, such as Notre Dame, Boston College, and Miami of Florida.

When I was in high school, all I knew about Notre Dame was that a guy named Knute Rockne had coached there and built a winning football tradition. I didn't know where it was, or how big it was. I had surely never been to Indiana, and I don't think I'd ever heard of South Bend.

All of that was changed by an Appleton restaurant owner, Russ Skall. He was an alumnus, and one of the thousands of arms in Notre Dame's national scouting network. He recommended me to Hugh Devore, the ND coach in 1963, and drove me to South Bend one Saturday morning in the fall of my senior year. Notre Dame lost to Wisconsin, 14–9, that day, but before the game, I was ushered into Devore's office. He tossed a lot of compliments at me, which was somewhat surprising to hear from a college coach, and then he promised I would be offered a grant-in-aid, which was downright astounding.

A few months later, in January, 1964, a rumor circulated in Appleton that Vince Lombardi of the Packers would become Notre Dame's new coach. I was in the bar when I heard it, and I promptly went from table to table, from stool to stool, announcing that if St. Vincent was going to South Bend, I was, too. Of course, the rumor was unfounded, and the Irish eventually hired Ara Parseghian from Northwestern. I'd never heard of him.

The next month, I got some advice that seemed logical from Dave Hurd, the Notre Dame assistant who was recruiting me. He said, "Rocky, you can visit all the schools you want. They all roll out the red carpet with dates and parties. You'll have a great time everywhere. But that won't help you make a decision. On the contrary, it'll only confuse you. Instead, why not pick three schools that interest you for solid reasons. Visit just those three, and then make your decision."

So I did. On consecutive weekends, I went to Notre Dame, Wisconsin, and Boston College. I did not, however, allow football to interfere with another of my loves. Here is a letter I sent to Dave Hurd in February, 1964:

Dear Mr. Hurd,

As you know, I am supposed to come down on the weekend of March 6–8, but I just found out that the school band is having their concert that weekend and I'll have to play. I was wondering if I could get the date changed to another weekend, maybe to the 14th, or to any weekend that you might think would be good.

Sincerely,

Rocky Bleier

I really did love playing my trumpet in the band. In fact, during my freshman year, when band practice and basketball practice conflicted, I went to band for an hour after classes, then to the last half hour of basketball. As you can imagine, Torchy was less than enthralled with my lack of devotion, and told me to make a choice. Luckily, band was changed before my decision was due. If he'd forced me, I don't know what I would have chosen. That's how committed I was to the trumpet.

Dave Hurd was more understanding, though. He rescheduled my visit for Friday, March 13 . . . a perfect day to meet the previously unknown Coach Parseghian.

Ara was overwhelming to me. He had that dark Armenian face, the firm chin, wavy black hair flecked with gray, and those piercing, deep-set eyes. He *looked* like a head coach. He had such presence in one-to-one conversation, especially on his own turf. He impressed me that day, and later, as being extremely well organized. All through the interview, he took notes in longhand on a yellow legal pad . . . notes which he filed and retains in his office today. He began the conversation rather dramatically.

"We offer less than the NCAA permits," Ara said, "so if you're looking for something under the table, I'll close my books right now and end the discussion. Once you sign the grant, it's yours for four years. We don't take it back if you're injured or don't play well. We give room, board, tuition, and books. We don't give the fifteen-dollars-a-month laundry money, but we have our own laundry on campus, and we'll give you tickets for it."

Not only did Notre Dame have its own laundry, it had its own barbershop for my crew cut, its own clothing store, its own bookstore and dining halls. It was a city within itself, and quite small—just six thousand undergraduates in those days. In fact, the campus even had its own movie theater, Washington Hall, where I went that Saturday night to be entertained.

Remember, 1964 was before coeducation. This was the social event of the weekend. The place was jammed with guys screaming epithets at each other and at the figures on the screen. That may seem a little childish to you, but I was a naive Midwestern kid from a Christian Brothers high school, and I enjoyed the camaraderie I found.

I was escorted around campus for the weekend by Tom Regner, an offensive lineman, and Kevin Hardy, a defensive lineman. They were both in the area of 6-feet-4, 260 pounds, both became All-America, and both had their heads shaved nearly to the scalp. They were truly imposing sights for this little lad, but they were genuinely friendly and I liked the way everybody on campus said hello to them.

I saw Coach Parseghian again before I left Notre Dame. In a rather forceful and persuasive manner, he offered me a grant-in-aid and asked me to sign it immediately. These are his notes from the earlier interview:

Rocky Bleier, Xavier H.S., Appleton, Wisconsin. 18. 5-10½, 177. Born 3-5-46. Ranked 18th in a class of 111. College boards: Verbal 435, Math 525. Wants liberal arts. Dad tavernkeeper. Averaged 12 points in basketball. Runs track: 100 . . . :10.3, 220 . . . :22.9, shotput . . . 46 feet. Scored 55 TDs in three years, scored 21 TDs in senior year. ND first school he has visited. Football team has won 34 in a row, 49 of 50 in basketball. This boy has good personality. Decided to pitch him. Will visit two others—Wis, B.C. Parents want boy to come to ND.

I really never had a chance. But at that point, anyway, I resisted and kept my promise to sign nothing until I'd visited the other two schools. The Wisconsin trip was heady stuff because the coach, Milt Bruhn, lavished me with praise. He said, "I've never seen anybody so quick laterally. You move faster laterally than most guys do forward." Bruhn promised to start me at halfback in my sophomore year, along with Tom Jankowski of Whitefish Bay, the stud fullback in the state. What he could not promise, however, was to reduce the student body by about 80 percent. There are nearly as many students on the campus at Madison as there are residents in all of Appleton. It's the biggest of the Big Ten, and I felt too small-town to be comfortable there.

Boston College was a serious alternative. I liked the city and the campus. It was different from anything I'd known in the Midwest.

I allowed one week to make a decision, and wore out my knees praying to the Lord for guidance. I knew my mother wanted me to go to Notre Dame ... for all the irrational reasons that most Catholic mothers want their sons to go to Notre Dame. While neither she nor Dad ever tried to exert an influence, Dave Hurd took one final precaution. On March 24, the evening I said I'd decide, he spent two hours talking on the telephone to Mom ... just to be sure the other coaches would get a busy signal. He really didn't need to. In the end, I was sure I wanted Notre Dame.

When I got there, however, I wasn't so sure Notre Dame needed me. The first order of business for freshmen in the fall was to be timed in the forty-yard sprint. As we assembled in the old Fieldhouse, it was all I could do to keep my jaw from falling open. These guys were monsters. I thought I was good-sized, at about 185 pounds, until I saw Ralph Moore, a fullback who went 6-feet-2, 220 pounds. He had a shaved head that made him look even meaner, and when he ran, he kicked his knees up near his chest. There was another behemoth named Jim Yacknow, a tight end with size, strength, hands, everything. He had a heavy beard and looked so mature that one player walked into the Fieldhouse and asked him, "Where do we go, Coach?"

I thought, "What the hell am I doing here?"

Freshman year was really not much fun. We had no games, so it was practice, practice, practice. We ran the opponents' plays against the varsity defense in what was supposed to be dummy scrimmage, but always turned out to be "live" contact. Those defensive linemen never missed a chance to cheap-shot the little freshman back with an elbow or a forearm. It grew cold and dark in early November on Cartier Field, our practice facility. For the first time in my life, I was eager for a season to end.

It was only small consolation that the varsity was having a great season, winning its first nine games with John Huarte throwing for a Heisman Trophy to Jack Snow. In the final game, they were knocked off, 21–17, in the last few minutes at Southern California. But 9–1 was cause for delirium, coming on the heels of 2–7 in 1963. It was Notre Dame's first winning record since the Terry Brennan era ended in 1958. We freshmen never felt part of it, though. We watched the varsity on television like the other fans.

Freshman life apart from football was not much fun, either. I didn't know anybody in South Bend—least of all, any girls—and there wasn't much to do on campus. I worked off most of my excess energy in impromptu wrestling matches with Chuck Grable, my roommate. We'd lock the door, strip down to our scivvies, and go at it for as long as an hour . . . amicably, yet intensely, with beds, desks, dressers, lockers, lamps, and chairs flying all over the room.

Drinking in the dorm was another occasional diversion. One night, we sat around like a bunch of cowboys, playing stud poker and drinking straight shots of whiskey. I finally passed out. Chuck and the others were caught by our floor prefect, a priest, who told me the next day, "I don't know how you can stand it, all that drinking and rowdiness in your room while you're trying to sleep." I agreed it was tough.

It was also a tremendous relief, our prefect thinking I wasn't involved with the card party. As in Appleton, I was very concerned with my image. I wanted everybody to think highly of me. To this day, in fact, I place a high premium on making a good impression.

At Notre Dame, I was always happy to join in the dormitory pranks, as long as I wasn't caught. The occasional drinking, shaving-cream bombs, setting wooden doors on fire with lighter fluid, hiding moldy bread in someone's room . . . we did lots of devilish things to entertain ourselves and kill time.

Those first nine months seemed like nine years. I actually hated Notre Dame. But, of course, I didn't tell anybody back home. They all thought it was such an honor for me to be going there . . . to the University of Our Lady, with all that wonderful tradition, and that quality education, and that sensational football team. How could I tell anybody I didn't like Notre Dame?

Plus I knew several guys from Appleton who'd gone away to school, then dropped out and returned home. I'd always considered that rather gutless. I was determined to stick it out at ND.

By sophomore year, I had my football confidence back and knew I would play in spite of my size . . . or maybe because of it. I have what I think is an interesting theory about Coach Parseghian and his offensive coordinator, Ton Pagna. Both were running backs at Miami of Ohio . . . the kind of running backs who survived on versatility, good hands, steady blocking, picking the right hole. Neither did it on exceptional size or speed. Consequently, I feel they recruited and played backs who were made in their image and likeness. They wanted all-around athletes and they wanted winners.

I guess I was their kind of guy. I had played basketball and football, and pitched four summers of Legion baseball. In track, I had run the 100, the 220, and the half-mile relay, put the shot, and long jumped. I'd won eleven high school letters, and my teams had won football, basketball, and track conference titles in each of my last three years.

In addition, I was compactly built, just as Ara and Tom were. That's the way they wanted their backs. They used to see a tall back on film and say to each other, "He's cut too high." Tom subsequently told me they'd made a study of the leverage principles involved in blocking, and the stride patterns of the tall runner versus the short runner. They'd had success with the versatile, smaller man, who might not have had breakaway speed, but never made a critical mistake or missed an assignment.

In the eleven years of the Parseghian-Pagna Era, therefore, the offensive backs looked like they came stamped out of a machine: Bill Wolski, Joe Farrell, Nick Eddy, Larry Conjar, Rocky Bleier, Bob Gladieux, Dan Harshman, Ron Dushney, Ed Ziegler, Jeff Zimmerman, Bill Barz, Denny Allan, John Cieszkowski, Andy Huff, Ed Gulyas, Bob Minnix, Eric Penick, Art Best, Wayne Bullock. Eddy and Penick may have had a little more speed, and Cieszkowski and Bullock a little more size than the rest of us. But essentially, we all had about the same tools.

"A halfback is half tank and half cat," Pagna used to tell us. We spent four years at Notre Dame trying to live up to that description . . . trying to become the complete players Ara and Tom had been at Miami.

My sophomore season began with a sprained ankle, but by the second game, I was ready for fourth-quarter duty with the all-sophomore backfield . . . Tom Schoen at quarterback, Paul May at fullback, Dan Harshman and me at halfback. After the upperclassmen had put the victory away, Ara would send us in all together. We'd rush onto the field with the fans screaming, "And they're only soph-ah-mores." The opposing defenses must have been pretty tired by the time we arrived, because I ended the season with the team's best rushing average, 5.6 yards a carry.

I got only one start that year. In a 69–13 victory at Pittsburgh, Bill Wolski tied a fifty-year-old record with five touchdowns. I don't know if he was injured or just exhausted, but he couldn't play the next week against North Carolina. I took his place and had a good day—eleven carries, sixty-six yards.

Yet I was suffering an identity crisis. I just couldn't focus a mental picture of running alongside Nick Eddy and Larry Conjar. Fortunately, Torchy Clark was in South Bend for that game, and he obliterated my identity crisis as only Torchy could.

"The hell you don't belong in that backfield," he said. "You're as good as any of those guys." So much for insecurity.

Two weeks later, we finished the season 7–2–1, which is about the record we deserved.

Spring ball before the 1966 season was tremendously exciting. A battle for the starting quarterback job developed between two freshmen—Coley O'Brien, who came heralded from Washington, D.C., and Terry Hanratty, who merely came from Butler, Pennsylvania.

Meanwhile, the coaches were installing a pair of new offenses. They conceived a two-back offense, basically for passing, which employed Curt Henneghan as a flanker. And there was a three-back offense, which called for me to replace Henneghan and function as both a runner and wide receiver. Ara seemed committed to using both systems until midway through spring practice, when I developed a respiratory infection and missed a week's work.

I quickly learned that "The Man" is short of patience on only two matters in life—missed assignments and missed practice, no matter how good your excuse. So, with the freshmen throwers coming along, Ara decided to junk the three-back offense and go exclusively with Henneghan. All summer, I cursed my misfortune. But then, in prefall practice, the situation turned inside out. Henneghan returned to campus with a pulled hamstring, and guess who became a starter?

So did Hanratty. In the final week before the opener, Ara decided he liked Terry's size and stronger arm more than Coley's polish. But what a spot for him: The first game of his college career was to be played on national television against Purdue, the intrastate rival, the Top Ten challenger, the team with Bob Griese. A year earlier, Griese had completed nineteen of twenty-two passes and beaten us single-handedly.

On the first series of downs, we drove to the Purdue 8-yard line. There, Hanratty made a bad toss on a pitch-sweep. The ball hit me on the right shoulder pad, and before I could control it, three Boilermakers hammered me. An unknown sophomore cornerback named Leroy Keyes caught it in midair and went ninety yards for a touchdown.

Leroy eventually became a sensational player on both offense and defense. But when I see him these days, I always say, "Leroy, I should get ten percent of your contract every year. I made you what you are. I made you an All-America in nine seconds." That was his first game as well, and I put him on display like a debutante. "Our play" made every highlight film and television show of the season.

On the ensuing kickoff, however, Nick Eddy matched Keyes's effort with a coast-to-coast run of his own. I didn't block anybody on the play, but I sure looked pretty leading Nick into the end zone. And I felt a whole lot better than I had a few moments earlier.

Later in the game, Hanratty atoned for his poor pitch. He and Jim Seymour connected thirteen times for 276 yards, and we won, 26–14.

Then they did it nine times against Northwestern and eight more against Army. All of a sudden, everybody was making up nicknames for these two sophomores, calling them the greatest playmates since Christine Keeler and Mandy Rice Davis. We were No. 1, and life was lovely.

The No. 2 team was Michigan State, and before long, the season became a pedantic countdown to our _____ (fill in the blank with your favorite adjective . . . cosmic, cataclysmic, monolithic) meeting on November 19. The Spartans beat all their opponents by an average of twenty-two points per game. We beat ours by thirty-four. In fact, it reached an absurd level against Duke on the Saturday before the "Big One."

Tom Pagna had always regaled us with heroic tales of his playing days. His favorite epic concerned a game at Miami of Ohio in which he was never tackled. Pagna said he ran the ball four times for four touchdowns. Then Ara, who was his coach at the time, took him out of the game because Miami was so far ahead. Just for effect, Tom told us he wore his uniform the next week without sending it to the cleaners. He was not bashful in mentioning that his feat would never be duplicated.

Well, against Duke, Nick Eddy duplicated it. And I almost did. Nick ran the ball once for seventy-seven yards and a touchdown. I ran the ball twice and had one TD. We scored every time we had possession in the first half, for forty-three points.

Then the weeklong buildup for Michigan State began. And it was at least equal to the game itself. Their students started things by dumping leaflets out of an airplane as it circled our campus. The leaflets were addressed to the "peace-loving villagers of Notre Dame." They asked: "Why do you struggle against us? Why do you persist in the mistaken belief that you can win, freely and openly, against us? Your leaders have lied to you. They have led you to believe you can win. They have given you false hopes."

Every night was occasion for a pep rally. The band marched around campus, playing the "Victory March" nonstop. Thousands of students fevered themselves, tossing around the rolls of toilet paper they would need the next morning. Ultimately, all would converge on a particular dorm and chant a player's name until he poked his head out the window and uttered a few incoherent phrases about the hated Spartans. It was great fun.

The newspapers spent all week informing America that Bubba Smith, State's pick-your-adjective defensive end, was slimmed down to 283 pounds with a 14D shoe, a 19½-inch collar, and a size 52-long MSU blazer. I didn't need to read it. I had seen the movies. Until then, the best lineman I'd played was Granville Liggins of Oklahoma, who was only 5-feet-10, 215 pounds. But *zip*, was he quick. Now here was Bubba in game films, jumping over linemen, splitting the double-team block . . . nearly as quick as Liggins. And seventy pounds heavier!

The train ride to State was another experience. Their fans were standing on the platforms in Battle Creek and Kalamazoo—some even stood along the tracks, in cornfields and on dairy farms—jeering and holding sheet signs: "Bubba for Pope," "Hail Mary, full of grace, Notre Dame's in second place." None of that, however, was as bad as our arrival in East Lansing.

As I disembarked, I noticed the metal steps were slippery with ice. Behind me, I heard a yelp. It was my roommate on the road, Nick Eddy. He'd slipped, missed his grab for the handrail, and reinjured his bruised shoulder. He was doubled over, crying with pain and with the instant realization that he couldn't play in the biggest game of his career.

People called it "The Game of the Century" that year . . . which was not especially important, because somebody makes that statement about one game in nearly every college football season. What *is* significant is that now, nine years later, some of the experts are *still* calling it "The Game of the Century."

In the pregame warm-up, I was entranced—almost dizzy, or high —at the sight and sound of the seventy-six thousand fans in Spartan Stadium. Nothing I ever experienced on a football field, before or since, has equaled it. The chants rocked and swayed at a deafening level. Try to imagine quadraphonic speakers blasting the Rolling Stones at full volume. It was like that . . . clearly, the edge of insanity.

The game started disastrously for us. Our center, George Goeddeke, separated his shoulder and exited on the first series. Next time we had the ball, a messenger lineman mistakenly brought in a quarterback-draw play. (Ara would never have taken that risk intentionally.) Hanratty ran it for four yards before George Webster pinned him and Bubba pounced on top, separating *Hanratty's* shoulder. State's offense, meanwhile, forged a 10–0 lead.

We came back just before the half on a thirty-four-yard TD pass from Coley O'Brien, Hanratty's substitute, to Bob Gladieux, Eddy's substitute. At the start of the fourth quarter, we got a Joe Azzaro field goal, and that was all the scoring. 10–10. The numbers will live forever.

There was plenty of postgame discussion about Ara's decision not to call time-out and not to pass when we had possession for the last six downs of the game. There was some discussion on the field, too. Bubba yelled, "Come on, sissies, throw the ball. I'll call time-out for you."

Charlie Thornhill, their linebacker, who had an exceptional game, screamed, "You don't *want* it."

I've always defended Ara's reasoning. We'd been stripped of our offensive weapons, we'd come back from a ten-point deficit, our defense had kept Michigan State outside our 45-yard line in the second half. Then, the critics wanted us to throw long, desperate passes into a prevent defense that was specifically designed to intercept them.

And consider our quarterback. Coley O'Brien is diabetic. He drank orange juice and ate candy bars on the sideline to maintain his insulin at a safe level. In this game, he was so tense that he recalls little or nothing of the action. Ara knew he'd done a great job bringing us back. He was not about to throw it all away with frivolous play-calling in the last minute.

I was our leading ball carrier, with fifty-seven yards. I wondered if I'd fulfilled the expectations of Larry Conjar, our senior fullback and one of the offensive leaders. Before the game, he'd said to me, "Nick isn't going to play. The responsibility is on your shoulders. You can't let us down."

I also caught three passes for sixteen yards, but I paid for those. On a catch over the middle in the third quarter, Charles Phillips, State's defensive back, speared me with his helmet in the kidney. After the game, I felt a rush of pain while standing at the urinal. I looked down and noticed I was passing pure blood. But at the moment, it didn't seem to matter. Conjar's arms were a mass of black and blue. Jim Lynch, our linebacker, had played with a monstrous charley horse. Don Gmitter, the tight end, gutted it out on one good knee. And Gladieux joined the others who were done for the season.

Almost everybody was crying, especially Tom Pagna. The emotion of the game, the hitting and violent contact, was converted into the emotion of the locker room . . . the tears, the hugging, the trite phrases. Then Ara spoke to us:

Men, I'm proud of you. God knows, I've never been more proud of any group of young men in my life. Get one thing

Ara Parseghian
(*Notre Dame
Athletic Department*)

The 1966 Notre Dame
backfield: Rocky Bleier,
Larry Conjar, Nick Eddy,
Terry Hanratty (*Laughead
Photographers*)

A tired halfback (*Notre Dame Athletic Department*)

straight, though. We did not lose. We were number one when we came, we fell behind, had some tough things happen, but you overcame them. No one could have wanted to win this one more than I. We didn't win, but, by God, we did not lose. They're crying about a tie, trying to detract from your efforts. They're trying to make it come out a win. Well, don't you believe it. Their season is over. They can't go anywhere. It's all over, and we're still number one. Time will prove everything that has happened here today. And you'll see that after the rabble-rousers have had their say, cooler minds who understand the true odds will know that Notre Dame is a team of champions. There will be moments when you'll want to blast out at something, or someone. But when we open these doors to the press and to some of our so-called well-wishers, remember one thing: Whatever you do, whatever you say, reflects on us, on your parents, on the team, and on Notre Dame.

Michigan State's season, indeed, had ended. We had one final game against Southern California in Los Angeles Coliseum. I was in the hospital with a lacerated kidney, but I got daily reports on practice. Pagna was at the top of his inspirational game, chastising the offense, "Why can't the Regners and Seilers and Conjars recognize that one more Saturday will immortalize their playing careers?"

To Pete Duranko, the defensive tackle, he noted, "Duranko, no two men should ever block you out."

But Tom's best was reserved for a mimeographed letter to the team, known as "The Phantom Speaks," which he wrote each week. This was the letter he circulated in the locker room a few days before the USC game:

Irish! You are hurting . . . but unbowed and unbeaten. There are no sophomores on our squad. Having lived and fought your way back against Michigan State made all of you grow up . . . beyond any point of inexperience.

I remember 1964 in this same Coliseum, the Irish squad walking the long, empty walk from the field to the tunnel after our defeat. I remember their full-grown bodies—shaking with sobs of dejection. I recall the fantastic turn of events that robbed us of a national championship. We never cried FOUL!

We're going back there. The odds are these: They are a good-wound, quick football team on their home field. We must travel there and play in warm weather. We must overcome their advantages.

We are fighters—hurt tho we may be! We are aware of all the obstacles, all the memories.

Go, Irish—become undefeated!!! The champions you are!

We did exactly that. We dismembered USC, 51–0.

Several weeks later, the Trojans' coach, John McKay, told a member of his staff, "We'll never be beaten that badly again." And he probably won't. Every working day in the off-season that followed, McKay left word that he was not to be disturbed, and locked himself in a dark room to watch a portion of that game. Every working day for six months.

When USC people asked to see him, his secretary would say, "He's watching the film." And everybody knew what that meant.

McKay got his revenge the next year. He came to South Bend with a tailback named O. J. Simpson, who turned us every way but out. He ran for 150 yards and two touchdowns. Before we could get him out of town, we were a 2–2 football team, and not looking very formidable.

I played Pagliacco that night—laughing outside, crying inside— the friendly, jovial host to five busloads of friends and relatives from Appleton. They left home at 6:00 A.M., armed with a Dixieland band, lots of liquor from Dad's bar, and my mother as a tour guide. After the game we took them to dinner in Niles, Michigan, just across the state line. It was a small, intimate affair for 150 people. We had a guest for every yard O.J. had gained in the afternoon. I saw him running across my plate all night.

Our team failures weighed more heavily on me in 1967 because I was captain. The captaincy at Notre Dame entitles you to do more than call the toss of the coin. It makes you part of Irish football lore, and compels you to maintain an ideal. It's not an honor you openly campaign for, but it's one I wanted very much. One evening at the Grotto of Our Lady, I prayed, "Lord, please make me one of two things. Make me captain, or make me an All-America." In His infinite wisdom, the Lord made me captain. I guess He was trying to tell me something.

I wanted to be captain so badly, I almost broke up with my girl friend over it. She kind of wanted to get married. But in those days, Notre Dame captains were always single. Not by any ruling . . . that's just the way it was. Of course, it was a good excuse to give my girl, because I really didn't want to get married. In those days, nothing was stronger than my desire to become captain.

Soon after I was elected, I went to seek advice from Jim Lynch in the traditional basement room of Sorin Hall, where nearly every Notre Dame captain has lived since they first teed up a football in 1887. Lynch was the '66 captain by unanimous vote, a guy who fairly gushed charisma. You have no idea how acute was the inferiority I felt. My election came on a second ballot. And when our picture appeared in the *South Bend Tribune,* the caption read: "Jim Lynch, square-jawed captain of the 1966 National Champions, passes the symbolic Irish shelalaigh to his successor, Rocky Bleier, the baby-faced running back from Appleton, Wisconsin." Baby-faced!

Now the contrast was even more stark. Lynch had taken us all the way in '66. A year later, we had won only half of our first four games. Worse than that, I didn't sense the same yearning for victory, the same electricity in practice that we'd evidenced a year earlier. I discussed it with Pagna several times. I thought it was my fault. I wondered if maybe the guys didn't respect me.

Tom said, "Nonsense. The problems are these: The team tasted success once, and nobody wants it as badly the second time. We've lost some good people to graduation. And we've got to make some technical adjustments. Hanratty's had such success with Seymour that now he's hunting him up. Defenses know it. That's why we've had so many interceptions. Seymour's breaking his routes too often, trying to go deep on every play. We're too much a passing team. We're not hard-nosed. We're not prepared to go the long, hard grind—four, five, six yards at a time. When we get behind, there's a feeling of, 'Well, don't worry, Terry'll throw the bomb and get us even.' "

So we went back to the running game, and back to scrimmaging in practice, despite the risk of injury. Most important, the coaches made an appeal to our pride. Notre Dame didn't go to bowl games in 1967, so we had no tangible incentive. There would be no National Champion-ship this time. But Ara insisted our own pride was a loftier goal. He was convincing, too, because we won our last six in a row for a very creditable 8-2 record.

I cherish three of those six in particular. Against Navy, I played the finest game of my college career—fifty-nine yards and two touchdowns rushing, a thirty-yard kickoff return, and a twenty-seven-yard punt return.

Two weeks later at Georgia Tech, I suffered torn ligaments in my left knee while scoring a touchdown just before halftime. That, nor-mally, is an incapacitating and immediately detectable injury. But the quadriceps muscles in my thigh were so taut that they did the work of the ligaments, holding my knee in place.

I played the entire second half . . . running, blocking, catching passes, and punting. I even did some dancing at a party Saturday night. The doctors blinked a bit on Sunday, when they finally made the diagnosis. Monday I entered the hospital, Tuesday I underwent surgery, Wednesday I rested with the help of my friend Demerol, and Thursday I hobbled onto an airplane. Our season finale was Friday night at Miami of Florida. I was still woozy from all the sedatives. But if I couldn't finish my career in uniform, I wanted, at least, to be on the field. Besides, this was a helluva game. Both teams were in the Top Ten, we at 7-2, Miami at 6-2.

Partly because of the medication and partly because my tear ducts seem to work overtime, I set an Orange Bowl record for emotion that night. It started before the game, my eyes moistening as I watched everybody suiting up. When I felt I couldn't control myself, I slipped into the bathroom for a good, solid cry. I made several trips.

I composed myself and stood near the doorway, off at a distance from the team, as Ara went into his pregame oration. He finished by saying, "Dave Martin and Dick Swatland will be cocaptains tonight."

That made me flinch, and I tried so hard not to cry again. But it was hopeless . . . especially when my teammates filed past me, one by one, at the door. Each man gave me a pat on the rump or a silent glance. Near the end came Danny Harshman, my former roommate and best friend at Notre Dame, who was starting in my place. He stopped and grabbed my hand. He squeezed it a second and said, "Remember, Rock, you'll always be our captain." Cue the tears.

We won, 24-22, in a kind of classic, gutty style that typified our whole season. Back in the locker room after the game, Ara quieted his noisy troops long enough to hold up the game ball and ask, "What should we do with this?" And in unison the team began to chant, "Rocky, Rocky, Rocky." Well, that's all I had to hear. Ara presented me the game ball, and I responded like Niagara Falls. I didn't stop crying for another twenty minutes.

Fortunately, I was in the kind of environment and among the kind of people who understood, and even appreciated, my emotional outburst. Given my background and personal makeup, Notre Dame was the right place for me. And that was true of my nonfootball activities, as well.

I dabbled in student politics and helped with retarded children a couple afternoons a week at Northern Indiana Children's Hospital. Those kinds of activities were well organized at Notre Dame, and available to be shared with fellows like me. I could cry in a football locker room, or cry after spending an afternoon with a retarded child

. . . because the people around me were just like me. They knew what I was feeling, and they empathized.

Yet, by a strange dichotomy, that great strength was also Notre Dame's greatest fault. We were *too much* alike in those days. We were 98 percent white and 98 percent Catholic. Too many of us in student politics had similar views. In the classroom, we needed more nonwhites and non-Catholics to expand our horizons. Our thinking was inbred, and therefore restricted.

There were more restrictions: no cars on campus, lights out at 11:00 P.M., confinement to the dormitory after midnight, coats and ties to dinner. (The rule of mandatory daily Mass had been lifted a few years earlier.) Those things don't exist today, I'm glad to report. But for the boy I was at ages eighteen to twenty-one, it was tolerable discipline and probably benefited me. I'm also happy to say Notre Dame has diversified its student body since I graduated. It is by no means a cross-section of American society. Yet I dare say it is more nearly similar than dissimilar to other major universities. The myth of Notre Dame, as something separate and apart from the mainstream of higher education, should be spiked and put to rest.

Academically, the university is probably a bit overrated. It is struggling mightily, but I don't think there is any present possibility that it will become the "Harvard of the Midwest," or the "Catholic Harvard," as some administrators have publicly hoped.

I opted for the School of Business, mainly because the foreign-language requirement in liberal arts frightened me. I graduated with a B average, though I must confess I have no particular aptitude for business. I cannot even keep my checkbook in balance. I guess if I had it to do over again, I'd take a broad-based liberal arts program, with emphasis on classical thought and literature.

While I'm expounding, permit me a few final words on the condition of college athletics and the practitioners at my alma mater.

I loved playing college football, and I'm distressed at hearing some of its problems. For instance, when a major state institution like the University of Vermont must give up the game for financial reasons, it's time to take corrective action. But more serious than the financial problem is the moral crisis.

Let's put this into perspective. We had our black eyes at Notre Dame, but they were mostly in the nature of pranks. In 1965, six of my teammates were seen hauling television sets from a Purdue University fraternity house to a waiting hearse, which they'd driven from South Bend. A few years earlier, some players were caught breaking into a cigarette machine they'd cleverly transported from the fourth floor to the baggage room of Breen-Phillips Hall. And yes, Rocky Bleier once sold his complimentary game tickets for $50 apiece when his pockets were empty. I don't condone those incidents, and Notre Dame didn't, either. The six television haulers were expelled, and I would have been disciplined if Ara had learned of my salesmanship.

But none of that chills me as deeply as a conversation I heard last year between a recruiter and the coach of a major Eastern college football team. The recruiter mentioned a high school running back whom he'd seen in the Deep South. Great burst, good moves, quickness . . . this kid had everything, the man said. The coach responded, "We'd love to have him. We need his kind desperately. But I simply don't know how to recruit a kid from that far away without cheating."

Capsulized, that is the crisis of college football today: Can the game expel outlaws who are polluting it with offers of cash, cars, and apartments to impressionable high school kids?

Luckily for the serious student-athlete, there are still universities like Notre Dame and men like Parseghian whose integrity is intact. Of all my teammates, I knew only one who received a gift from an alumnus. It was a suit of clothes for a young man who had never owned one. But if he'd found out about it, I'm sure Ara would have disciplined the player unsympathetically.

Notre Dame people are not the only ones still playing within NCAA rules. I'm heartened, for example, by the beautiful story of Earl Campbell, a fantastic fullback who, in 1973, became *the* most actively recruited player in the glorious history of Texas high school football. Campbell visited Austin one afternoon for an interview with Darrell Royal, coach of the University of Texas.

Royal began, much as Ara did, by mentioning that he'd close his books and stop wasting everybody's time if the player wanted more than the standard grant-in-aid. Understand, Campbell is a black man of some considerable pride. He looked sternly back at Royal and said, "My people were bought and sold when they didn't have a choice. Now I have a choice, and nobody's buying me."

4] Pittsburgh

In the fall of 1967, my senior year, Dan Harshman and I took a walk through downtown Pittsburgh the night before our game with the Panthers. As we circled back to the hotel, I mentioned to Dan, "It's not a bad city. It's not as bad as people say."

After a lifetime in the flat, monotonous Midwest, I was struck by the strong character of Pittsburgh's Allegheny Mountains. The hillsides were colorful with turning leaves . . . not in splashy, picture-postcard shades, but in a rugged, burnished bronze. And they were hung with sturdy old frame houses, like ornaments on a Christmas tree. Everywhere you looked, across a river, over a ridge . . . there were houses clinging, at some impossible angle, to a rustic hillside.

Sections of the landscape carved by man had that same quality. Crossing the bridges, I could look up and down three different rivers, but always to see the same picture . . . railroad tracks paralleling the water on either side, flanked by steel mills and foundries and power plants. A rugged picture that I liked.

The next scene is three months later in the South Bend living room of Joe and Mary Hickey, the best friends a Notre Dame football player ever had. Joe is class of '56 and president of the family construction company. His father helped Rockne sell football tickets and keep the ship afloat back in the twenties. It probably seems that long ago since Joe and Mary ate dinner without an Irish player at their table. But they ask for it.

This night in late January, 1968, I'd had a few beers, which, considering my infrequent indulgence, about zonked me. I figured I had one coming, though. Football pressure had ceased, and it was too early in the second semester for any exams. Besides, this was the final day of the NFL college player draft, and I was tired of waiting by the telephone for a call that didn't seem to be coming.

Joe turned on the ten o'clock news. And was I hearing correctly? . . . or did that sportscaster really say, "Rocky Bleier, the Irish running back, went in the sixteenth round to the Pittsburgh Steelers."

Considering the condition I was in, and considering the condition the Steelers were in, I didn't know whether to laugh or cry. I hadn't gotten a questionnaire from Pittsburgh, hadn't heard from them all season. I didn't know whether to be disappointed that I'd gone so low, to such a lousy team . . . or happy that at least I was drafted by somebody.

Playing at Notre Dame had made me visible to every pro scout in the business. I only hoped that while they were evaluating the Kevin Hardys and Alan Pages, they'd noticed No. 28, too. At the same time, I knew I had several liabilities.

First, I'd never been a standout. Early on, Conjar and Eddy were the stud runners. Then, in my senior year, a sophomore fullback, Jeff Zimmerman, and junior halfback Bob Gladieux each gained more yardage than I. Second, my speed was suspect. I was timed only once in college—that first day of freshman year. I ran forty yards in 4.8 seconds, which is slow for a 180-pound back wearing full football gear. I was running in shorts and T-shirt. As long ago as high school, there had been doubt that I was fast enough. When Dave Hurd graded my Xavier films for Notre Dame, he gave me A in every category but speed. Third, I was known to have suffered serious injuries. They went as far back as seventh grade, when I sailed over the landing area in a practice long jump, straining all my ankle ligaments. I didn't think the pros had me scouted *that* well, but I was certain they knew about my lacerated kidney and ruptured knee ligament. I was also told the pros sometimes fear a back is physically "used up" after absorbing three years of punishment from major-college defenses.

As I subsequently discovered, all my fears had some basis in fact. Here are the Steelers' scouting reports on me:

FALL '66 REPORTS

"Bones" Taylor, Steeler coach: Makes the big play for Notre Dame without much credit . . . catches the ball in crowds and runs the ball well . . . keep an eye on this boy, he is a classy ball player . . . he has the potential for running back or flanker . . . size big problem . . . 5-11, 185.

Ralph Kohl, super scout for BLESTO-V [a scouting service to which the Steelers subscribe]: Good speed and hands . . . speedy, dependable receiver.

SPRING '67 REPORTS

Don Heinrich, Steeler coach: Not a great prospect as running back, but his best spot is flanker . . . captain . . . estimated 5.7 in 50 . . . good speed and hands . . . adequate size . . . average balance and quickness . . . straight-line runner as a ball carrier . . . not good, quick change of direction . . . doesn't appear to accelerate like he should or could with his speed . . . average blocker . . . fair prospect . . . rate 2.3.

Art Rooney Jr., Steelers' chief scout: Good blocker . . . really belted Alan Page of the Vikings in ND Oldtimers' Game . . . good downfield blocks . . . seems maneuverable . . . picks well as a running back . . . hits into the line hard . . . runs under control . . . gets off line good, tough . . . question overall speed and hands . . . might be a defensive back because he hits . . . 2.4.

Ralph Kohl: Prospect . . . slim chance on account of size and lack of great speed . . . not a very tough kid . . . good college back, but little pro potential . . . will be drafted in middle rounds . . . punts, too, but just fair . . . little pro potential . . . 1967 captain-elect . . . rate 2.4 . . . draft sixth to tenth . . . 4.9 estimated in 40.

Ken Stilley, BLESTO-V scout: I don't think this boy can make a pro club . . . not tough or strong . . . maybe a flanker, we'll watch in the fall . . . not what we are looking for.

FALL '67 REPORTS

Ralph Kohl: Prospect . . . catches well, but lacks size and great speed . . . good athlete and good college ball player . . . can't win in the NFL with this kid . . . will be drafted in the middle rounds, though . . . rate 2.2.

Ken Stilley: This boy is not a great runner . . . he has fair hands . . . might be a flanker, but he does not have that kind of speed . . . will have a tough time making it . . . rate 2.2.

Art Rooney Jr.: Did not play against Miami . . . supposed to have had a bad knee . . . no rating . . . against Michigan State, showed movement, balance and second effort as a runner . . . caught the ball well short . . . runs under control . . . strong . . . inconsistent blocker . . . could develop into a blocker as a pro . . . a com-

petitor . . . does not have one great, special talent to make him
an outstanding pro prospect.

Clearly, the Steelers were not ecstatic about me. At their annual
draft meeting that year, they posed this question: Presume Bleier, at
185 pounds, is now a true 4.8 seconds in the forty-yard dash. If he gains,
say, twelve pounds to 197, will he then be a 4.95 or a 5.0 in the forty?

Projections like that are what scouts get paid for. At 197 pounds and
4.8 seconds, they figured I was worth a gamble. Any lighter or slower, I
couldn't play in the NFL.

On the second day of the draft, two men pleaded, and eventually
sold, my case. One was Don Heinrich, the Steeler backfield coach who
had rated me so highly in his report. The other was Ken Stilley, who
wrote: "I don't think this boy can make a pro club." Ken was, however,
a Notre Dame man who allowed himself to stray from objectivity on
occasion. He was also the BLESTO-V scout assigned to phone the
Steelers periodically during the draft and give his opinion on the talent
still available.

Stilley began his pitch low-key on the tenth-round conference call.
"This kid Bleier," he said, "is not a bad pick now."

After the thirteenth round, he mentioned, "Don't forget Bleier."

After the fifteenth round, Stilley let his voice rise a little. "Holy
heck, this guy's a steal now. He's a steal."

That's when Heinrich picked up my banner. "The kid has all the
intangibles," he said. "Let's take a chance on him. Maybe he can take
the twelve pounds without losing the step. Hell, this is the sixteenth
round. We can take the kid on his heart alone." So, one round before the
end, as the general managers were yawning, almost falling asleep after
twelve hours' work, an NFL spokesman stood at the front of a New York
hotel ballroom and droned, "Detroit takes Robert Rokita, defensive
end, Arizona State . . . Pittsburgh takes Rocky Bleier, running back,
Notre Dame . . . Miami takes Henry Still, defensive tackle,
Bethune-Cookman. . . ."

You'll notice that scouts have peculiar ways of talking to each other
and to their computers. They rate college players according to their
deficiencies. The poorer players, with more deficiencies, put more
"weight" into the computer. Consequently, they have higher ratings.

The cutoff point is 1.8. A player rated higher should not play in the
NFL. Anybody from 1.2 to 1.8 should make the team. From 0.9 to 1.2,
he should start as a rookie. From 0.7 to 0.9, he should play very well as
a rookie. From 0.0 to 0.7, he should be an NFL star in his first year. This

year's No. 1 draft choice, for instance, was a 0.6, Randy White of Maryland. The last man picked, 441 players later, was Stan Hegener of Kearney State in Nebraska, whom the Steelers rated 2.1.

I was rated between 2.2 and 2.4. The worst rating they assign is 2.5. Of our Pittsburgh starters in the Super Bowl, nobody was rated as poorly as me. For example, Terry Bradshaw was a 0.9, Franco Harris 1.0, Larry Brown 1.5, Frank Lewis 1.0, Ron Shanklin 1.3. Only Jim Clack, our left guard, was even close to my rating. He was a strong 2.2, and signed as a free agent . . . a player not drafted. I probably would have been a free agent, too, if not for the exposure Notre Dame gave me.

The scouts put me in that category of competent, hard-nosed, productive college players who have glaring physical weakness. Dick Haley, the Steelers' director of player personnel, explained it to me this way: "Every year, there are fifteen wide receivers, for instance, who have the intangibles, but not the size or speed. Only one or two of them will overcome the physical handicap and play five or six years in the league. At the time of the draft, we don't know which one . . . the one who will become a Raymond Berry or a Howard Twilley. I often say to myself, 'Will the real player please stand up?' "

So those were my odds of making it in the NFL. About 1 in 15.

At the time of the draft, I was riding around campus with my injured knee propped up in a golf cart. That was the symbol of a fallen warrior at Notre Dame. The university maintained a fleet of carts, ostensibly to give comfort to athletes wearing leg casts.

Frequently, however, athletes would respond to the university's generosity by racing their vehicles through the bushes and across the well-manicured lawns of the main quadrangle. At midnight, so no one knew. Just for something to do. And between you and me, Terry Hanratty won most of those races.

It may also be revealed, for the first time in print, that Chuck Landolfi's cart lies rusting and corroded at the bottom of St. Joseph's Lake on campus. Landolfi was a running back from Ellwood City, Pennsylvania, who broke his leg as a freshman. One night, while slightly under the influence, he drove his cart off the dock, bailing out just in time to see a big splash.

I guess the worst thing I ever did was ride eight guys to class one morning. I was more interested in relinquishing my golf cart. I couldn't wait to have the cast removed and start working out again.

Once I regained full range of motion in the knee, I started doing leg raises to strengthen the quadriceps. It had atrophied badly during the six weeks' encasement. At first, lifting ten pounds was difficult. But I stayed with it, exercising every day. By May, I could lift 100 pounds in three sets of ten repetitions apiece . . . with each leg.

For my upper body, I undertook a heavy weight program. I lifted every afternoon with Steve Quinn, a center who was on his way to the Houston Oilers. Though we both made hefty gains, neither of us reached our mutual goal . . . a bench press of 300 pounds. After lifting, we ran several laps around St. Joseph's and St. Mary's lakes. How well I remember that picturesque setting . . . the late-afternoon sun gleaming off the water, with the Golden Dome and Sacred Heart Church in the background. I might have appreciated the beauty a little more if I weren't hurting so badly. Those runs destroyed me . . . just burned out my cardiovascular system and left me for dead. Worse than that, Steve always beat me with a big, finishing kick. I worried, "I must really be in bad shape if this two-hundred-fifty-five-pound lineman can outrun me."

After graduation, I returned to Appleton and ground out six weeks of solid, uninterrupted, undistracted workouts. I got up each day at ten o'clock, and went to the YMCA to lift. At noon, I ate lunch . . . always a steak and malted milk. After a quick nap, I went to the Appleton High track and strapped on ten-pound ankle weights.

Struggling with that extra burden, I followed a running program the Steelers had sent me. Every day for the first two weeks, I ran a mile, followed immediately by four forty-yard dashes, four thirties, four twenties, and four tens. The next two weeks, I ran a mile and a half, then six forties, thirties, twenties, and tens. The last two weeks, I ran two miles, then eight forties, thirties, twenties, and tens. All that with no rest between intervals.

I was in the greatest shape of my life, up to that time. I even made the 300-pound bench press, and, naturally, called Steve Quinn with the good news. He was furious. The bad news came a few days later in the mail . . . my last-semester grades from Notre Dame. The English professor, whose four o'clock class I had cut to lift weights, gave me a D for my sketchy efforts.

Not even that, however, could depress me during the final week in Appleton. I was feeling confident and enthusiastic as I packed my '66 Mustang convertible for the drive to Pittsburgh. I took everything I owned—clothes, guitar, golf clubs. If I didn't make the team, I figured I'd take a drive South, stop a week or two in Florida, see some friends, then return to Appleton and plan the future. I had some vague notions about law school, but I hadn't applied anywhere, nor had I taken the law boards. All I really wanted to do was play pro football.

Two minutes into downtown Pittsburgh, I was rudely introduced to the fact that none of the streets run parallel. God's three rivers made the land a triangle, so man constructed his streets the same confusing way. And left me hopelessly lost in search of the Steelers' offices.

Finally, I found them, parked across Sixth Avenue, and checked into the Roosevelt Hotel. Next morning, I met the coaches, took a physical, weighed in at a beefy 205 pounds, and agreed to arrive at training camp in the evening. I walked across the street, and lo and behold, there in the parking lot was an empty car. Mine.

Devoid of my belongings. Everything I once owned was stolen. I mean everything, including all my football shoes.

Bad as that was, there was worse news awaiting me at St. Vincent College, our training camp in Latrobe, about seventy miles east of Pittsburgh. The Steelers were trying to field a squad for a rookie scrimmage with Cleveland in two weeks. They were short on receivers, so they made me a flanker. I was bulked up to 205, thinking I'd be a running back . . . and here they were looking for the quick cuts and deft moves of a receiver. The extra weight had slowed my forty-yard time to five seconds flat. There was no way I could make the team as a flanker.

I got a break within a few days, however. One of the rookie running backs, Jay Calabrese of Duke, had stepped on a piece of glass in a swimming pool the week before we reported. Now it was bothering him, so the coaches substituted me for Jay. I was the leading ball carrier in the Cleveland scrimmage and scored a touchdown . . . offsetting one by my old teammate, Tom Schoen, for the Browns.

But I was still light-years away from making the team. There was a superquick rookie named Byron McCane running beside me. And the veteran backs were coming in—Dick Hoak, Willie Asbury, Earl Gros, Don Shy.

The arrival of the veterans also meant the resumption of a fine old Steeler tradition . . . happy hour before dinner. During two-a-day practices, we were off the field at four thirty, with dinner scheduled for six. So, if you showered in about a minute and fifteen seconds, dressed on the way to the parking lot, and drove the country roads of Latrobe like Jackie Stewart at Monte Carlo, you'd have exactly one hour of heaven in a little pub called The Nineteenth Hole.

It was Paul Martha, a defensive back and off-season attorney, who first explained it to me. He said, "Bleier, I like you. You're a good kid. You worked hard out there today, and I think it's time you replaced some of your natural body fluids. Besides, the biggest hell-raisers in the NFL have consistently come from Notre Dame—great names like Paul Hornung, Monty Stickles, Myron Pottios, Mike Lind. I'd like to see you uphold that tradition. I never met a man from Notre Dame who couldn't drink beer, and drink it well, in large quantities. I'm betting on you this afternoon at The Nineteenth Hole."

The veterans would bet each other which rookie could drink the most beer. (You can imagine the pressure it placed on us rookies.) But in Martha's case, this was an act of sympathy. The first day he saw me, he was convinced I couldn't make the team. He thought I was too slow, top-heavy from all the weight lifting and prone to muscle pulls in my legs. He was just trying to show me a good time before I was cut.

What he didn't know was that I hadn't had more than one drink per evening since my little spree on the night the Steelers drafted me. I guess I was still inhibited by my ideal of the Notre Dame captain. It was simply understood that he didn't smoke or drink in public. My good friends Tom Schoen and John Pergine would hide beer under their beds and crush out cigarettes when I'd come into their room. That's how strong the captaincy image was.

But I didn't feel I could explain it to Paul Martha. So I dutifully drank every beer he placed in front of me that first evening. Which was thirteen. (Another night, a big rookie tackle named Ernie Ruple of Arkansas drank that many shots of whiskey, and favored us with a like number of "sooooooooooooooooey pig" hog calls before passing out in a contest with Ben McGee.) I was also assigned to take the little aluminum ring-top from every veteran's beer can and fasten them into a chain. They cut my fingers a thousand different ways, but I was too drunk to care.

Martha told me that when he was a rookie, in 1964, the place to drink was Iggy's, in Warwick, Rhode Island, near the old Steeler training camp at the University of Rhode Island in Kingston. Bobby Layne, the grizzled quarterback, would load his rookies into the back of a pickup truck for a night on the town. Then, after they'd drunk to Layne's satisfaction, he'd drive them back to camp, as they barfed over the sides of the truck.

We heard lots of stories about those great old days in Rhode Island. Martha told me that, if anything, they were understated. The coach, Buddy Parker, told his players he didn't care what they did off the field. And the players took Buddy at his word. They were on campus with thousands of URI coeds, and fifteen minutes away from a beautiful summer resort, Narragansett Bay. It was an early night for Bobby Layne if he found his dorm room by 4:00 A.M.

On the field, things weren't much different. Parker insisted the team run a two-mile trail through the woods every day after practice. The veterans would run until they were out of his view, then sit down on tree stumps and pull out the cigarettes they'd hidden under their jerseys. After the rookies had run the outlying section of the course, the vets would get up and rejoin the pack as it headed back toward Parker, who stood with stopwatch in hand, screaming for a final sprint. Layne would pant breathlessly, "Goddam, Buddy. That gets tougher every day."

Not even the rookies got in shape in those days. In 1966, Pittsburgh's first draft choice was a fullback from West Virginia, Dick Leftridge. He was a local boy, and supposedly the big, fast back who would give oomph to the offense. Well, Dick showed up in Rhode Island plenty big, all right. He was 250 pounds, thirty pounds over his playing weight.

After a hot afternoon practice, he'd always be the last man staggering off the field. By the time he got undressed, everybody else had showered. And as the drinkers sprinted off to Iggy's, they would stop for one final look at the spectacle of their No. 1 draft choice. Leftridge would have all the shower nozzles pointed to the middle of the floor, the water turned as cold as possible. He'd be lying on the floor in the midst of this torrent, his great, oversize body gasping for air and moaning with relief.

Pittsburgh never won anything in those days, of course. In fact, until 1972, the Steelers had been in the league forty years without winning so much as a division title. They came close, however, in 1963. Entering the final game, they were 7–3–3, a bizarre record befitting a bizarre team.

Parker had spent the season shuffling his personnel in fits of rage and superstition. For instance, he cut a very good offensive guard, Lou Cordileone, on the flight back to Pittsburgh after a defeat. Somebody told Lou a joke, Buddy heard him laugh, and he was gone. Eventually, players took to hiding in lavatories or under blankets to avoid Parker's tantrums. But for Lou, it was too late. The next day, as the Steelers watched film, Buddy spotted several good blocks and asked, "Who was that?"

Each time came the answer, "Cordileone."

Somehow, despite all that, the Steelers had only to beat the Giants in New York to win the Eastern Division. But their quarterback was not up to it. Ed Brown was thirty-five years old by this time . . . a nervous type, a bachelor, and a drinker of no small capacity. He'd had several bad games late in the season, so he decided to go into serious training for the Giant game. He went "on the wagon," and his system couldn't take the shock. By kickoff, his hands were shaking visibly and he was feeling slightly irritable. Bobby Layne, the quarterback coach that year, called down a play to him from the press box in the first quarter, and Brown knocked the headset off Bobby's ears by screaming, "That's the dumbest play I ever heard of." Pittsburgh lost the game, 33–17.

Parker did not have what you would call a strong staff. His receiver coach, for a prime example, assigned to convert Martha from a college running back to a pro flanker, handed him several thousand feet of film.

"What's this?" Martha asked.

"Film of Buddy Dial, the best receiver we ever had here," the coach replied. "You study those films and you'll become a great one, just like him."

"But, but, but," Martha stammered. "Aren't you going to show me some moves and techniques on the field?"

"Oh, no," said the coach. "I don't know any more than you do about this stuff. We're going to have to learn it together."

Layne, meanwhile, would disappear Sunday night, after each game. Parker would tell the team he was scouting college players. When Layne reappeared on Wednesday, *he* would tell the team what a great time he'd had in New York raising hell with his good buddy, Mickey Mantle.

Layne and Parker were amusing, but of all the characters of that era, they tell me the Hall of Famer was Bill Saul. He was a kid from a coal-mining family in Butler, Pennsylvania.

Saul was simply bigger than, was stronger than, was tougher than, smoked more than, drank more than, played cards better than, shot pool better than, and buried his helmet in your numbers harder than anybody around. We don't have people like Saul in the NFL any longer. He could, literally, drink a case of beer and smoke a pack of cigarettes until two in the morning . . . then come to practice at ten o'clock and perform better than anybody on the field.

That first night at The Nineteenth Hole, Bill showed me his famous no-hands trick. He fit his mouth firmly around a glass of draft beer. Then, without using his hands, he raised the glass, opened his gullet, and chug-a-lugged the whole thing. Incredible!

It was an incident with Saul, they told me, that led to the demise of Bill Austin, the Steelers' head coach from 1966 to 1968. Late in the preseason of 1967, Austin exploded at an afternoon practice. It was hot and humid, threatening rain, and the players were weary of two-a-days. Austin raged, "Goddam it, we'll run 'live' goal line till I see something I like." He pitted his No. 1 offensive unit against his No. 1 defense for a series of running plays. In the National Football League, that is positively unheard of. Forty-five minutes later, everybody knew why.

The first man injured was Saul. He tore up his knee so badly that he never played again with any effectiveness. Then Ken Kortas, a defensive tackle of huge dimensions and potential, hurt his ankle. Then Jim "Cannonball" Butler injured his knee, and the team had lost its outside threat on offense. Then Martha made a hit, and the suspension in his helmet collapsed. The helmet split, leaving him with a concussion and a bad cut over his right eye.

Finally, Austin put an end to this "game." But the damage was done. It was too late to replace any of the four injured, especially Saul. He was a true leader and the hub of a defense that had jelled near the end of '66. With that defense and Austin's abilities as an offensive coach, the Steelers had come to camp in 1967 thinking they might have a good year. But after the senseless carnage of that scrimmage, the feeling was gone. And so was all respect for Bill Austin.

When I arrived in 1968, he was in the last season of a three-year contract. It seemed the players sensed his vulnerability and exploited it. Roy Jefferson, in particular, used his leverage as player representative to defy him.

One evening in camp, several guys had a playful battle with water buckets and fire extinguishers. Austin was infuriated when he heard of it, but Jefferson persuaded him not to discipline the players involved. The next day at a team meeting, Austin said, "I know about last night. I know some of you don't have the maturity to handle professional football, but I wish you'd try. I think you should stop acting like little boys. Isn't that right, Roy?"

Jefferson jumped up and screamed, "You said you wouldn't mention this. I thought we agreed to handle it man to man."

Austin was silent for a second as his face flushed. Then he said, "Talking back to the head coach will get you a hundred-dollar fine."

Jefferson screamed again, "Why don't you make it two hundred?"

Austin said, "Okay, two hundred dollars."

Jefferson bid one more time. "Make it three hundred."

Austin screeched, "You got it." But nothing was ever done about the fine.

Jefferson got the best of his coach another time. In a film session, Austin ordered several replays of Jefferson dropping a long touchdown pass from Dick Shiner. He said, "With performances like this, we'll never win in the NFL. These are important plays. These are plays we have to make if we want to win."

Jefferson finally snapped, "Go to hell. I couldn't reach the fuckin' ball. Nobody could. If you were a better coach, you wouldn't have to rely on me to catch the bomb every down."

Ironic, isn't it, that they're together again with the Washington Redskins.

Jefferson wasn't the only player who flaunted Austin's authority. Don Shy listened to a critique of his running one afternoon in the locker room, then turned away from Austin and said, over his shoulder, "What the fuck do you know about it?"

That sentiment was completely foreign to me, after playing for Ara Parseghian. He was man of such passion for winning that our respect for him was automatic. At squad meetings, he'd lionize teams like Iowa and Army, making us feel we'd have to play the game of our lives to beat a thirty-point underdog. And in pregame speeches, he'd fire us like a blast furnace. Ara would cock his head to the side, work over his chewing gum, and pace among us. I don't remember many of the words he used, because they didn't seem important. It was his tightly drawn posture, the cords that stood out in his neck, the desire that seemed to run through his fibers and fuel his body. If Ara had a fault as a coach, maybe it was this intensity. Sometimes he'd get us so high and so tight before a game that we didn't relax and play naturally until the second quarter.

With Austin and the Steelers, however, no such danger existed. The first time I started in a training camp scrimmage, I rushed into the huddle, bubbling, "Come on, guys. Let's go, let's get after it."

One of the veterans looked at me and said, "Cut out the college rah-rah shit. Just do your job, kid. That's what you're getting paid for."

There was also a big difference in technique between Notre Dame and the Steelers. Pagna and Parseghian had analyzed and refined their offense so thoroughly that they had a method for everything.

Not so with the Steelers. One morning in camp, Heinrich, the backfield coach, asked me how we ran an off-tackle play at Notre Dame. So I showed him: crossover step, step, plant, and hit the hole. Each was a precise movement.

Heinrich then told the backs, "Try Rocky's method to see if you like it. We don't really care how you run it. Just do whatever feels natural."

I liked the new freedom to express my creativity as a runner. In an exhibition game at San Diego, I actually reversed my field on a sweep and gained thirteen yards . . . something I never would have done at Notre Dame. I suddenly realized Ara and Tom had made me a mechanical, rigid, structured runner. While there may be debatable merit to that, it cannot be argued that their teaching made me the Steelers' best-prepared rookie in 1968.

None of the Steeler receivers, for example, could take their three-point stance left-handed. Coach "Bones" Taylor once tried to explain how they could save a step by taking a left-handed stance when throwing a crack-back block from the right. But none of them could do it. "Bones" asked if anybody on the team could, and I was the only guy who raised his hand. That's the first thing we learned in freshman year at Notre Dame. And it's a technique I still use—lined up on the right side of the center, I take a left-handed stance; and vice versa.

Those kinds of fundamentals, probably more than anything else, are what helped me make the team. I got a big chance during that preseason game in San Diego when Shy hurt his shoulder on the first snap. I played the rest of the game and outgained all the Charger rushers combined, with sixty-one yards.

I started the next week against Cincinnati. Then, against Washington, I scored my first professional touchdown on a marvelous evening. I felt quick—diving, twisting, jumping—and fast in the open field. One run, I broke for thirty-six yards. I had a nothing-to-lose attitude as the final cut drew near, so I played with the kind of abandon that reminded me of my high school years.

Alas, once the season began, I found myself on the bench. If this was to be Austin's last year—and it was—he was going down with veterans. Rookies were strictly for the special teams, in his view. I ran the ball only fourteen times all year, for fifty-three yards. Even more frustrating was the specter of Earl Gros, our starting fullback. Rightly or wrongly, I felt I could fall forward farther than he was running.

It was a dismal year. While the players spent their time pointing fingers at each other, Austin lost trust in all of us. They say the ultimate, in that regard, was Joe Schmidt, the Lions' coach, who once accused his players of talking about him in the huddle. Well, Austin was not far behind. He charged that some players were not putting out intentionally . . . as a means of getting him fired.

Bill was from the Vince Lombardi school of coaching, which favors ranting and raving, pushing and cajoling. With Lombardi, there was a loving personality under the crust, which came through to his players. With Austin, there was nothing. Often, we'd see him after he'd had several drinks, scratching the middle of his chest in a nervous habit. That '68 season, he nearly scratched a fracture in his breastbone.

The first victory of our 2–11–1 year came in the "O. J. Simpson Bowl." We entered the game 0–6 against Philadelphia, which was 1–5. At that time, it seemed the loser would finish with the NFL's worst record, and therefore earn the right to select O.J. in the college draft.

The game was just what you might expect . . . sloppy tackling, poor execution, and stagnant offense directed by two of the greatest dink-shot passers of our time, Dick Shiner and Norm Snead. It was humiliating to be a party to it. We finally won, 6–3, on two field goals by Booth Lusteg, our eccentric kicker.

Booth warmed up for his game-winning boots by kicking paper cups along the sideline. One of his practice kicks, in fact, took with it a glob of mud and struck Ben McGee in the face. Ben would have killed Booth, except we didn't have another field-goal specialist. So we beat the Eagles, which prompted some fans to complain, "The Steelers can't do anything right. They can't even win O. J. Simpson by losing."

I understood their complaints. Sometimes I even agreed with them. Except for the guy who broke into my car, I came to enjoy the people of Pittsburgh that year. They are honest, hardworking folks, ethnic and blue-collared, much like the people of Appleton. And they're astonishingly small-town, considering they're the tenth-largest market in the country. That's because the city is not large at its urban center. Pittsburgh is really Baldwin and Shaler Township and Creighton and Elizabeth and West Mifflin and Natrona Heights.

Liking them as much as I did, I was a little disappointed that 'Burghers did not feel more civic pride. Their city is beautiful, especially downtown . . . not at all the smoking, smoggy dungeon I recall from my grade-school geography lessons. Perhaps their sports teams had given them the loser's syndrome. Whatever the cause, I was sorry they didn't defend themselves against the sick jokes which might be applied rightfully to places like Buffalo and Philadelphia.

I was as fascinated to hear them talk as they must have been to hear me. We Wisconsinians have a distinctive dialect. "Fine" comes out "fie-in." "Band" is "bay-ind." "Hot" is "hut." "Gag" is "gaig." "Yard" is "yerd." "Roof" becomes "ruuf." "Their" is "thur." Long *o* comes from deep in the throat and acquires a *w*, such as "no-w" for "no," and "go-w" for "go."

In Pittsburgh, long *e* becomes short *i*. So the "O. J. Simpson Bowl" was the "Stillers" against the "Iggles." If you wanted me to tackle the ball carrier in that game, you screamed from the stands, "Git 'im, Blire." In Wisconsin, my name is the full, two-syllable "Bligh-er." In Pittsburgh, it's "Blire."

Long *a* becomes short *e* in Pittsburgh. "Sale" is "sell." Even short *a* becomes short *e* sometimes. As in the "Ellegheny River." The plural of "you" is "y'uns." "Couldn't" is "coun't." "Up there" is "up-air," and "down there" is "dahn-air." "Sewer" is "sore," and "we'll" is "wool."

But the most fun about Pittsburgh is its zany characters. Larry Merchant of the *New York Post* once wrote, "Pittsburgh has more characters per square inch than any other city in America." Most of them, it seems, are found in the Oakland section of town, where I lived for several years, and where the University of Pittsburgh is located.

The boys from Oakland are like this: In the fifties, several of them got roles as "extras" when the movie *Angels in the Outfield* was filmed at Forbes Field. After shooting was complete, the production manager distributed $15 envelopes at an exit gate. But the Oakland boys, not satisfied that their thespian talents had been justly rewarded. slipped back into the stadium and rejoined the line. Some of them went through three and four times, until the Hollywood paymaster threw up his hands and exclaimed, "Jesus Christ, we got more extras than *Gone with the Wind.*

Most any time of the day or night, the boys can be found discussing Pitt football. They're true fans. When Dave Hart walked into the Oakland Cafe after accepting the head coaching job in 1966, one of them said, "Congratulations, Dave. We not only hope you win, we hope you beat the point spread."

The sports publicity man at Pitt in the sixties was a fellow named Carroll "Beano" Cook. Among Beano's classic stories is a tale from 1963. Pitt was in the midst of a 9–1 season, its best in many years, led by the ubiquitous Paul Martha. One afternoon, Beano saw several assistant trainers carrying an athlete on a stretcher from one of Pitt's practice fields. Rushing to the scene, he was confronted by a gentleman, obviously panicked, who told him, "This is John Simons, the star of our soccer team. He just broke his leg in practice."

Beano gazed down on the young man writhing in pain and biting his lip. Nonchalantly, he observed, "Better he than Paul Martha."

The gentleman gasped a moment before displaying his indignation. He was Mr. Simons, the soccer player's father, and he was on his way to the administration building to withdraw his considerable financial support of the university.

For his part, Beano was admonished loud and long by a Pitt vice-president and the athletic director. Asked if he had any defense whatsoever for his ignorant behavior, Beano replied, "Yes. I still maintain I'm right. We have to play Syracuse this week. It *is* better that a soccer player break his leg than Paul Martha."

Oakland also had its share of Notre Dame fans. Primary among them was Joey "Big Face" Diven, once the world's greatest street fighter according to the legions who felt his right hand, but now a law-abiding county detective. Pittsburgher Billy Conn—himself a pretty good street fighter before he became middleweight champion of the world—scored the most devastating punch of his career against Joey

. . . verbally. "County detective?" he said. "Joey, you couldn't find a bottle of ketchup in the Heinz plant."

Joey is a big, lovable guy who looks like Rodney Dangerfield, and he's nearly as gentle. There was a day, however, when he could be stirred into action. In 1951, for instance, a center for the Pitt football team, Harold Hunter, picked a "hey-rube" (as the 'Burghers refer to it) with a friend of Diven's. Joey retaliated by pounding Hunter and a large portion of the Pitt team into submission, three days before their game with Notre Dame. It became kind of a tradition. Just to be sure the Panthers wouldn't bother any more of his friends, Joey beat up half the team for three consecutive years . . . always in the week of the Notre Dame game. So the Irish would get full benefit.

Joey used to stand on the ND sideline as a combination inspiration-security man. After every Pitt–Notre Dame game for twenty years, he'd walk to the center of the field and shake hands with George "Yutzie" Pascarelli, the greatest Panther fan in town. Just like the coaches did.

Yutzie was a Pitt student during the Depression. He worked all night selling newspapers, then came to class exhausted and fell asleep. The professors asked him why he couldn't stay alert, and Yutzie told them he couldn't afford to give up his job and the $12 a week it earned him. The profs said, hell, at those wages, he was wasting his time in college. So he quit. Yutzie spent the next forty-five years selling newspapers at the corner of Forbes and Atwood in Oakland. And shaking hands once every football season with Joey Diven.

Another Notre Dame diehard is Charlie "Lump" Jones, who earned his nickname by choking on two free throws in the final minute of a high school basketball game. With absolute precision, Lump imitates Joe Boland, the radio voice of Notre Dame in the fifties:

> Good afternoon, ladies and gentlemen, from South Bend, Indiana, on a cold and cloudy day, with the wind out of the northwest at fourteen miles an hour and the Golden Dome in the background. The Irish are poised in the tunnel, garbed in their green jerseys with white numerals, and when they come down that ramp, they'll run a little faster and tackle a little harder for Our Lady. Notre Dame football is brought to you by Codine, the amazing cold remedy that stops colds fast. And by Pontiac, the only car with wide-track wheels.

Lump can give you starting lineups, complete with heights,

weights, and hometowns, from the famous 1957 Notre Dame–Oklahoma game . . . and play-by-play on the eighty-yard, twenty-play drive in 3:19 that broke Oklahoma's forty-seven-game winning streak. All of it from memory.

He can also rend your heart with a song or a verse. Here's an old Irish lyric he adapted to describe my football career through one year with the Pittsburgh Steelers:

> You may treat him with scorn and derision,
> You may bring a hot tear to his eye.
> You may say with a sneer, when a running back appears,
> That the Rock need not apply.
>
> But when I think of the heroes the Dome has produced,
> And the glorious deeds they have done,
> He'll still play his part and say from his heart,
> He's proud he's a Notre Dame son.

5] *Drafted Again*

I found out I'd made the '68 Steelers in a strange way. Near the end of training camp, Bill Austin sent word he wanted to see me. Normally, in pro football, that can mean only one thing . . . you're about to be cut. I was positively terrified as I went to see him, trying to recall what I'd done wrong in practice.

Austin said, "Rocky, we got a notice from your draft board in Appleton, Wisconsin, today. Your student deferment has expired, so you're being reclassified 1-A." I didn't understand. What did he care? Austin smiled at the puzzled look on my face.

"We'll get this taken care of," he said. "We think you're good enough that you'll make the team."

If he said anything else, I don't remember it. I tried to act calm, floating out of his office. But once I got outside, I cut loose a big "Yipeeeee!" A couple nuns passing on the sidewalk looked at me like I was crazy. In that moment of euphoria, I never dreamed that the next few months would be such a bureaucratic tangle.

Our business manager had, as an ancillary duty, the task of keeping us in black-and-gold uniforms, and out of drab, olive green. His job had grown increasingly more difficult, though. With the Vietnam War at its hottest, National Guard and reserve units were jammed with applicants. And the Steelers had recently lost their two primary contacts for placement . . . a congressman who was defeated in the '68 elections, and an Army general who passed away.

In September, the Appleton board ordered me to take a preinduction physical. I passed, of course, which meant I had three weeks to file for deferment, or to find a reserve unit. If not, I was subject to be called for induction immediately, depending on the needs and wishes of the Appleton board.

I had never thought much about military service. I guess I regarded it like a lot of unpleasant things in life . . . if I had to do it, I had to do it. No sense complaining.

But the Steelers told me not to worry, they'd get me into a reserve unit. A month went by without any word. Then, in October, I discovered there was an opening in New Kensington. I went to see the commanding officer, but he said his meetings were on Sundays, game days for me. He was sorry, he couldn't help me.

Later that month, another letter came from Appleton. This one contained the chilling phrase, "Greetings from the President . . ." I was drafted. And a little frightened. The Steelers told me to transfer my records to Pittsburgh. That would buy me thirty days, at least.

In a week, the club found a spot in a Washington, Pennsylvania, National Guard unit. "Go down there and get into this outfit, no matter what," were the business manager's directions. "Even if you have to lie, just get into it. We'll handle it from there."

The commander in Washington asked me the magic question: "Have you received your draft notice?" I said no. And he swore me in. He also agreed to ignore the fact that I played football on Sundays and couldn't begin attending meetings until the end of the season.

Meanwhile, notice of my membership in the National Guard was passed from Pittsburgh to Madison to the Appleton board, which did not take it sitting down. Appleton retained ultimate jurisdiction over my case, since it had drafted me. When the board learned I'd contacted the National Guard, it responded by serving me an induction notice.

That notice was lost in the mail several days and did not reach me until November 27, 1968. It was lying on a table in the locker room at Pitt Stadium, the Steelers' home in those days. I opened it gingerly, as if I expected it to explode. And it kind of did.

It read, "You are ordered to report at 7:00 A.M. on November 28, 1968, at the APO Station in the Federal Building, Grant Street, Pittsburgh, Pennsylvania, to be inducted into the armed service of your country. Bring this notice with you."

The next day! Eighteen hours from now!

My mind was spinning as emotions gushed through me in a whirlpool—anger, fear, uncertainty.

The Steelers sent me to see Colonel Donald Neff of the Marine Reserve, a longtime football and basketball official, and friend of the Rooneys. Colonel Neff advised me to become an officer in the Marines. He said he could get me into the next class, which didn't report until January, 1969. If we could get the Appleton board to agree, I could play the season's last three games.

I said okay. He called Appleton to confirm it. But the board demanded a written guarantee from Colonel Neff that I'd have a place in the January class . . . a guarantee he couldn't give.

The next morning, before I went to face the music, Colonel Neff called me again. He said, "Rocky, don't you have an old leg injury that we can mark on your records? All football players have some kind of leg injury. That way, they'll hold you over for consultation, which is another thirty days. You can finish the season, then go to basic training on Parris Island, and transfer to the Marines' Officer Candidate School."

"Sure, I've had leg injuries," I replied, "but none that is bothering me now. Besides, the Appleton board would probably want me to fly out to be examined by their doctors."

"I guess you're right," said Colonel Neff. "All we can give you is twenty-four hours for high blood pressure."

I told him that would be no exaggeration. I did, indeed, have high blood pressure. I'd have to report the next day, Friday.

Thursday night, I called Tom DeRosa, a golf pro from Greensburg, Pennsylvania, who had won a tryout with the Steelers in 1968 as a kicking specialist. He had been in the Army Reserve for several years, so I valued his counsel. Tom said, "Whatever you do, don't join the Marines, and especially, don't become an officer. Go in as a draftee. You might be able to get an 'early-out' in the summer of 1970, because your occupation is seasonal. Then you'd only miss the 1969 season."

Friday morning, another conversation convinced me Tom was correct. The doctor who'd examined me Thursday took me aside and asked, "Rocky, do you really want to go into the Marines?"

I said, "Gee, I really don't know. The colonel's been pretty good to me."

He said, "Yeah, but one thing you have to realize is that the colonel's not going to be with you on Parris Island. Another thing, the Marines are a fighting unit. They'll be in Vietnam for sure. In the Army, at least you have a chance of getting an MOS [Military Occupational Specialty] other than infantry. You might get clerk-typist, or something else here in the States."

You must be getting the notion that I was like a piece of tumbleweed on this matter. And I was . . . pushed and pulled, at whim, by all sorts of forces. I followed everybody's instructions . . . the business manager's, Colonel Neff's, Tom DeRosa's, the doctor's. I was so disoriented by the swiftly moving events, I never sat down and asked myself, "What do *I* want to do?"

Worse than that, I never asked my conscience, "How ethical is this?"

On the question of placing players in reserve units, Dan Rooney, the Steelers' vice president, maintains this rationale: "The government has designed its own military system and made these spots available. We think we have excellent people, who can enhance the quality of these military units. So we're actually doing a favor for the Army and Navy and National Guard, while keeping our players available for football."

But in retrospect, it seems more a question of influence. Is it right for the Steelers—or for any group or individual—to use the influence of a congressman and a general? Especially when it's clear that not everybody has access to them?

Besides, I had another reservation. Recurring through those hectic weeks of maneuvering was a question: If I ever get married, what will I tell my son when he asks where I was during the war? Will I have to tell him I was playing football? That I had somebody sneak me into a reserve unit so I wouldn't have to fight? What kind of a thing is that to tell your son? Looking back from current perspective, I'm glad I don't have to face that problem.

On the question of lying to the National Guard commander in Washington, Pennsylvania, there's no doubt I was wrong. At the time, I convinced myself that I was Steeler property, and that I should lie if they told me to lie. But as far back as grade-school religion classes, I can recall the relevant Catholic teaching: No superior has the moral right to direct you to sin.

With respect to Colonel Neff and the doctor, I was again guilty of subverting my conscience. I told myself everybody was pulling strings, nobody wanted to go to Vietnam, the colonel and doctor were doing these things on their own. And there may have been some truth in that. But the essential fact is this: I knew they were violating *my* moral standards and *their* moral standards on my behalf. And I did nothing to stop them.

I did what I did because it all seemed so monstrously unfair. Almost nobody had given me a chance to make the Steeler team. I had lifted weights, I had run sprints, I had studied the playbook, I had blasted the blocking sled, I had sweated, I had worked my ass off. *I* had done it. I had become the only thing in life I really wanted to be. I was a professional football player . . . and then, suddenly, it was over.

The day before induction, I stopped at the stadium to say good-bye. The team was in a film session, and I didn't stay long, because my emotions were near the surface. Tony Parisi was the last guy I saw. We shook hands as he let me out the door. His eyes were sad and full of empathy. He said, "Jesus, Rock, you worked so *hard.*" Before I could react, or he could say more, I turned and ran out.

I remember the opening kickoff against Cleveland in late season, when I knew I'd been drafted. I raced downfield, wanting to be injured. I saw their kickoff wedge form, and I hurled myself into it. Three of the Browns hit me, and then one ran over me. He actually stepped on my leg with one foot and my chest with the other. Shots of pain went through me in all directions, but I didn't wince. I almost smiled. I lay there for a second, thinking, "I hope I broke a bone, or cracked a rib. Maybe it'll be bad enough that I won't pass my Army physical." No luck.

I recognize it might make a better story if I'd been more heroic. But let's tell it like it is: I wanted to keep playing pro football. I don't submit that as a defense for my attempts at draft evasion, because I regard those as indefensible. I just wanted to keep the position I'd earned.

Once I took the oath, however, I committed myself fully to the Army life-style. Sure, there were moments on that flight to Fort Jackson, South Carolina, when I thought, "Rock, yesterday you had a three-hundred-dollar apartment, a month-old Corvette, and a place in the National Football League. Tonight, you are US 52861914."

I thought about it plenty as we arrived and were herded like convicts into buses by military police . . . as we were processed until 4:00 in the morning . . . as we stood in formation, shivering in a freezing rain, waiting for the induction center to be opened . . . as we gave up our civilian clothes and personal articles . . . as we were ordered to fall out at 6:00 A.M. after one hour's sleep. But from that morning forward, I refused to let myself look back. I was in the Army, and I was determined to start liking it.

I assure you, however, it took considerable effort. Especially the third night when I drew "fire-guard" duty. That's an honor which entitled me to stay awake all night, carrying buckets of coal to the furnace. In the morning, of course, I was expected to act like I'd had my normal eight hours' sleep. It was the kind of ordeal only Bill Saul could have enjoyed.

After a week at Fort Jackson, we were told to expect our drill instructors, who would take us to Fort Gordon, Georgia, for eight weeks of basic training. As we waited in the barracks, my imagination began to manufacture characters like the one played by Jack Webb in the movie *The DI.* Funny thing. The two guys who showed up were everything I had imagined.

One was about 5-feet-10, 230 pounds. All chest. Squat, blocky son of a bitch. The other guy was taller, about 6-feet-3, and meaner. I'm sure he must have practiced those faces in front of his mirror every morning. Two tough-asses. Cold-blooded. Right out of the stereotype. Tight crew cuts. When they walked into the barracks, it nearly scared us off our duffel bags.

"All right," the little one said in a very indifferent tone. "We're here to pick you up. We're not on a vacation. So when you get your ass into that bus, I want to you to get in there quick. All I want to see are elbows and assholes." I was so scared, I had to change my underwear twice along the way.

At Fort Gordon, we pulled up to our company barracks, C-42, and it was more of the same . . . except louder. "All right, this is your new home," the little guy screamed. "When I tell this bus to unload, I want to see everybody moving all at once. I want everybody off this bus within thirty seconds. I want you to line up in formation. All right, now move. Move! Move! Move! Move, you guys! Hurry up! Get those legs up! Get those bags up!"

From that point, it was everything I'd heard about the Army. Clean your weapon this way, polish your shoes that way, arrange your locker with the socks here and the handkerchiefs there, make your bed with square corners. Eventually, I used a sleeping bag on top of my bed, leaving those beautiful square corners untouched and ready for inspection at any time.

Harassment was a way of life. There was to be absolute silence in the chow hall, except for drill instructors who would prowl among the tables, yelling, "You're done, mister. Come on. Let's go, get out of here." We were to be given precisely two minutes from the time we got our food until our last bite. In the chow line, we were not to speak or move or look to either side. Any violation would precipitate this kind of scene with the DI:

"Mister, what's distracting you?"

"Nothing, sir."

"Mister, you were looking at something. Ten push-ups, and count for me."

"One, two, three, four, five, six . . ."

"I can't hear you."

"One, two, three, four, five, six, seven, eight . . ."

"What are you saying, mister? I can't hear you."

"One, two, three . . ."

It all began at 5:30 A.M., each man startled into a new day by the harsh overhead lights and a gravel voice that demanded, "All right, you guys. Get up, get up, let's go, let's move it."

Inside the drafty cinder-block barracks, twenty-five pairs of feet stepped hesitatingly onto the cold concrete floor. Then, with a rush, they all scurried to one of two potbelly stoves in either corner. We huddled together like a bunch of refugees, slipping our cold arms and legs into icy fatigues.

On the off-chance that hot water might still be available, we'd sprint outside to the lavatory. Showering and shaving in cold water was not fun, but it was the only alternative.

At six o'clock, we fell into formation, then moved to breakfast, platoon by platoon, according to neatness displayed during inspection. In eight weeks, our platoon never went to chow first. Never. Our captain actually ordered the sand and red Georgia clay around the barracks raked into neat little furrows. Still, we couldn't rate the top inspection grade.

After chow, we'd clean up once again before stripping down to T-shirts for morning physical training. PT began with this dialogue between the sergeant and his shivering men, who responded in chorus:

"Gentlemen, we're having PT this morning."

"Yes, sir."

"You guys want more PT?"

"Yes, sir."

"You guys *love* PT?"

"Yes, sir!"

The rest of the day was spent practicing your salute or about-face, forced marching, presenting arms, or firing your M-16 on the rifle range. There was no free time. We were in bed, and glad to be there, at eight thirty.

Things were a shade easier for me, because I was named assistant platoon sergeant. It was a dubious distinction, because it compelled me to listen to everybody's gripes. The benefits were two . . . a chance to march outside formation, and no KP.

My problems were one. Nerves. I couldn't handle all the screaming and regimental nonsense, so I began smoking for the first time in my life. With a ten-minute smoke break every hour and cigarettes at nineteen cents a pack, I couldn't afford not to.

But that's about all I did by way of indulging myself. Occasionally I'd get a terrible craving for chocolate candy or ice cream, two items not scheduled in our diet. I satisfied those urges by hiding a Hershey bar in my locker, and once, by sneaking off to a Dairy Queen, which stood just off base, temptingly within view of the barracks.

Television was also a small pacifier for the troops on Sunday afternoons. That is, if you liked the religious shows offered in the Bible Belt of northeast Georgia. We did get the Jets–Colts Super Bowl in January, 1969, and I watched it longingly as I spit-shined my marching boots.

After basic, we took a two-week leave before returning to Fort Gordon for AIT (advanced infantry training). Ninety percent of us had been assigned infantry as our MOS, thus ensuring a tour in Vietnam.

The major difference between basic and AIT was the thickness of our beds. In basic, we had only an inch-and-a-half mattress. During AIT, we had a box spring and mattress which totaled eight inches. Just like civilians have.

Most of the harassment stopped, as we began concentrating on the essentials of war. There was a "jungle school," for instance, which taught us the kinds of booby traps to expect in Vietnam. Officers showed us the poison-tipped "pungy sticks," sharp enough to puncture a boot, which were hidden deep in a hole, covered by bamboo grating and vegetation. They also showed us trip wires connected to hand grenades.

We played "war games." A sergeant dropped off a whole platoon in a field and told us to find our way to an imaginary base. He gave us each a compass and told us to beware a group of infiltrators, whose parts were played by other officers. Platoon members who were caught by infiltrators were often tortured—tied to a pole for several hours or physically abused.

They taught us survival techniques, as well. We learned that rattlesnake head can be eaten if it's been broiled sufficiently to kill all the poison. (You'd be surprised how tasty.) The most resourceful trick, however, was done with a chicken. Step by step, here is your own handy guide for chicken dinner with your bare hands:

Take the live chicken by the neck and wring it around several times before snapping its head off. Then reach into its rectum and find the point where all its skin comes together. Unfasten it and pull off the epidermis, including feathers, in one big sheet. That leaves you with a naked bird. Bite the chicken in its stomach. Now reach inside and clean out all the organs from the breastbone down to the intestine. If a freshwater stream is nearby, rinse thoroughly. Now fry or boil if a fire is available. Otherwise, raw chicken will fill you, if not delight you.

We spent lots of mornings on forced marches (running, jogging, fast walking) of eight and thirteen miles. The sergeants led us in singing old paratrooper songs: "I want to be an Airborne Ranger, I want to live the life of fun." Other days, we sang the very upbeat "Fort Gordon Boogie."

This soldier had his own ditty, sung privately and endlessly on afternoons when the sun was hot, the M-16 was heavy, the feet were sore, and the base was still five miles away. It's a tune I'd heard lots of years ago:

> That's okay, Rosie would say,
> Don't you worry none.
> We'll have good times, by and by,
> Next fall when the work is all done.

AIT ended with a "fire show" in a vast, empty field. They demonstrated how a squad could attack with several M-16 rifles, an M-60 machine gun, and an M-79 grenade launcher. Then they fired several rounds with an M-105 recoilless rifle, an M-155 cannon, and an M-175 artillery gun. We saw tanks and flamethrowers. Next, a Cobra gunship flew over and strafed the area with grenades and rockets. Then several jets flew by, dropping conventional bombs and napalm.

It was absolutely devastating. Grenades belched from the gunship at a rate of four per second. *Poof, poof, poof, poof.* The rockets appeared just as quickly, but came with the sound of a lasso spinning overhead. The napalm finale, though, was easily the most horrifying . . . a sheet of flame and smoke hundreds of feet in length and breadth. We spectators looked at each other in disbelief. Some guys cheered and applauded.

Impressive as it was, I took the awesome display of firepower to be poor substitution for a convincing, rational argument about Vietnam. In truth, I would have been satisfied with less. I would have been happy if somebody, anybody—a lieutenant, a general, a sergeant —had taken us into a room for half an hour and said, "Men, here is why we're going to Vietnam."

He could have spewed propaganda. He could have parroted the Johnson-Nixon line about fighting for the principle of self-determination in Southeast Asia. He could have told me the Communists were at our back door, and had to be stopped. No matter how faulty his reasoning, he would have pleased me. But we got nothing of the sort. Just a show of force to buck up our confidence.

While the lack of a sensible explanation disappointed me, I never let it affect my outlook. More than anything else, an attitude of complete acceptance got me through Vietnam. I never questioned. I kept my emotional stability. I simply did each day's work in an unthinking, detached, unemotional way . . . never debating my part in the cosmic issues of war and peace, life and death, American and Vietnamese politics.

We had young guys of seventeen or eighteen in Vietnam who

allowed their philosophies to rip them apart. Some of them went three months without smiling. They never got up and stretched in the morning, and said, "Gee, it's good to be alive," even if they *were* climbing out of a bunker.

Somebody had put a bug in their ears. They spent their days and nights in depressing, circuitous arguments about their own unfortunate fate and the hopelessness of the war . . . "Why do I have to fight? I don't hate these goddam gooks and dinks. I'm thousands of miles away from home, on their land. Why am I here?"

During my twenty-nine-day leave before shipping out to Vietnam, I made a conscious decision not to fall into that morass. Bitching while I was overseas wouldn't help, I knew. If I wanted to change the status quo, the time to do it was before my Vietnam tour.

But I never did much of that, either. I never filed an appeal with the Appleton board. It never occurred to me to apply for conscientious-objector status, as my brother Dan did several years later. I was in the mainstream at Notre Dame, which meant I was apolitical. I heard about peace moratoriums and demonstrations at the ROTC building, but that was something for the extreme Left. It all seemed very distant while I was in college.

In November, 1968, one of my Steeler teammates told me, "Why don't you sound off about it? Make some noise. Get some shit in the papers. You shouldn't have to go."

In basic training, a few guys recognized my name. One of them said, "Rocky, why don't you get your ass into Special Services like all the other celebrities in the Army. You don't think Elvis Presley ever did any fighting, do you?"

One of the guys who were inducted with me in Pittsburgh made several phone calls to a general and eventually became assistant soccer coach at West Point.

But that wasn't me. If I had to go, I was going like everybody else. I didn't want to disgrace all that I stood for. I was an eldest son, steeped in the American tradition. "God, Country, Notre Dame" is the inscription above the doors of Sacred Heart Church on campus. I believed in that. And you can add one more . . . "Family." I didn't want anyone to be ashamed of me.

In retrospect, there's one additional factor which didn't occur to me in 1969, but makes a lot of sense now. Deep in Catholic teaching, there is a doctrine that God wants—indeed expects—man to find adversity. The Bible refers to this life as a "vale of tears." The Gospels speak of each man carrying his own cross. Al Lison, my counselor at Xavier, calls it the "theology of suffering." When someone was done an injustice in our family, my mother would always say, "Well, you'll be a stronger person for it."

In a subliminal way, I think I accepted military service—almost welcomed it—because life had been so fruitful for me, to that point. Perhaps I was actually feeling guilty about my athletic and academic success. My subconscious may have *needed* a setback.

The last words I said to my mother in California before shipping out were, "I think it was meant to be this way."

That's the attitude I took with me, away from Travis Air Force Base, and out over the Pacific Ocean. The Lord wanted me to be inside that big troop carrier. He had an assignment for me, and he expected me to do it. I never questioned. I didn't think about getting shot or killed. The Lord would worry about that.

Most of my thoughts during the flight were directed toward my father. I hoped I hadn't embarrassed him during the twenty-nine days in Appleton. I'd had several drunken good times with my old high school pals. Nothing destructive, just several late evenings. The last one, in particular, was full of pathos.

In 1966, I'd gone out with Paul Schreiter on his last night before leaving for Vietnam. I watched with a mixture of sadness and pity as he began the night on beer, switched to ginger brandy, and finished on tequila at my dad's bar. At 3:30 A.M., he asked the group if we'd have one last pizza with him. Poor Paul, he wanted to make that night continue forever. I think his heartsickness was worse than his hangover when he staggered onto an airplane without any sleep at 7:00 A.M.

Now, three years later, Paul was back from Vietnam. He was among the crowd at *my* going-away party, probably thinking the same thoughts as I went from martinis, to ginger brandy, to a zombie with a martini chaser. I hoped my father wouldn't find out how sick I was.

More significantly, I hoped Dad wouldn't feel compelled to support my judgments and willingness to go to Vietnam. Several of my friends in Appleton had applied for conscientious-objector deferments. Soon, their parents adjusted principles and personal views, in order to justify the actions of their sons. In my case, I hoped the reverse would not be true. I hoped my father wouldn't feel obliged to defend my participation to everybody who came into the bar and asked.

I really didn't know how Dad felt about it. We hadn't ever talked very much about the war. Or about anything. He was a strong paternal figure who radiated a quiet kind of love and support. But we didn't often engage each other in serious dialogue. He had to spend so many hours in the bar, providing for us, that we never had much time to talk.

As we began the last leg of our flight, from Guam to Saigon, I thought about him, and realized I'd never verbalized my feelings. If something happened in Vietnam, I wanted to be on record. So I took paper and pencil out of my duffel bag:

Dear Dad,

First of all, let me wish you a Happy Father's Day. I know this letter will be a little late, but I want you to know the thought is there.

Many times I've wanted to sit down and talk to you and to let you know exactly what you mean to me. This is like coming in the back door, but I thought it would be a good opportunity. Now, if only I had a couple martinis, the words would come a little easier.

I don't think I ever told you I love you—not as a son to his father, but as man to man. I say this in the respect of the image you gave me to follow, and just being the man you are. You have meant a lot to me and you always will.

Another thing on my mind that I wanted to say is this: Most parents are proud of their children, which is natural. But for some, their children can't do wrong. Well, I can do wrong. What I'm trying to say is I don't want people to say behind your back what a rotten guy I am for one reason or another. But I would like you to realize it, and not be naive like a lot of parents. The reason I write this is because my actions at home weren't the most ideal, and this bothered me. Well, at least, at this particular point, I tried to bring it out.

But enough of this. I just wanted to wish you a Happy Father's Day, and whatever happens, you mean a great deal to me.

Love,

Rocky

6] *Vietnam*

I don't know why, but I figured the runways in Saigon would be under attack, and we'd have to dodge antiaircraft fire. Instead, our arrival was tranquil and fairly pleasant.

As we drove through Saigon, I got my first look at the poverty and suffering wrought by two generations of war. I didn't know if the bars on our bus windows were designed to keep the troops in or the South Vietnamese out.

We spent the first week in a Saigon "jungle school" that was more advanced and more relevant than the one we'd known at Fort Gordon. The week was uneventful, except for a late-night incident over a loud stereo. It was keeping the whole barracks awake. Twice, I asked the owner to reduce the volume, before reporting it to a lieutenant, who ordered him to turn it off. I nearly came to blows with this music-lover.

"Once you get out in the field, you'll learn you have to depend on your buddies, not squeal on them," he said. "Besides, I've been out fighting the damn war. What have you been doing?"

That was an attitude I found several times in the ensuing months. Guys back from a tour would spend hours regaling each other with stories of "The Nam." They'd use it as a crutch, asking special treatment on the theory: "Hey, man, gimme a break. I just did twelve months in The Nam."

We helicoptered three hundred miles up the coast of the South China Sea to Chu Lai, where I visited the rear base of my newly assigned batallion, the 196th Light Infantry Brigade. Three days later, I joined the 120 men of my company—Company C (or Charlie)—on LZ (landing zone) West, forty miles west of Chu Lai. They were just coming back from the field and looked rather bedraggled . . . dirty, unshaven, weather-beaten, and older than their years. I met Jim Britton of upstate New York, who became my sergeant and bunker mate, and

Captain Tom Murphy of Savannah, Georgia, our commanding officer.

Companies A, B, C, and D worked as a unit on LZ West and LZ Siberia. The landing zones were situated on two hills about five miles apart. In between was Hiep Douc (pronounced "hep-duck"), a valley which stretched down five hundred yards from the summits. It was the prettiest landscape I'd ever seen. In the morning, clouds hung down to the tips of the mountains. Into the valley, we could see miles and miles of green foliage, dotted with rice paddies that looked like miniature lakes. If there hadn't been a war underway, Hiep Douc would have made a nice resort.

The landing zone was a permanent installation, complete with helicopter pad, mess hall, officers' quarters, and lavatories. We "grunts" slept in bunkers dug three to four feet into the ground with a wooden frame for support and sandbags on top for protection. Along the front, we hung ten hand grenades. Against the side, we leaned our weapons. Inside was a dirt floor, covered with cardboard, which became a quagmire during monsoon season. Bed was an air mattress laid on a wooden pallet. Each bunker accommodated three or four men.

I spent about half my days on the landing zones . . . cleaning the area on garbage detail, repairing bunkers, loading and unloading helicopters, pulling guard duty, reading the collected works of Ernest Hemingway, writing letters, and taking naps. If nothing else, days in camp kept my stomach happy. We got three hot meals a day. In addition, we could sample cartons of chocolate milk and ice cream while we unloaded them from helicopters.

Base was mostly boring in terms of fighting action, except for one particular night when I was pulling guard. I put my ear to the transistor and turned it on just loud enough to hear the Armed Forces Radio Network. I cupped a cigarette in my hand to hide the red glow. It was particularly chilly on the hill that night, so I wrapped up in a poncho liner.

It was also very dark, and still, and lonely . . . good climate for an active imagination. As I stared out at the front of the camp, I began to wonder what would happen if the Vietcong sneaked around back. If they broke in through the rear, who could stop them? They'd stab me in the back before I could turn around. I took a few peeks over my shoulder, and lit another cigarette.

At that instant, I thought I heard a noise near the ten-foot barbed-wire fence in front of me. Then silence. A minute later, I heard it again. I reached for the M-16 leaning against the bunker. I thought I saw movement. There was no moonlight, so I couldn't be certain. I unlatched the safety and aimed the rifle. Suddenly, an object bounded

NORTH
VIETNAM

Demarcation
Line

Mekong

River

L
A
O
S

THAILAND

Da Nang

Hiep
Douc

Chu Lai

C A M B O D I A

SOUTH

VIETNAM

Mekong River

SAIGON

S O U T H   C H I N A   S E A

SOUTH VIETNAM
1969

0   50   100

Scale of miles

toward the left. I wheeled to fire. . . . It was the German shepherd dog who'd become our company mascot. I came within a hairbreadth of pulling the trigger on him.

I put my heart back into my shirt, my M-16 back against the bunker, and marked the incident down as a highlight of camp life. Normally, the day's most challenging decision would be where to sleep . . . inside the bunker where there was no breeze and the rats were biting, or on top of the bunker where the risks were rain, wind, and cooling temperatures.

Days not spent on the landing zone were devoted to either sweeps or patrols. A sweep was simply the exploration and policing of a given area, known as a "grid square" on Army maps, by a group no larger than a full platoon (twenty-five men). Usually, these sweeps turned out to be useless exercises in hiking. The primary difficulties were two: First, returning to camp meant struggling uphill after a long, exhausting day in midafternoon temperatures of 110 degrees or more. Second, everybody would be irritable—in the vernacular, "have the ass"—about the possibility of missing chow or perhaps an occasional USO show. The lieutenant often compounded that problem by losing the path back to camp, which meant cutting through dense thickets and crawling straight uphill on hands and knees.

Patrols were more extended visits to the field. A company normally "humped" for a week. Again, the purpose was to reconnoiter an area designated by battalion headquarters, perhaps because of suspected enemy activity. We never knew for sure.

One's companion on these patrols was one's "rut sack," a canvas bag stretched over an aluminum frame. Contained therein were a small hammock, air mattress, a couple pairs of socks, sandals, poncho liner, mosquito netting, mess kit, iodine pills for purifying water, calamine lotion, several cans of fruit, beer or Coke or both, and several "lurps" (dehydrated food ration taken on an LRRP . . . long-range reconnaissance patrol). Additionally, each man packed his own personal effects . . . in my case, a diary, a camera, Hemingway, and a large wooden cross that Al Lison had carried in World War II. Each man also carried as much water as he wanted and his weapon. For me, it was five quarts and an M-79 grenade launcher.

The launcher looked like a snub-nosed rifle. It had a sight and range finder for accuracy. The grenades were shaped like giant bullets, five inches long, three inches in diameter. They weighed about one pound apiece, and I was required to carry sixty rounds. I loaded them into two ammo bags . . . one mounted atop my rut sack, the other slung over my shoulder as a bandolier. I draped a towel over my neck to prevent the straps from cutting and digging. My shirt I tied at the bottom of the rut sack, along with the five canteens. The launcher I nestled in my hands. Loaded for humping, I looked like a packhorse . . . and felt like one. Carrying one's home on one's back was a heavy proposition. My gear weighed about 100 pounds.

The load got to be oppressive for some guys, late of a hot afternoon. Occasionally they'd vent their frustrations on the rut sack. It was a catharsis, made all the more refreshing when the sack had a living, breathing identity.

"You goddam green monkey," someone would scream during smoke break, kicking his sack across the grass. "You son of a bitch, you've been kicking my ass all day. Now I'm gonna kick yours. You've had a free fucking ride since seven thirty this morning. When are you gonna get off my back?"

In the field, there were moments, like that one, of true levity. Another involved the dreaded "wait-a-minute vine." If rut march was proceeding smoothly for half an hour or more, we were soon due to have somebody catch his rifle or the edge of his pack on an overhanging vine. They were shaped like little fish hooks, and their grip was so tenacious, you'd swear they had hands. When they grabbed somebody, you'd hear, "Wait a minute. The wait-a-minute vine's got me."

In the field, I found that certain items I'd deemed "necessities" in life were really not necessities at all. Toilets, for instance. Thus culminated a gradual progression, which brought me "back to nature."

In American society, of course, one has an apartment with his own bathroom, where he may go in quiet privacy to read, or think about the world's problems, or whatever. He can close the door and get away from it all.

Then he gets into the service, and the situation is kind of semi-private. Some lavatories have stalls with no door. Some have no stalls . . . just a long white row of porcelain. Solitude is not issued by the U.S. Army. But if a man really values his privacy, he can have it at a price. He can sneak around the corner and get the last john in the back. Or he can hold it all day and go at two o'clock in the morning, when everybody else is sleeping.

Then he goes overseas and finds the old wooden "outhouse," like his grandparents used to have behind the barn. Walk in, step up, and there's a plank of timber with several holes cut in it. On rare occasions, there are also a few roughly hewn toilet seats. A man might exchange pleasantries with the man beside him, but there's not much thinking, or reading, or solving of the world's problems now. This is all business. He does what's necessary and leaves.

(On very unlucky days, the serviceman may draw "shit-burning detail," which means just what it says. He pulls big tins out from under the wooden planks, drags them a short distance, douses them with gasoline, and sets the whole mess aflame. That normally leaves him sick to his stomach for a week.)

Then he gets out into the field and learns a new, free-form method. A john is where he finds it. He walks away from the group, to a spot behind some bushes perhaps. In his first endeavor, he is introduced to the pain that squatting produces in the legs. He may also fear for the continued cleanliness of his pants, which he's pushed down around his ankles. But he learns.

His toilet paper comes, like food and cigarettes, in his C-rations. He carries it in the strap of his helmet, so it's within easy reach, never to be lost or stolen. Also so it won't be crushed by nonessential items in his rut sack. Like food. He's careful not to lose his toilet paper, because nobody loans it. Camaraderie and fellowship have their limits.

Life in the boondocks, indeed, belonged to the resourceful. Shaving was done out of the helmet. Showering was done only when God ordained it; rain was our shower. Occasionally, a briskly flowing stream became our bathtub. But we were careful to be equally brisk. Leeches in the water were a hazard, and besides, if we had to move out quickly, one did not want to be caught with one's pants down, as they say. Up on the hill, things were not much better for our personal hygiene. A shower in camp required filling, bucket by bucket, a fifty-five-gallon drum on top of the shower stall. Cold water, of course.

Eating in the field got better as the day went along. Breakfast and lunch came out of the rut sack. A hot dinner was flown in by helicopter from battalion headquarters, and it was decent . . . chicken, steak, roast beef. More important than the food, they brought us a huge container of Kool-Aid, swimming around a block of ice one yard square. Just looking at it reactivated the salivary glands.

For late-evening snacks, we had a special treat. Pizza. Here's the recipe: Take a biscuit tin and peel back the lid about halfway. Reach in with a knife and slice the biscuit; remove the top half. Take a wedge of cheese, crumble, and sprinkle inside the biscuit tin. Now take a ration of dried beef, cut into small pieces, and drop those into the biscuit tin. Close lid on the biscuit tin and place inside a cardboard box. Set fire to the cardboard box. By the time it burns out, the biscuit will have been toasted, the cheese melted, and the beef fried. A delicacy.

An average day in the field might go like this: Rise at 6:30 A.M. Eat a can of fruit for breakfast. March in rut formation (single file, more or less) perhaps five thousand meters to a day position. Sweat, sweat, sweat. Set up a "day logger," a perimeter configuration of men designed to protect us from attack. Set up the poncho liner for a sun shield. Sweat, sweat, sweat. Mix a lurp for lunch.

At this point, one platoon would make a sweep of the immediate vicinity. The other two platoons would remove their perspiration-soaked boots, socks, and fatigues, to dry them in the sun.

Eat dinner and guzzle Kool-Aid. March another five thousand meters or so to a night position. Set up a "night logger." Inflate the air mattress and build a tent with mosquito netting . . . which blocked the breeze and sometimes made me unbearably hot, but not as unbearable as ten million mosquito bites.

If you think that sounds more like an agenda for the Boy Scouts than the U.S. Army, so did I, at first. We moved twice a day, so the enemy couldn't get a fix on us. In fact, it seemed that's all we did. I felt so silly, "playing soldier." But I came to understand and appreciate the fact that Hiep Douc was simply quiet.

The lack of activity persuaded some guys to cut corners. Night guards fell asleep in the field. Other guys just refused to fight the war. "Short-timers" (those who had a short time of service remaining) played it extra cautious and spent most of their days inventing excuses to get to the rear. Guys dispatched on a squad sweep would convince each other that they didn't have enough manpower, then kill four hours sitting in a point bunker, radioing in fake messages about their progress. It was a ludicrous way to run a war.

Meanwhile, our officers were feeling pressure. Even though ours was a relatively cool AO (area of operation), they felt the demand for production, which came in only one form . . . enemy KIAs (killed in action). Statistics. Officers' careers and promotions depended on them: "How many KIAs did you get last week?" "What's your percentage?" "Did you get any action?"

Those were the operative questions. Nobody talked about methods. Only results were important. Pressure came from above and multiplied geometrically at each level, until it reached the lower echelons with a massive weight. There, on the bottom, were lieutenants and sergeants, young and maybe impetuous. In their early and mid-twenties. Ambitious. Eager to distinguish themselves and establish a good record.

Below them were the "grunts," the privates. Guys who knew what went on above them. Some of whom wanted to move up. All of whom knew that the soldier with the most KIAs each week went on "stand-down" . . . a three-day orgy of barbecues, drinking, floor shows, and pornographic movies in Chu Lai. Kind of like an incentive clause in a football contract.

It was this sort of mentality that led to the creation of a destructive form known as the search-and-destroy mission. The My Lai massacre of 1968 resulted from such a mission. In my tour of duty, thankfully, there was only one search-and-destroy. And I think I can characterize the basic conversations that brought it into being.

Battalion headquarters might have called our commanding officer and said, "All right, we have a mission here for you. We have this area that has to be covered. A lot of enemy activity has been in that position. And we've known it's been there. It's been there before, and goddam it, let's do something about it, because it's in my AO. I want this shit cleaned up, and I want to get it out of there. Use whatever means you need. Burn everything that's standing. I don't care what you do, just clean it up."

In turn, the commanding officer might have gone to his lieutenant and said, "All right, tomorrow at 0700 hours we're going down into the field. Get your men prepared. There's a lot of enemy activity in this area. The old man wants it cleaned out once and for all. And it's our job."

Then the lieutenant would have gone to his platoons and said, "Okay, the whole company is moving out tomorrow. The CO wants to get the shit off his back, and it's up to us. This whole area is just infested with VC. It's a goddam hideout for them. They're all Communist, and it's our job to clean them out. I don't want any prisoners, no matter who they are. I don't want to hear about it. Don't take anybody alive."

Lastly, on the bottom level, there were the members of the platoon. They were twenty-five men chosen at random from this country, a representative sampling of American society. Of the twenty-five, you might have had a couple with quick tempers, maybe a teenager who saw himself as a young Audie Murphy, maybe a guy from an under-privileged background who thought he could make a name for himself, maybe a guy who thought being in the Army was license to kill any-body, maybe a guy who was truly hateful, maybe even a manic-depressive.

So they took this collection of fallible human beings, pumped them full of that rhetoric, applied all the pressure from the military hier-archy, filled them with anticipation, and then turned them loose in a Vietnamese village. How did they react?

We were informed one morning of a suspected enemy concentra-tion in an area below LZ Siberia, called Happy Valley. Orders came to search-and-destroy. We helicoptered into a rice paddy and set up a defensive position. As we moved out, our point man shouted, "I see somebody running across the ridge." So the whole platoon raced up a steep hill, there to find a village of four to five "hootches" (grass-and-bamboo huts).

Frantically, guys went searching for underground shelters. Without pausing to check for someone inside, they exploded the shelters with grenades.

Somebody yelled, "Burn them. We have to." Immediately, guys set fire to the pitiful little shacks that contained these people's every earthly possession. The women shrieked hysterically at us. It was absurd. There were no VC anywhere. Nothing but a few harmless villagers, whose lives we annihilated, simply because "search-and-destroy came down."

During the melee, a "papa-san" (Vietnamese adult male) appeared. The man was about fifty years old, had no weapon, and obviously was no threat to us. Yet one of our young kids, an eighteen- or nineteen-year-old, rushed up to him, kneed him in the groin, and cracked his skull with the butt of an M-16. The old man dropped to his knees in agony. The kid dragged him by his armpits twenty yards. Then he stopped. In a fury, he stood over the old man, screaming, "You motherfucking, slant-eyed dink. You're the reason we're over here."

Any male in the general age bracket of twelve to forty was suspect as an NVA (North Vietnamese Army) soldier or Vietcong, although he might also have been a South Vietnamese soldier on leave. Even though this man was past the age of suspicion, we were instructed to ask him for an ID. If he could not produce it, we were to hold him for interrogation by the commanding officer. Under search-and-destroy pressure, though, some of our young guys didn't have the patience to follow regulations.

In order to avoid such confusion, the U.S. Army got into the housing industry. In a move of ultimate arrogance, Uncle Sam ordered the natives of Hiep Douc to leave their homes and move into a compound at the base of the valley. It was called "Tin City," because these people were offered tin and wood to build new homes. The Army warned that anybody caught outside Tin City, especially males twelve to forty, could be shot on sight.

In actual practice, however, it did not work that way. Tin City was filled with little boys and girls who greeted us by saluting and reciting their only English phrase: "Hi, GI Joe. Hi, GI Joe." But many of the older Vietnamese people refused to leave their homes. They took no side in the war, and merely dug bunkers for protection from attack. We were constantly finding little villages tucked here and there in the woods.

We discovered one such village on a sweep in July. A check of the hootches uncovered nothing. Three of us were going to find water when, from out of nowhere, there came a little man, less than five feet tall. Our point man yanked the shotgun to his shoulder, then stopped before pulling the trigger, because he thought it was a little boy. He was wrong. It was a man about thirty years old.

My two buddies grabbed him by his black pajamas.

"You VC? You NVA?"

He said nothing.

"Papa-san, you VC? You VC?"

We didn't know what to do with him.

The point man said, "Fuck, let's kill him. Then we wouldn't have to worry. I don't know why I hesitated. I should have just shot the bastard."

The other guy said, "Maybe we should tell him to *di di mau* [get out of here]. Then we can shoot him as he's running away."

The point man replied, "Aw, shit. Let's just tie him to a tree and shoot him right here."

It was a few incredulous moments before I realized what they were saying. "What the fuck are you guys talking about?" I asked them. "We can't shoot this guy. Let's take him back to the lieutenant."

"No," the point man insisted. "The lieutenant said he doesn't *want* any prisoners. What the hell's he gonna do with him? We'd just have to guard the fuckin' gook and take him back with us. The lieutenant doesn't want to be bothered."

I said, "Let's take him back and let the lieutenant decide. It's his decision. If he wants to kill him, that's his business."

"Well, shit, I don't know. The lieutenant said he doesn't want any prisoners. He might be pissed if we bring him back."

"Well, let him be pissed," I said. "In clear conscience, I can't shoot him. He doesn't have a weapon. He hasn't tried anything. He just showed up."

Finally, we took him to the lieutenant, who checked him out and freed him.

It was that kind of war. There was no demarcation between residential areas and battlefields. There were no fronts or flanks or tactical moves, like the wars we studied in history books. We were just a bunch of guys wandering around in the woods, looking for that nebulous "activity." We didn't even know how to recognize it if we saw it. The first one hundred days I was in Vietnam, I never even *saw* a Vietcong or an NVA.

The lack of a clear objective or goal and the mounting anxiety worked a hardship on us. Each guy coped in his own way. Some were tempted by Tin City, which was generally off-limits for a few very good reasons. First, we didn't know the Vietnamese language or customs . . . patting a young boy on the head, for instance, is a sign of disrespect. Second, anti-American sentiment sometimes took cruel forms . . . one GI was given a Coke with finely ground glass mixed in the bottle; it killed him.

Still, those deterrents were not enough for the foolish. I heard about one young guy in our company who spent an entire afternoon boasting that he was going to Tin City to get drunk and laid. He was found dead the next morning in a stream.

Other guys found their release in drugs. The soft drugs, marijuana and hashish, were available. I never saw hard drugs, but we heard stories of heroin dealers and addicts. Actually, drug use on LZ West and Siberia had declined by the time I arrived. A few weeks previous, an enemy squad had penetrated the barbed wire and killed several GIs by tossing grenades into their bunkers. A large section of camp had been stoned on marijuana during that attack, and they were frightened into kicking the habit.

On my first day in camp, several guys took me aside and asked if I was "a head or a boozer." I said, "Well, I like to have an occasional martini. You know, on the rocks with an olive." They chuckled. In Vietnam, where necessity was a strange bartender, drinking meant something else.

The ingredients were beer, issued twelve cans a week to each man; Coke, issued six cans a week; and Scotch, vodka, or whatever each guy received in his "care package" from home. Their idea of a mixed drink was to take a sip of warm Coke, then a belt of warm Scotch, swish it around in their mouths, and swallow. Ugh.

The heavy drinkers were exploited occasionally by the entrepreneurs in the group. We always had guys who'd disappear to the rear base. When next seen, they'd be packing several cases of beer and Coke in the field, offering them at outrageous prices. The standard trade was two beers for a Coke. But the entrepreneurs would rather have your money.

I was more than content with my weekly ration, thank you. The warm Coke was merely unpleasant. The warm beer I drank only with a grimace . . . but I drank it. That was the only remedy for the dusty, biting thirst that choked me on scorching afternoons.

My favorite beverage, however, was cocoa. Mom sent the mix in my care packages, and I hid it from the company vultures, who liked it equally well. Nothing warmed a chilly night on the hill like a hot cocoa. And nobody could interfere with it . . . not even the enemy.

I had just finished mixing a fresh cup one evening on top of my bunker at LZ Siberia, when I heard the alarm, "Incoming rounds! Incoming rounds!"

We dove into the bunker as the first mortars struck camp. "Son of a bitch," I said to Jim Britton, "I don't mind those guys taking this war seriously, but couldn't they wait until I've had my hot chocolate?"

As the NVA attack continued, I noticed that the rounds were seven seconds apart. So, between blasts, I bounded up the steps, speared the cup, and sprinted back to safety. Without spilling a drop. "Britt" offered to nominate me for a medal, but I declined.

"All in the line of duty," I said.

Insignificant as it seemed at the time, that mortar attack marked the end of tranquillity in Hiep Douc. It came in late July, and was repeated the next two nights. Seven harmless mortar rounds, seven seconds apart, at about seven o'clock each evening. What was the NVA's fascination with the number seven?

The fourth night, our platoon was dispatched to the base of a long and narrow fingerlike appendage that extended down into the valley from Siberia. We were to set up an OP (observation post) and get a fix on the origin of those mortar attacks. Hopefully, we could radio that information to our artillery, which would knock out the NVA position.

But seven o'clock came and went without a sound this night. Eight o'clock, nine o'clock . . . still nothing. At ten o'clock, I fell asleep. I was feeling tired from a head cold I'd gotten several nights earlier, pulling guard on a rainy, chilly, breezy night. When I awoke at two in the morning, the rest of my platoon told me what I had missed. LZ West was under attack. Flares and gunships had lighted the sky so brilliantly, my platoon mates had been able to watch the battle, five miles away. Kind of like having "nickel seats" for a heavyweight boxing championship. We trudged back up the hill with our own mission unaccomplished.

The next morning, we heard that a regiment of three hundred NVA had surrounded West in a "zapper attack." A zapper was a commando unit which usually attempted to cut its way into camp, drop pack charges into several bunkers, then exit before we could react. This time, they made too much noise and tipped their entry. Our guys were waiting for them and killed fifty NVA. More than one hundred were wounded. There were no American casualties.

A couple days later, we got word that the Marines and the South Vietnamese Army had some action on a hill adjacent to ours. They were pushing NVA down into Happy Valley. We were assigned to act as a restraining force to catch the NVA in their retreat.

Our 155s and 175s "prepped the area," blasting it with hundreds of rounds of artillery. Then aircraft dropped gallon drums of gas to kill the foliage. An hour later, we landed by helicopter. We crossed the Song Lau River near Tin City and entered a narrow path on our way to the far side of the valley. The path was strewn with trees and brush knocked over by our gunners. As we picked our way among them, I brushed an insect from my eye . . . and went instantly blind.

It must have been the defoliation gas, or maybe some gunpowder residue from the artillery. The medic told me the terrible burning would eventually subside. But for several hundred meters, I kept my eyes tightly shut. I grabbed the shirt of the guy in front of me and played follow the leader.

My eyesight had just returned when we came upon a clearing with several hootches set on the left side, across a small stream. We walked single file, a little slower now, scrutinizing this little village.

Something moved. In front of me, one of our guys opened fire. Then he tossed a grenade, which devastated a hootch. He had seen the front door crack open slightly, then slam shut.

We sloshed through the stream to find that the hootch was no NVA hideout. It was the home of a Vietnamese family. The father was dead, the mother was bleeding badly, and the three children were wailing in terror. We left them and pressed on. Everyone was feeling edgy. There were signs of recent activity, but still no NVA.

With combat duties occupying base personnel that evening, no hot dinner was planned. They helicoptered C-rations to us, but not enough to go around. Three of us who got none were left to share a single-portion lurp.

I had the water, another guy had a can of Sterno, and a third guy had a ham-and-lima-beans lurp. A vicious Vietnamese downpour was pelting us, so I draped a poncho liner over me, lit the Sterno under it, and boiled water in my mess kit. Then I dumped in the lurp and invited the other two guys to join me under the poncho. We sat there on our rut sacks, watching ravenously as the spoon and serving pot were passed from man to man. First the lurp owner took his three bites, then the Sterno owner, then me. And that was dinner. We agreed it was better than nothing . . . but just barely.

We spent a full week in Happy Valley . . . looking, looking, looking. Nothing. So on August 9, we were to be replaced by B (or Bravo) Company. We set up the standard defensive perimeter, allowing our helicopter to land in the middle. All but fifteen of us departed on the first two loads. We expected to see the others soon. But it wasn't until eight o'clock that night, some five hours later, that they returned to Siberia, looking shaken and feeling pissed off. What had happened?

"You won't believe it," one guy replied. "After you left, the colonel of the goddam battalion showed up with his own personal helicopter to bring us back here. Except there was one problem. The goddam thing didn't have enough fuel. So the colonel and his command sergeant major got out . . . you know, roughing it with the grunts for a change. They sent their chopper to Chu Lai to gas up, and told the pilot we'd meet him in two hours at Bravo's defensive position.

"Okay, so we'd gone about a klick and a half [fifteen hundred meters] when our point man came face to face with three NVA. I'm telling you, he could see the dinks' faces. They were twenty-five yards away. Our guy raised his gun and . . . *click* . . . nothing. The round didn't chamber. So our second guy came up to support, and we were in a damn firefight. Bullets were flying everywhere. I don't know how we missed each other.

"Most of us took cover behind stumps and trees. The colonel tried to dig himself a hole, he was so scared. But the sergeant major was a big dude, maybe six-three, two hundred and fifty pounds. Everybody's sergeant . . . tough-ass, part Indian, World War II hero, and probably hadn't been in one of these things for thirty years. He was so excited, I thought he was going to have a heart attack.

"He pulled his hand gun, a forty-five . . . *a forty-five*, mind you . . . and started hollering, 'Come on, you guys, let's go get those bastards. Fuckin' gooks. This is what we're here for. You on the right, when I say charge, you charge. On the left, when I say pin 'em down, you open fire.'

"The son of a bitch almost got us killed. What's worse, we missed dinner, so that's two nights in a row without anything to eat."

That's how we came to know for sure that there was "shit in the valley." We didn't know how many, or where they were coming from, but it was certain that the enemy was concentrating in our AO. Later we learned that it was the Thirty-first Regiment of the Second NVA Division, a force of eight hundred to nine hundred men. We were put on twenty-four-hour alert to move out on one hour's notice.

On Friday, August 15, I stretched out inside my bunker, and wrote:

My dearest sister Pam,

This is another letter from your brother, the war correspondent. Please share with other members of the family.

First of all, the good news. You may have my guitar for your birthday present. I heard you've been playing it, so you might as well keep it. It may be slightly used, but it's the best I can do. I can't get to a gift shop over here. Happy Birthday!

What exciting, captivating experiences have I to relate to you? Well, LZ West got probed extensively the other night, and another hill almost got overrun. We thought the next night that we'd get hit, but nothing happened except for a few mortar rounds coming in. No damage. If the NVA or VC ever had the equipment or fighting power we have, it would be twice as bad.

Mortars are the scariest, because you don't know where they are coming from, or where they are going to land. If you hear one screaming overhead, you might think it's one of our mortars, on its way to an enemy position. Then you hear it whistling down, and you know it's not.

I'm going to Leadership School on Aug. 24, so I'll be out of the field for two weeks. I should be able to make sergeant and, besides, it's a good time to take a break from this routine. Army life is worse than ever.

I've been talking to God a lot, and He's taking good care of me. The other thing I think about most of the time is R & R—rest and recreation. I can go to Bangkok, Hong Kong, Sydney, Honolulu, or Tokyo. What do you think?

Stay tuned for another adventure from the land of the big sun. We'll keep 'em coming.

Thanks for the pictures. They looked so natural. Take care and remember my platoon motto: Eat shit; a million Vietnamese flies can't be wrong.

Love,

Rocky

7] *August 20, 1969*

On the night of August 17, while I was writing that letter to Pam, word came that B Company had been hit. The NVA whom we'd been expecting to catch in Happy Valley had somehow slipped into the adjacent Que San Valley and taken up residence there. An NVA came into Bravo's perimeter during the afternoon, screaming, *"Chieu hoi, chieu hoi,"* meaning, "I surrender." He said, under interrogation, that he could lead them to a cache of weapons and rice up in the hills.

One platoon maintained the camp, while two others followed the *"chieu hoi."* He took them farther and farther up a mountain range, until, from the camp below, they heard a barrage of everything the NVA could muster . . . rockets, mortars, machine guns.

They shot the *chieu hoi* (although the Army after-action report indicates he was accidentally killed in a gunfire exchange) and hustled back to the perimeter. Too late, they found the other platoon annihilated, and a firefight waiting for them. The enemy ambush had succeeded. Now Bravo was waiting for us to bail them out.

On the morning of August 18, Company C sent two platoons into Que San Valley by helicopter . . . second platoon and my platoon, the first. The ride was an adventure in itself. We were so loaded—ten men and all their gear—that the chopper barely rose off its pad. We seemed to plummet straight down the side of the mountain, until an air current caught us and yanked us back into the sky.

We spent most of the afternoon tense with anticipation, waiting for third platoon, which was already in the valley, coming from a position near Tin City. They arrived about 5:00 P.M. We set up a night logger and made plans for retrieving Bravo.

At 8:00 P.M., three-fourths of us moved out, including twelve men of my platoon. We took only our weapons, our ammunition, and a poncho liner to carry the dead. It was an eerie night, black and cold. The evening temperature was still 70 degrees, but that seemed chilly in the damp valley, compared to the dry, searing 110 degrees we'd experienced on the hill that morning.

I don't know how far we walked, perhaps a few miles through elephant grass, scraggly bushes, and dense underbrush. I do know it was a long, increasingly frightening journey. At first, the only sound was our marching boots on the soft earth and the rustling of bushes. Then we heard on the radio that Company D had been attacked in the jungle below LZ West. Two men had been killed and five wounded.

The farther we went, the darker it got, the smokier it got, and the more it smelled of gunpowder. We heard firing . . . first at a distance, then seemingly closer. At one point, I saw an American helicopter lurch as it was struck by green tracer bullets. The chopper gave off puffs of smoke, spun a moment as if to crash, then circled and limped back to safety.

Finally, at 10:00 P.M., we arrived. The men of Bravo were lying in a ditch at the side of the road . . . ten dead, twenty wounded. The ones still alive were enormously relieved to see us. I felt we should stay the night. We had plenty of manpower to protect ourselves, manpower that was in need of a good sleep. But our officers decided to return immediately to the night logger.

It was an hour of confusion before we'd gotten the dead and wounded lined up. As we began to move out, I noticed one corpse lying unattended in the ditch. I turned to one of my platoon mates and said, "C'mon, let's take this guy."

"Hell, no," he said. "Our platoon's got rear security."

"But there's nobody left to take him," I argued.

"I don't give a shit. Let him lay there."

Another fellow, however, was willing. We found a bamboo pole and tied the dead man to it with his shoelaces. I gave my grenade launcher to another soldier, and we moved out.

Five minutes later, the guy carrying the front end of the bamboo pole slipped off a narrow dike between two rice paddies and fell into two feet of water. In doing so, he pulled the back end out of my hand, and the corpse landed on top of him. Rigor mortis having set in, that stiff, lifeless form must have filled him with a macabre sensation. He jumped back onto the dike instantly, and looked at me with big, terrified eyes before resuming our march.

We went only another hundred yards before hearing small-arms fire. It came from the front, where our point men were attempting to cross a small stream. The NVA had set up a machine gun on the water's edge, and spotted us through the darkness.

We tossed the corpse into a ditch and rolled in beside it. I was exhausted to the point of nearly falling asleep. I had no weapon for protection. I wondered how large a force we'd encountered . . . and how many other ambushes would be waiting along our route.

The two sides fired back and forth for an hour. We were too far back in line to see the NVA, but I could hear our guys yelling: "I see somebody over here. They're over here." "Throw a grenade over there." "Watch it, watch it."

Then the NVA ceased firing. We didn't know if they'd been wounded or simply decided to retreat. On our side of the stream, word filtered back: "Leave the bodies. We're moving out." I waited for my platoon to come up from the rear, and recovered my grenade launcher.

The others had crossed, and our unit was just entering the stream, when the NVA machine gun opened up again. We dived for cover, panicked at the thought of being separated from the others. I lay on my side in a tangle of weeds, muddy water oozing and seeping through my fatigues. I unclipped the scatter round on my grenade launcher, and for fifteen minutes, we returned fire. Then it ceased once more.

Now we stepped warily into the ankle-high water, and crossed without further incident. But on the other side of the stream, we didn't know which way to go. The fifty men ahead had broken contact. Nobody among the twelve of us could remember, for sure, if the night logger was to the right or left. Several of us argued for the right, and eventually convinced the others.

We moved cautiously along the path. A thick cloud still blotted out the moon, leaving us to navigate in blackness. The cold was more bracing, the quiet more frightening. We strained our eyes, looking for another ambush along the stream to our right or the hillside to our left. Two well-placed grenades and a volley of machine-gun fire could kill us all. And we didn't even know if we were headed toward the night logger. We could be wandering deeper and deeper into enemy territory.

Unexpectedly, mortars. A salvo landed behind us with that distinctive, piercing report. *Poom, poom, poom, poom.* Right at the spot where we'd crossed the stream . . . not five minutes earlier. The NVA had pinned us down, then sneaked away and radioed our coordinates to their artillerymen. Those mortars were meant for us.

We realized it instantly. The same twelve men who had been inching along so tentatively, suddenly broke into a terrified running stride. I thought I was pretty fast, but guys were passing me on all sides.

The fellow who, supposedly, was in charge of us was named Williams. He was a legend in Charlie Company. Twice, he had escaped death with near-miracles. The first time was several months ago, when NVA zappers tossed a grenade through the peephole of his bunker. It landed on his bed . . . but did not explode until he had jumped up and run to the doorway. He was not wounded.

The second incident was more recent. His squad had run across an enemy force in the field, and engaged in a firefight. The NVA heaved a grenade which hit Williams smack in the chest, fell to the ground in front of him, fizzled, and died. Twice, he'd caught lightning in a bottle. But apparently he didn't want to go for three in a row with this mortar attack. He zipped past me with arms pumping and legs churning. I couldn't decide if his eyes or his mouth were open wider. We hustled all the way back to the night logger, arriving about 3:00 A.M.

At 7:00, I was awakened by rifle shots. I knew it was NVA fire, because the shots had that peculiar clacking sound. Another ambush? Another firefight? Were they going to rush our camp? Did they have enough men to overrun us?

Fortunately, it was none of the above. At the stream-crossing the previous night, we had left one of our men behind. In the darkness and confusion, he had missed the signal to move out. He crawled all night on his hands and knees, a distance of more than two miles. He slipped around the machine-gun position, and heard NVA talking. At daybreak, he was sighted by other enemy soldiers, who shot at him. That was the firing I heard. But he escaped and got into camp safely.

That afternoon, August 19, we moved a short distance. Nobody told us, but apparently our objective was still the same . . . to pick up the dead bodies of Bravo. This time, we were joined by another B Company, that of the 198th Light Infantry Brigade. Now we had enough manpower to handle almost anything . . . a company and a half, nearly two hundred men.

On the way to our new position, we tromped through rice paddies with mud up to our thighs. My platoon had lead position for both companies. We were crossing a paddy which descended and turned to the left, when word came from our point man: "Freeze."

Orders were passed back from man to man: "Activity up there at the end of the rice paddy. Break up into two factions."

We took the left side, second platoon took the right. It was the first time I'd ever seen coordination between two lieutenants. By radio, they supervised the placement of machine guns, grenade launchers, and M-16 riflemen. It took fifteen minutes to put everybody in position. We must have had fifty different weapons at the ready. We stayed low and kept our voices down.

Our target was a lonely little hootch which stood alongside a large tree at the far end of the rice paddy. Nothing else was around . . . no people, no other hootches.

The lieutenants counted down on the radio: "Five, four, three, two, one. Fire!"

Simultaneously, from both sides, we rained a volley on that hootch like I have never seen. It was like the grand-finale fire show back at Fort Gordon. Tracer bullets and small-arms fire ripped through the bamboo supports. Just knocked the hell out of it. In less than two minutes, we felled the tree and set the roof ablaze with our grenades. As we ceased fire, I could see smoke billowing from the sagging walls. I heard someone shrieking. Through the settling dust, I could make out a figure.

It was a mama-san. Then another mama-san. Then two papa-sans and a few little kids. Their bunker had saved them. Now they were crying and screaming in such forceful combination I thought they might kill all two hundred of us with their bare hands. A mama-san rushed up to our lieutenant and stood toe to toe, looking up at him. Her face was contorted in rage as she cursed him at the absolute top of her voice. He tried apologizing in Vietnamese, but it was no use. The rest of us shuffled around, almost feeling embarrassed in front of these poor people. I realized we must be a little jumpy . . . attacking that little hootch with enough firepower to knock out half a regiment.

As our two platoons finished searching through the ashes of the hootch, Company B of the 198th set up the night logger on a nearby hillside. By the time we arrived, all the good sleeping positions had been taken. Only a section of jungle, briars and elephant grass was left for us. So our platoon walked shoulder to shoulder, trampling it into a makeshift mattress. I fell asleep next to a tree, with one of its roots jabbing me in the back.

The next morning, I reached for the tree, steadying myself to get up. I felt something tingly on my hands. I scratched my neck, then my arm, then my back and legs. I looked at the tree. It was the Santa Monica Freeway . . . for ants. They were going up and down, up and down . . . millions of them. They were little and red, the ones we called "piss ants." They were acrobats. Just before biting, they'd stick their hind legs in the air, balancing on their front legs and head. They barely pinched the skin, not hard enough to hurt, just hard enough to piss you off. On the morning of August 20, I was plenty pissed off.

This was the plan for the day: Company B of the 198th and our third platoon were to set up a secured landing position north of Bravo's dead, so helicopters could fly them out. Second platoon was to drop back in reserve to "Million Dollar Hill," an area so named because a million dollars' worth of American helicopters were shot down there in one day. (That's right, taxpayers. One day.) We of the first platoon were to approach Bravo's dead from the south, pick them up, and carry them to the waiting helicopters.

We humped until about ten o'clock, then took a five-minute smoke break. I sat down in the shade with two of my closest friends, "Doc," the medic, and "Hawaii," a fellow nicknamed for his home state and a bunker mate to Britt and me on the landing zones. Nothing important was said. Just the regular small talk.

"Saddle up," said Captain Tom Murphy, the CO. "Be careful. We'll be in open territory. Stay about eight yards apart." He didn't want to lose everybody to one round of artillery.

We moved out, forty yards through a wooded area, toward a clearing, and then onto a dike which separated two dried-up rice paddies. I was eighth from the front. Behind me were a fellow named Dave, then Doc, then Hawaii.

I had just stepped out of the woods when I heard our point man shout, "Gook, gook." He fired a couple shots and started chasing. Everybody followed, running down the dike, which dipped twice to lower levels.

Suddenly, that chilling, repeating sound of an automatic weapon. *Chch-chch-chch-chch.* An NVA machine gun. We dived off the dike into the rice paddy, most to the right, some of us to the left. I was halfway onto the paddy.

I rolled onto my back and tried to flip off my pack. The Army's easy-snap shoulder flaps would not come unfastened. I struggled, and finally slipped my arms through the loops.

I grabbed my launcher and the grenades, and crawled on my stomach twenty yards to the front of the paddy. In the two lower-level paddies ahead of me, I could see our point man was no more than twenty yards from the NVA machine gun. It was about forty yards from me, sitting in a wooded knoll just before the front rice paddy. I could see where it was rustling the bushes.

I rolled over on my side and breeched a load in my grenade launcher. Just as I rose to sight the weapon and fire, I heard Dave yell from behind me, "Hey, Rock." At the same time, I felt a dull thud in my left thigh. I thought he'd thrown a stone at me to get my attention.

But it began to sting. I looked down, and saw blood gushing through two neat holes in my pants . . . one in the front, one in the rear.

"Dave, I'm hit," I screamed back over my shoulder.

"Do you have a sterile bandage?" he asked.

"No, I left my pack back there."

He tossed me a gauze patch, and as I turned to catch it, I noticed that everybody else had disappeared into the jungle on either side of the paddies. I lobbed in a few rounds, then crawled with the launcher back to where my pack lay.

The radio man hollered, "I'm going over to the other side where the lieutenant is." He slipped around the back of the paddy.

In fright, I realized I was the only target out in the open. I crawled directly to my left, behind a row of hedges ten feet high. A minute later, I saw a volley of four or five machine-gun rounds go ripping through my pack.

Dave had fallen back behind a rock about fifteen yards away from me. He yelled, "Rock, you okay? You okay?"

"Yeah, yeah. I'm okay."

"I'll tell Hawaii to send word back that you've been hit," he said.

"Okay, okay," I said. "Get a medic up here."

The others had maintained their relative positions when they jumped into the brush. Thus, Dave expected Hawaii to be just behind him. He yelled, "Hawaii."

There was no sound or movement.

"Hawaii, Hawaii."

Still no response. Dave turned and saw Hawaii lying face down.

"Rock," he screamed over the clattering of gunfire, "I think Hawaii's been hit."

Now I tried. "Hawaii, Hawaii."

Dave said, "Rock, Hawaii's not moving. I think they got him."

The injustice of it all began to wash over me. Here was a kid nineteen years old. He was drafted soon after high school graduation, and shipped to Germany. He had slightly more than six months to go in the service when he came due for reclassification. If he'd had six months or less, he'd have been discharged. But he had slightly more, so they transferred him to Vietnam. By the time he'd been reprocessed, gone through jungle school, and been assigned to a company, he had only four months to go. On the day he was killed, Hawaii had less than three months to serve.

We used to sit on top of our bunker at LZ West and Siberia, smoking cigarettes. He'd tell me about his girl friend back in Hawaii. They were engaged, and she wrote him every day. How he loved those letters. They were going to get married as soon as he got home.

Doc yelled up to me, "Hawaii got it. He's dead."

I looked down silently and asked the Lord to take care of him.

"How do you feel?" Doc asked me.

"I think I'm okay."

"You think you'll be able to walk?"

"I don't know. I've never been shot before."

I lay there, dry and parched from the exertion, planning my next move. I could try to retrieve my pack, lying out in the open about ten feet away, but I didn't know how quick I could be on my feet. More critically, I was afraid of giving away my position.

The lieutenant called everybody over to the right side of the dike, leaving only Dave, Doc, and me on the left. He was trying to set up machine-gun and grenade-launch positions of our own. The four point men needed help badly. They were pressing themselves against the front dike wall of the first paddy. It was only two feet high, so they were digging furiously with their hands into the sun-baked dirt, trying to get lower.

The lieutenant yelled across to us, "Who's got the grenade launcher? Who's got the grenade launcher?"

Dave screamed, "Bleier's got it, but he's hit."

"Well, you get it from him."

"I can't. I can't reach him. There's too much open space."

"Well, we gotta get some grenades on that machine gun," the lieutenant said, "until we can get our own machine gun set up."

I had carried my launcher and the grenades with me. Blocked by the hedgerow, I couldn't see the enemy position. But Dave could, from behind me and slightly to the right. He had a view just beyond the hedges.

I said, "Okay, Dave, I'll lob some grenades on them. You tell me where they land."

I lay on my back and fired the first grenade.

"Too far," he said. "Bring it back a little."

Again, I fired over the hedgerow.

"Still too far," he said. "Bring it way back."

I fired again.

"All right. Just a little bit more. Bring it back a little more."

My fourth grenade was in the general vicinity, Dave said. I fired three dozen rounds, hoping to keep their heads down for a few seconds while we got a counter-offensive organized.

After I ran out of ammo, I lay still for an hour and a half. I was tired from two consecutive nights without much sleep. I was thirsty. It was another cloudless, arid day. The sun withered me. It was always there, always blazing . . . a constant among the jungle's variables.

My leg was burning. I took off the sterile gauze and found a gash four inches long and one inch deep on the outer edge of my thigh, about halfway from the knee to the waist. There was no bone damage. The bullet had simply sheared off a piece of muscle and flesh.

I never thought about my football career. It was all I could do to consider the immediate options. What if the enemy saw the lieutenant yelling to me? They could tear up that hedgerow in a hail of machine-gun fire . . . and me with it. I was well within their range at seventy-five yards.

What if they surrounded me? Or overran us? Or flanked us on my side? I could hear them chattering. What were they planning?

I could hear our guys, too. There was a radio lying near my pack, and I heard our lieutenant say, "Christ, they're all around us. There's no place to hide. There's no cover over here. They're everywhere."

A minute later, I heard somebody scream from the other side of the rice paddy, "Jesus Christ, they . . . goddam it. Those fuckers. They just shot Jim. He's got three of their bullets in his stomach."

Up front, the clatter of machine gun and rifles continued. Our four point men were yelling, "Jesus, they're moving. I see them. Get that fuckin' machine gun set up."

I began thinking about a short story I'd read in my bunker a few weeks earlier. It was about an Air Force colonel during World War II. When his plane got shot down by the Germans, he popped his ejection button and parachuted into a clump of trees, unconscious. When he awakened, an enemy tank force was bearing down on him. He made a promise to God that if he escaped with his life, he'd become a priest. Somehow, he did get out. After he was discharged from the service, he went to the seminary and kept his promise to God.

During my Catholic education, I'd heard plenty of stories like that. Small miracles, the nuns used to call them. Pray to God, we were taught, and He'll get you out of any situation. I stared up at the cloudless sky, felt the scalding sun. I reached into my pocket and grasped the wooden cross Al Lison had given me.

Dear Lord, get me out of here, if You can. I'm not going to bullshit You. I'd like to say that if You get me out of here alive and okay, I'll dedicate my life to You and become a priest. I can't do that, because I know that's not what I'll do. I'm not going to be two-faced about it. I don't want to promise something now, and then change my mind later when things are going good. I don't want to come to You with a tight-situation prayer, if I can't be honest.

What I will do is this: I'll give You my life . . . to do with whatever You will. Here it is. I'm not going to complain if things go wrong. If things go good, I'll share my success with everybody around me. Here it is. Whatever You want to do, wherever You want to direct, that's fine. This is the best I can do

That's all I said at the time. Later, after it all worked out, I began to reflect: Why does man put himself in such a position of dependency? Why does he turn to God at moments like that and say, "Please take care of me, because I can't take care of myself"? Why? Maybe that's the kind of animal God has created. That might be the most conclusive proof I know for the existence of a Supreme Being. Perhaps if I hadn't spoken to God behind the hedgerow, things would have worked out the same. But one matter is for certain: When my self-preservation instinct came to the fore, I said the most fervent prayer of my life.

It was answered within five minutes. Doc had joined Dave behind his rock. He yelled across the fifteen-yard distance to me, "Rock, you and I are getting out of here."

Just as Doc took his first step toward me, I heard him scream, "Owwwwww." I looked back to see him doubled up with his hands at his waist. I thought he'd been hit in the stomach.

"You okay? You okay?" I asked.

"Yeah, I got shot in the hand," he said. A bullet had torn open his thumb.

A minute later, he scurried away from the rock and flung himself toward me. I took a gauze pad from his pack and bandaged his thumb.

"Let's get out of here," he insisted.

We crawled down the hedgerow, then turned along the left edge of the rice paddy. We did not stop or swerve for anything . . . thickets, briars, mud. We went directly through them all. The other men were hollering to us, checking our condition. But we didn't respond, for fear of revealing our position to the NVA.

If we'd met so much as one enemy soldier along the way, we'd have been helpless. Neither of us had a weapon. Thankfully, we met nobody. We scrambled across a little road. Then we came to an open field. Doc went first, I hobbled behind. It was about 150 yards from the hedgerow to the wooded area where we'd taken the morning smoke break. There we found Tom Murphy. He had tried unsuccessfully to flank the NVA, then fallen back with his squad to wait for the others.

"How you feeling, Rock?" Murphy asked.

I couldn't have communicated it. I felt relieved beyond anything I'd ever known. And protected, like I was back in my mother's womb. But I kept the stiff upper lip.

"Fine, sir," I said.

"Do you think you can hang on for a while?"

"Yes, sir."

"Well, good. I think you're lucky. It looks like you've got a million-dollar wound there. It'll get you out of the field for a month or so, then you might have to come back."

I was kind of pleased about that. I took a quart canteen of water and inhaled it in twenty seconds. I bummed a cigarette and lit up. Actually, I'd stopped smoking three weeks ago, after feeling sick and reaching an all-time high of a pack and a half per day. But now I felt I deserved a cigarette.

About twenty minutes after Doc and I arrived, the rest of the platoon returned, low-crawling in a row. The four point men who'd been pinned down finally escaped. There was just one problem. Most of us had left our packs in the rice paddy. In some of them were special self-contained rockets which had been issued to us recently. They were deadly accurate at long range. We could only hope that the NVA wouldn't find and use them on us.

Murphy's options were these: Move back to the day logger and risk another ambush along the way. Or stay and defend this position in the woods, hoping that reinforcements would arrive soon. He guessed we were comparable to the enemy in numbers and, after consulting by radio with battalion headquarters, decided to stay.

We set up an L-shaped defense, which fronted a pathway and faced the rice paddy we'd just left. Murphy spotted guys fifteen yards into the woods and told them to dig foxholes. We'd left three dead in the earlier skirmish, so there were now twenty-two of us, including five wounded. We didn't know exactly how many NVA there were, or what they might do.

The second question was answered shortly. The enemy followed us across the rice paddy, spotted our command post, and spread themselves over the edge of the woods.

About two o'clock, the firing resumed. Murphy was in the middle of our defense, lying on his stomach, propped up on his elbows to look over a small bush. He was working three radios and a pair of binoculars simultaneously. I was six feet to his right, sitting on a two-foot ledge at the side of the pathway. I was holding the gauze to my wounded leg, resting it on the path. Two feet above and behind me was a fellow named Tommy Brown. He was sitting on a hillside of rocks.

Pop. Immediately, we recognized the sound of the old "potato masher" grenade . . . an explosive head attached to a stick-handle with a pull string at the bottom. We called them "Chi-Com," or Chinese-Communist, because they were made somewhere in Red China.

"Grenade!" Murphy screamed and ducked his head. I rolled into the pathway on my right side. It landed about two feet behind me, almost in the lap of Tommy Brown. He dived over me, just as the grenade detonated.

665802

The "potato masher, Chi-Com" hand grenade (*U.S. Army photograph*)

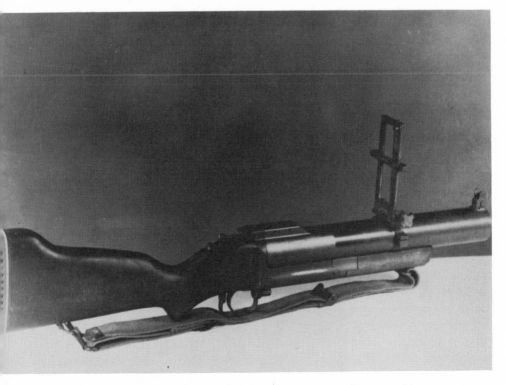

My weapon, the M-79 grenade launcher (*U.S. Army photograph*)

Tommy landed eight feet to my left, face down. He was conscious, groaning in deep tones. His back and legs were splashed with shrapnel holes. His blood mixed with the dirt and sweat, pasting the clothes to his skin. His moaning grew deeper.

I had been knocked out for a few seconds. When I awoke and looked back to the spot where I'd been sitting, I saw a hole two feet deep.

My ears were ringing. I couldn't hear at all. This was a cheap, concussion-type grenade, so the noise was actually greater than the damage. Except in Tommy Brown's case.

As I regained my hearing and full control of my senses, I realized I hadn't been hurt. Still, I stayed in a prone position on the pathway. Small-arms fire was flying over me. I was a spectator, though. I had no weapon, no mobility, no capacity to join the fight. I kept my head down and didn't really know what was happening. Five minutes passed before I looked up . . . and I was terrorized by what I saw.

A grenade was flying toward Murphy. He didn't see it. It hit him in the middle of the back, but didn't go off.

The grenade deflected toward me, bouncing crazily with its top-heavy shape. I had a millisecond to decide. Should I go backward? Or jump over it?

I crouched to spring forward.

The grenade was at my feet . . . and it exploded.

I landed on top of Murphy, both of us unconscious. He woke up after a few seconds. The first thing I remember, he was pushing me off.

He had caught it between the legs. He was moaning, having trouble staying conscious.

I was lying on my back, looking at him. Then I looked at my own legs, and saw the right one was quivering uncontrollably. It scared me. I grabbed it to stop the shaking. I felt my pants. They were full of blood. The pain in my right foot pierced me. I could see other places on both legs where shrapnel had shredded my fatigues.

Since Doc was wounded, too, we had only Murphy's medic from company headquarters to treat the entire platoon. He cut off my boot and tied a sterile gauze around the foot. "That's all I can do for you right now," he said, and low-crawled away like an alligator down the pathway.

Murphy was dragged away to the most secure position, the corner of our "L" perimeter. He had lost consciousness again. I was left lying among his three radios. One of them was communication to the *Blue Ghost*, our Cobra gunship overhead.

"Pop smoke, pop smoke. Mark your position," I heard the gunship demand. But nobody could find a canister of smoke. We'd left them all in our packs.

"Well, what are your coordinates?" the gunship asked. I tried to recall if I'd heard Murphy mention them. I couldn't. This was hopeless. The *Blue Ghost* couldn't help us if we couldn't locate ourselves.

Finally, somebody calculated our azimuth with a compass and range finder. We radioed it to the gunship, with specific instructions to strafe the open area around the rice paddy—so those special rockets would be detonated—and the edge of the woods, no deeper than ten yards.

Somehow, somebody miscalculated or miscommunicated. As the *Blue Ghost* peppered the NVA position, it fired rockets too deep into the woods, hitting our farthest foxhole. One of our men, a short-timer with twenty-eight days left, was killed. The other man had a piece of shrapnel break his collarbone, nick his heart, puncture his lung, and settle in his spleen. He was our second grenade launcher. When they pulled him back, he was in delirium, wailing grotesquely.

The NVA, incredibly, weathered the half-hour assault from above. Perhaps they had reinforcements. Or maybe there were more of them than we thought. Regardless, near 4:00 P.M., they came with another attack. It was a clear attempt to overrun us. They flanked our perimeter on three sides, and all hell broke loose. Mortars, grenades, machine guns, small-arms fire. Our guys were tired, wounded, probably outnumbered, desperately in need of assistance.

(The Army's after-action report of this period reads: "At 1545 hours, the *Blue Ghost* received extensive ground fire while supporting Company C. At 1645 hours, Company C received incoming mortars, resulting in numerous WIAs [wounded in action]. The enemy was on all sides of Company C and closing in.")

It was then, Murphy later told me, that he was convinced we would all die. From his own observation, from the reports of his men, and from gunship sightings, he estimated the NVA force to be 130 men. At the beginning of the day, we were thirty-two . . . the twenty-five men of my platoon and seven of Murphy's command group. If he'd known the manpower odds earlier, we would have retreated. But now it was too late.

He called his "Kit Carson scout" (former NVA soldier who had defected to our side) over to the corner of the perimeter and told him, "If they make an assault, we won't be able to hold them. When that happens, I want you to get away. Take this radio and put it into the hands of an American officer. Do not give it to anyone else. If it looks like you're in danger of being killed, destroy it."

Murphy's radio scrambled its waves into the air, so they could not be intercepted by the NVA. Only a special unit like the one he carried could send the scrambled signal and receive it intelligibly. If one of them had fallen into enemy hands, it would have destroyed our communication system in Hiep Douc.

Murphy's special radio was bringing him ominous news. Second platoon had twice set out from Million Dollar Hill, trying to rescue us. Each time, the NVA had allowed them to march into a clearing at the base of the hill, then driven them back with accurate mortar fire. Their casualties were almost as great as ours. They weren't going to be any help.

Third platoon and B Company of the 198th had evacuated the dead of Bravo-196th, as scheduled, in the morning. But now, as they tried to hump back up the hill to reinforce us, they had met an NVA ambush of their own. They couldn't get through, either.

Murphy looked over his troops . . . dirty, tired, hungry, wounded, and outnumbered four to one. He was convinced these men were about to die. When the final assault came, he was sure we could not defend ourselves. He called one of the lieutenants over and said, "Make sure each man has his weapon and all his ammo within reach. I want you to take every man who's able to hold a rifle, and prop him up against a rock or a tree stump. We're going to need everything we've got."

We had only two assets: first, the gunship. It could circle thousands of feet up, well out of view, then roar down without warning and strafe the hell out of the NVA position. Second, the enemy didn't know how weak we were. They didn't know that most of us were dead or wounded. They had no line of sight in the thick woods. There was only one pathway to get through to us, and we had it blanketed with a machine gun on either side. For a handful of guys, we were still putting out a lot of firepower. The NVA must have been deceived.

Still, we were theirs for the taking. Our left flank, for instance, was virtually unprotected. Most of our wounded were on that side, adjacent to an open field. I thought, "If the enemy sneaks around that way, they can enter this camp without the slightest resistance."

I found an M-16 lying in the dirt. I didn't know how accurate I could be with it. I hadn't fired one in earnest since AIT back at Fort Gordon. I rested it across my chest and crawled on my back thirty feet to the left, down a little slope in the pathway. I had almost no immediate cover . . . just a thin-trunked tree and three small rocks. But if the NVA were surrounding us, somebody had to guard that left-flank position, vulnerable as it was.

I began to consider the possibilities. If they found out how depleted we were, they could circle the woods and attack from behind, catching us in a cross fire. We would have absolutely no chance. We'd never see them coming over the hill to our rear.

Suddenly, there was another problem. Our rockets had started a fire in the woods. Most of the bushes and grass were burning, threatening to catch the trees ablaze. The wind was blowing it our way. Thick smoke rolled at us.

For me, the possible consequences were dire. If fire swept into our position, the other guys could run. But I couldn't even walk. And I couldn't blame them, if, under the pressure of the NVA and the fire, they left me behind.

The fighting continued sporadically. Murphy had ordered us to hold our fire, conserving it to defend against the final assault. The enemy kept it up, pelting us with automatic weapons and grenades. Several more guys were wounded. Our radioman, "T," was shot in the throat. Of the original thirty-two, nine were now dead, two missing in action, and the rest seriously wounded.

I never knew why the NVA didn't mount a concerted thrust. Murphy later speculated that we'd killed or wounded their commanding officer, leaving them without leadership. Whatever the reason, their late-afternoon maneuvers lacked the decisiveness they'd shown in the morning. They never pressed their advantage, limiting themselves to a few probes and long-range grenade assaults. About five thirty, they fell back, out of the woods.

A few minutes later, with the fire literally ten feet from our perimeter, I got my miracle. The third platoon appeared out of nowhere, and I heard a sergeant say, "All right, let's get the fuck out of here."

I closed my eyes for a moment and praised God.

My prayer was interrupted by a guy who came running up and dropped to his knees at my side. He couldn't contain his excitement. "Rock, Rock, we heard you were dead."

"No, I'm not," I said, a little stunned. "But what do you say we get my ass out of here."

They began to carry us out. Murphy went first, then me. It took four men apiece to hoist us, each grasping the corner of a poncho liner. They told me a medevac helicopter was waiting two to three klicks away (roughly two miles), back on Million Dollar Hill.

My four bearers tired quickly. They'd spent the day in a firefight of their own, before humping up the hill to get us. Several times they dropped me to rest, each time pleading, "Rock, can't you walk?" or "Let us drag you by your shoulders." I begged them to carry me. But after half a klick, the poncho liner broke.

I draped my arms over two guys' shoulders and continued, pivoting on my "good" leg, the left one that had been shot through the thigh. We went another klick that way, until my arms and shoulders gave out. I collapsed onto the ground and said, "I can't go any farther this way."

Now a guy said he'd carry me fireman-style, over his shoulder. I never knew his name, and I don't think he ever knew mine. I didn't know anything but nicknames for most of the guys. But the Army had a beautiful way of making names seem unimportant . . . and race, and color, and creed, and social status. We never looked for any of that in each other. The Army is a great equalizer.

I was white, this guy was black. We had each traveled thousands of miles to meet in a jungle. After this night, I would never see him again. We both knew that. Yet here he was, offering to pick me up bodily and help save my life. That's a special kind of love.

It was an ordeal for both of us. He struggled under my weight. I pushed against his back, to relieve the pressure of his shoulder digging into my gut. My dangling legs caught on trees and bushes, sending shots of pain up through my body and knocking him off balance. We could go only thirty yards at a time before resting. I stood on my left leg, clinging to him. We panted at each other, trying to catch our breath. Then he'd pick me up. We'd go some more. Then we'd rest, and pant again.

Meanwhile, the others were passing us. We had been ordered to stay in formation and keep contact. But every time we stopped to rest, two or three men passed us. We were slipping farther and farther back toward the rear. I was still without a weapon or mobility to defend myself.

I was physically drained. I hadn't had food all day. It was dark. I didn't know where we were. I knew it was open territory. NVA were everywhere in the valley. We could have been staggering into another ambush.

With half a klick to go, I collapsed again, this time onto the side of a little road we'd been following. I looked up at this guy, blinked back a few tears, and said, "I can't go this way anymore. Get me a stretcher. It's not that much farther. Get me a stretcher." My friend stopped a third-platoon radioman, who called ahead to the helicopter.

That's when it really started to hurt. *Thump, thump, thump.* With every heartbeat, the agony surged through my right foot. I lay there gritting my teeth, ripping clumps of grass with my hands. And crying. It hurt so bad.

Our position was more perilous than ever. That radioman represented the rear element of third platoon. Once he went off toward the helicopter, we were by ourselves. We had broken contact completely. We could only hope that he'd send a stretcher back to us. My friend and me. He stayed at my side, holding my hand, telling me, "It's all right.

You're okay. We're going to get there." With each new rush of pain, I squeezed him tighter. We were both covered with my blood. I was sobbing louder now. We were so *alone.*

Finally, four guys came with another poncho liner. They were too weak to lift me into the air completely, so they sort of dragged me the last five hundred meters. I knocked against rocks and tree stumps, my bleeding legs banging against each other, inside that little piece of plastic.

When we came within sight of the medevac, there was one final difficulty. It was sitting on top of a ridge, the access to which was a narrow, rocky path. It was not wide enough that my bearers could carry me two abreast. Two of them, positioned front and back, tried hoisting me. After a few steps, the front man lost his grip, and I fell backward, bouncing down the hill. I screeched with pain.

They tried again . . . I fell again . . . I screeched again.

In my clouded mind, I kept thinking the helicopter would leave without me and never come back. I was crying, babbling, whimpering about that. Finally, the four of them grabbed corners of the poncho liner and forced their way through the underbrush, up the pathway. They slipped and stumbled, jostling me against the rocks. I shrieked again.

They set me down on top of the ridge and sank to their knees, exhausted. I looked up at the helicopter's turning blades. "Thank you, Lord."

I was the second man to leave the firefight, and last to arrive at the secured claiming area. It had taken six hours to move two miles. It was midnight. August 20 had ended.

8] Rehabilitation

The first two medevac runs were full of the earlier arrivals, so I waited two hours for a third. In that time, I got a shot of morphine. It was the only pain-suppressant of any kind that I'd gotten since the rifle-shot wound fourteen hours earlier. It did nothing to relieve my misery, however. The confusion, pain, fear, panic . . . the darkness, the adrenaline, the thumping . . . all of it conspired to prevent the morphine from taking effect. I was still in shock, and not behaving very heroically.

"I gotta get another shot," I screamed at the medic.

"No, I can't do that," he said.

"Why not?" I raged. "I'm in pain. Do something!"

"It might knock you out, or disguise the seriousness of your wounds. The doctors at the aid station will want to know where it hurts."

"I don't give a shit. Now give me another fucking shot."

"No."

"Well, then, get the fuck out of here."

At 2:00 A.M., I boarded next-to-last, and Murphy last, for the flight to an aid station, the Twenty-third Medical Company at LZ Baldy. The medevac pilots were so harried, after ducking antiaircraft fire all night, and the flight was so quickly loaded, Murphy almost fell out as we were taking off.

The bottom third of his legs dangled outside the doorway. I held him by the shirt, but there was no room to pull him farther inside. The aircraft was jammed wall-to-wall.

My admiration for Murphy at that moment was total. He had gotten to Million Dollar Hill about ten o'clock, and could have gone on the first medevac run. But he waited four hours while the rest of us straggled back, insisting that he be the last man evacuated.

Now he was flying to the aid station with his shrapnel wounds exposed to the violent force of the cold winds. His legs banged against each other and against the helicopter door, buffeted by the air currents.

The pain registering in his face was inhuman. He later told me it was twice as painful as the wounds which ended his first Vietnam tour. He said it hurt so much, he felt like somebody other than himself. The agony was so different from anything he'd known, so far outside his personal experience, he felt it must have been happening to someone else.

I knew what he meant. Once he said that, I recalled having the same sensation . . . wondering, in my delirium, "Who *am* I? Who is this happening to?" The pain was so powerful, it changed my mind and body, and *made* me a new person. That's the only way I can explain it.

At the aid station, they put clean dressings on the wounds and gave me the second shot of morphine I craved.

Before they wheeled me out, I asked a favor. I'd felt stickiness, like dried blood, on my buttocks. So I told the doctor, "Check one more thing, please. I think I got my ass shot up."

He turned me over, slit my pants, made the examination, and sent me out. Never said a word about it. They left me on the stretcher in that position . . . lying on my stomach, my bare ass sticking out of my pants. The helicopter rose again into the clear, crisp night. The stars and moon looked so beautiful. I was feeling better after the second shot, kind of drowsy.

They rolled us into the Ninety-fifth Evacuation Hospital in Da Nang at 5:00 A.M. Everybody else was lying on his back. My position was unchanged, and now it was kind of embarrassing, because there were nurses around.

One of them walked over to me, looked at my naked bottom, and asked, "What's wrong with you?"

"I think I got my ass shot," I said rather sheepishly.

She said, "Oh," kind of matter-of-factly, and walked away.

After that, I forgot about it for more than a year. The damage to my leg, knee, and foot consumed my attention. Then, one day, while watching television, I scratched my rear end, as most TV-watchers do occasionally. I felt a little nick. And it dawned on me. That was the "big wound" I'd bothered everybody with. It was no wound at all. A small blood vessel might have been scraped. That was it. The embarrassment and cold air had been more painful than the little scratch.

Once I'd been admitted, a fellow came to my hospital room and said, "Let me take your personal articles. I'll keep them safe for you." I gave him my large wooden cross. That's all I had.

Then, ten minutes later, a Red Cross volunteer came by and said the same thing. The first guy was an impostor. It happened all the time, the lady told me. Somebody had stolen the wooden cross that had gotten Al Lison through World War II, and gotten me through Vietnam.

I was wheeled into a waiting room, where I met all the guys of my platoon who were still alive.

Murphy called out, "Hey, Rock, how are you?"

"Fine, sir. How are you?"

"Fine, fine."

(That was the last I saw of Murphy for several years. We were transferred to different hospitals for further treatment. Ultimately, he had five operations performed on his legs. He's now stationed at Fort Monroe, Virginia, awaiting an imminent promotion to major.)

An orderly shaved me, agreeing to leave my recently grown handlebar moustache intact. At six o'clock, I underwent surgery to clean out most of the shrapnel . . . tiny, circular-shaped bits of metal. I had more than a hundred pieces in me. And because the shrapnel was sulfur-coated, the doctors left my wounds open, hoping the pus and infection would drain out.

White sulfur is what caused the pain to become most intense several hours after I was hit. Like the "tiny timed pills" you find in that well-advertised cold remedy, sulfur has a delayed effect. After several hours' exposure, it begins eating away the skin. Doctors, in fact, can't see where the sulfur has lodged until this eating-away process has begun, three hours or longer after the blast. That's another reason they don't suture such wounds immediately after surgery.

In wars previous to Vietnam, the standard treatment involved washing the wounds with a copper solution. That caused a chemical reaction with the pure sulfur, yielding copper sulfate, which medical science thought was harmless. After World War II, however, research suggested that copper sulfate caused damage to the brain and kidneys.

In Vietnam, therefore, scalpels were the basic treatment. Once it had taken effect, sulfur left the skin looking like it was burned with a flame. Surgeons simply scraped away the burned and discolored tissue . . . plus two or three surrounding layers of tissue which may have appeared healthy but actually were infected with the quickly moving sulfur.

After a while, they learned how deep to cut. The hospital I visited in Da Nang performed this sort of operation twenty times a day. They came to understand shrapnel as a threefold problem . . . the burning caused by sulfur, the infection introduced through open wounds, and the holes resulting from surgery.

When I woke up in the afternoon, I wouldn't have known it was August 21, except that another patient handed me a copy of that day's *Stars and Stripes*, the Army newspaper. Irony of ironies, there was a story about "Rocky Bleier, ex-football player, now serving with the 196th LIB in Hiep Douc." They were one day late. And there was an implication in the term "ex-football player" that I did not want to consider.

The pain, fatigue, lingering shock effects, and general hospital atmosphere left me without appetite. I spent three days in Da Nang with an upset stomach. I ate absolutely nothing, no solid food, while I was there. When they lifted me onto an airplane bound for the Philippines, I was no burden at all. I weighed 160 pounds, forty-five pounds under my normal weight.

One night later, it was on to Tokyo. Camp Oji Military Hospital welcomed me on August 25, in the person of Dr. Anan Laorr, a native of Thailand who had studied at Syracuse University.

As he made rounds among the new patients, he stopped at my bed, barely introduced himself, and said, "Scissors." He cut the five-day-old bandages, which, for infection prevention, had not been changed since my night of infamy. Then he ripped them off . . . and watched me levitate off the bed.

Next he grabbed my foot and began examining it while mumbling little American colloquialisms to himself. "Mmmm, Uh-huh. Okay. Pretty good."

Meanwhile, I was jamming my fingernails into the headboard and breaking out in a cold sweat. Finally, I could take it no longer.

"Jesus, Doc, that second toe's broken," I said.

"I know," he said.

"Well, so do I. Could you be a little more gentle?"

He looked away from me and said, "Forceps."

Now try to imagine this. All the skin near the base of my first three toes was laid open. He took those forceps, inserted them through that opening, and reached them four inches into my foot, looking for more broken bones. It hurt worse than anything the NVA had done.

When he finished, he explained the damage to me. The steel plate in my combat boot had saved my foot. Infection had spread all the way up to my calf, but he would leave the wounds open and hope they'd heal from the inside out. Most of the shrapnel had been removed, but there might be pieces so deeply embedded that they'd take a year or more to work themselves to the skin.

The blast had gashed my foot in three places principally . . . along the instep, extending to the ball of the foot; alongside the big toe, reaching the bone; and under the second toe, shattering the bone. Damage to my legs and knees would leave an imprint, but this would heal. The flesh wound in my left thigh was stitched, and would leave a permanent indentation. He said he thought, with therapy, I could learn to walk normally.

That afternoon, Dr. Laorr's associate, Dr. John Baughman, came through the ward.

"So you're Rocky Bleier, huh?" he said amiably. "Notre Dame, right?"

"Yes, Doctor, who are you?"

"Never mind who I am. It's where I'm from that's important. I was at Southern Cal in 1966 when you guys creamed us 51-0, and I haven't forgotten." He raised his fist, but he was smiling.

"Listen, Doc," I said, "don't take it out on me. I wasn't even there that day. I was in a hospital in South Bend. Honest, Doc, honest."

We laughed about it for a moment before I got serious.

"Doc," I said, "you know I made the Pittsburgh Steelers last year, and I'd like to go back. What do you think my chances are?"

"You want an honest opinion?"

"Of course. Give it to me straight."

"Rocky, you won't be able to play again. It's impossible."

He said it positively, without equivocating. Kind of sadly, but assertively. I don't think it registered with me at the time. I didn't argue with him. But I didn't repeat his opinion to anybody, either.

On August 29, the effects of sedation had subsided enough that I felt able to call home. In case of injury, the Army had given me the option to inform my parents personally, or let them do it. I elected to do it myself. The call went through to my dad at the bar. I stammered and talked too fast, the speech pattern of my youth. The last thing I mumbled was, "Tell Mom not to worry. I'm all right." I guess she didn't believe it, because she called back the next night.

On August 20 at 5:00 P.M. in Appleton, Dad had been playing golf. Mom was watching the evening news and saw a graphic, detailed account of the action in Hiep Douc. The reporter said B Company had been hit, C Company had gone to help, and was ambushed with more than half its men killed. She sat on the sofa in our apartment, shivering with fright. When my dad came through the door, her first words were, "Rocky's been hit. I just know he's been hit. Now what are we going to do?"

She called my uncle, Lieutenant William Marshall, at Fort Riley, Kansas. He told her, "If Rocky's been killed, you'll know within forty-eight hours. And the Army will come to you directly. They won't send a telegram."

My mother spent most of the next two days in the apartment. She did not answer the telephone, and she prayed there would be no knocks at the door. By the time I spoke to her from Tokyo, she was wrung out. After I hung up, I found some Red Cross stationery and tried to reassure her:

Dear Mom and Dad,

By now, you've received my first letter. I can't remember what I said, except not to worry, and that still goes.

When I called, we had a bad connection, so I hope you got everything straight. Yesterday, they closed up the wounds on my legs, but they left the foot open. Still infection in there. I get it irrigated every four hours, so it should drain pretty soon. When it does, they'll sew it up.

Have been having quite a bit of pain, relieved only by a shot of Demerol every four hours. But today I feel better and it doesn't hurt as much. They change the bandages twice a day. And sometimes, when the doctor starts digging around, I could climb the walls. You can always tell where he is in the ward, because guys are crying, "Goddam it, Doc. Son of a bitch." Some days, I'd just like to kick him in the face with my good foot.

Can't wait to get home. Getting on my nerves over here. Would like to see some friendly faces. Don't worry, I'll be okay. Will write later.

Love,

Rocky

P.S. Boy, I have to mention the papers making a big deal out of this. Talked to both AP and UPI over here. Also did an interview with NBC—if you see it, notice I still have my handlebar. Thought they forgot about me after I came into the service.

The Army allowed wire services to release the story soon after I'd called my parents on the twenty-ninth. That's how most of my friends learned of it. Chuck Noll, the new Steeler coach, told the team during its evening meeting at training camp.

Actually, the first news reports made it sound more serious than it really was. AP quoted a letter I'd written to my father, saying I was "pretty lucky" to be among the survivors. I guess everybody thought the worst. A friend of our family, in fact, got confused and sent a sympathy card. That really jolted my mother.

Two days later, September 2, AP carried a picture of me sitting in bed, my right leg suspended for the infection drainage. My left leg was not visible under the covers. Like all good mothers, when their sons are in danger, Mom jumped to conclusions. "He had his leg blown off and didn't tell us," she said to my father. "Or else they amputated it. He's being brave about it and not telling us."

I, meanwhile, was talking to reporters in a half-drugged stupor and promising them everything but a Super Bowl title for Pittsburgh in 1970. I don't recall those earliest interviews, but I was quoted as saying, "I'll be off my back in two or three weeks. The doc informs me there'll be no problems. I'll be back with the Steelers next year. This is no big deal. I was never very fast, anyway."

I wasn't thinking seriously about the words of Dr. Baughman while I was in Tokyo. I just wanted to get out of there.

Oji was enough to make me count my blessings. In the bed next to me was a Bluegrass native whom we'd nicknamed, naturally, "Kentucky." He was hit by a bunker rocket, a special kind that is designed to burn through a bunker before exploding, rather than exploding on impact. His bunker mate was killed, and he was knocked unconscious. He awoke and crawled out of that burning hellhole, only to find Vietcong running through camp. He lay there, half expecting to be shot through the head, when another American soldier spotted him and dragged him into the safety of a different bunker. "Kentucky" had large holes in his legs, shoulders, and wrist from rocket shrapnel.

I met another fellow who'd been through a rocket attack. He was on a personnel carrier when an NVA rocket tore off a heavy metal door. It hit this guy with an impact so great, the doctors had to split him down the middle to check for internal injuries. He had a scar from his breastbone to his groin.

There were the other kinds of stories, too. A guy woke up one morning in the field with a lump on his forearm. His medic said it was probably just a spider bite, but he should go to an aid station to have it checked. The aid station said the same thing and sent him to Saigon. Saigon said the same thing, but they didn't have time to treat him. The hospital wasn't safe from attack, so everybody was being moved to Tokyo. Tokyo finally lanced it, gave him some antibiotics, and told him not to play with spiders anymore. When they attempted to reassign him, they found he had less than six months' duty, so they discharged him.

Our ward was entertained each night by a fellow named Joe. During the day, he was normal as could be. But at night, he'd march around the beds, carrying a broom over his shoulder like an M-16. We never knew if he was putting us on or not.

"Hup, two, three, four. Hup, two, three, four." He kept time for himself.

"Hey, Joe, what are you looking for?" someone would ask.

"Rats. They're everywhere."

He'd low-crawl under the beds, as if in combat.

"I see 'em. I see 'em," he'd scream. "Pow, pow. There goes one now. I'm going to get him."

"Nu-u-u-urse," a patient would moan.

"What do you want?"

"Joe's out of bed again."

"Where is he now?"

"He's on the floor. Looking for rats. Under my bed."

The nurse would find him and say, "Now, Joe, you're doing a very good job. But let's go back to bed. You killed all the rats last night."

"Yeah," he'd say, "but they're everywhere. They're all over."

"C'mon now, Joe. Go to bed."

"Well, okay. Hup, two, three, four. Hup, two, three, four."

I didn't know whether to laugh or cry. He probably should have been in a psychiatric ward.

I looked all through the hospital before finding some friends from another platoon in my company. I asked a sergeant, an E-6, what happened in Hiep Douc after I departed.

He told me, "We really got into a lot of shit when we went back to LZ Siberia the night you were shot. I don't know where they got them, but the dinks brought in 105s. They pounded Siberia, just pounded it, knocked the shit out of it.

"We were out in the field the next day, and they kicked the shit out of us, too. We had an E-7 with us, a platoon sergeant who'd been in twenty-two years, done two or three tours of Nam. He was really gung ho, always looking for some action. Well, a .50 round caught him in the head and just skipped him down the rice paddy. I caught a .50 in the legs, and it knocked the pins out from under me. And our machine gunner—I think he was a friend of yours—nice kid. He caught it right in the chest. I don't know how many of us are left."

I subsequently checked with the Pentagon, and found a more complete report of the action in Hiep Douc. The official battalion summary dates the NVA offensive on LZ West and LZ Siberia as August 11 to 29. The enemy concentrated southwest of West, where local water supplies were located, and attacked with 60-millimeter mortars, 75- and 82-millimeter recoilless rifles, 122-millimeter rockets, and 127-millimeter antiaircraft guns.

The nightly shellings of both bases closed the mess halls and confined our guys to their bunkers, where they mixed lurps for every meal. With the air base threatened, it was impossible to resupply, by helicopter, essentials such as food, water, medicine, and ammunition.

When bandages ran out, the medics used old shirts to bind up shrapnel wounds. Food rations and ammo were hauled in overland. But water was too heavy, and besides, the Army considered it a luxury. For eleven days during the height of the NVA offensive, water was rationed on West. No shaving or bathing was permitted. Finally, when the pressure eased on August 28, a half-million gallons of water arrived by airlift in five days.

Despite the limited air traffic, there were several helicopter crashes during the month—some of them attributed to enemy ground fire, others attributed to mechanical failure in the official Pentagon reports. One such disaster, the crash of a Command and Control helicopter, killed eight men, including our battalion commander, his command sergeant major, and an Associated Press newsman. Worse yet, the NVA set up an ambush near the crash site and annihilated two recon patrols. As our company could attest, that was an old, reliable maneuver by the enemy . . . based on the Americans' constant practice of returning to pick up their dead.

The command on West and Siberia had a fourfold problem: Secure the bases; defend the people of Tin City, as promised; drive out the NVA positioned southwest of West; eliminate another, smaller enemy force northeast of Siberia. Our guys finally accomplished the task by importing the 90-millimeter recoilless rifle, an antipersonnel weapon that devastated the enemy's well-dug bunker positions. Pentagon reports put the number of NVA dead at 540 to 682 for the period August 11 to 29 in Hiep Douc. Wounded were estimated at more than 1,000. American casualties were listed as fewer than 200 dead, fewer than 500 wounded.

I considered myself fortunate to be in the latter group. Some others in Tokyo hospitals felt the same way. The E-6 told me, as he was leaving for physical therapy, "We were really in a lot of trouble. I think I was kind of lucky to be wounded and get the hell out of there."

That's the thought I took with me September 14 when I flew off for Fort Riley, Kansas. Maybe I couldn't play football again, but how could

I bitch? A lot of guys wouldn't return to the States at all. I recalled the story a corpsman had told me in Da Nang: On one of his medevac runs, a guy was being loud and obnoxious because he had lost his arm. He screamed and carried on for a few minutes until another guy crawled off his stretcher and punched him out. That guy had no legs.

Sure, I had some physical wounds, but it could have been worse. Besides, I had no emotional scars. My grenade launcher being accurate up to 150 yards, I was never involved in close combat. I shot only at targets. I never knew if I killed anybody. The only time I was in contact with a dead man was that night we were ambushed at the stream-crossing. Even then, it was dark, I didn't see his face, I didn't know him. So I came back home without fearing nightmares or mental illness. Twenty percent of Vietnam veterans cannot make that statement.

Fort Riley was as sweet as Army life can be. Everybody was extra nice to Vietnam casualties. They bent certain rules and offered us favors. I imagine the brass knew about it, because they were nicest of all.

A retired general in the next room befriended me. Every morning he'd bring his newspaper over to me, and we'd spend a half hour or so talking about sports. One day he bounded into the room and asked me the name of a Notre Dame receiver whose brother had played at Army.

I said, "That's my old teammate, Jim Seymour, General. His brother John was a running back at Army in the early sixties."

Then the general went out and returned with the new commanding general of the post! We spent a half hour talking about the brothers Seymour, about my wounds and my progress toward recovery.

I saw the commanding general again two weeks later. I was on crutches, stepping from my therapy room toward an elevator. The general was on an inspection tour, surrounded by an entourage of colonels, majors, and captains, all hustling around him. He saw me and stopped.

"Hi, General," I said. "How are ya?"

The entourage looked at me, aghast. Then they looked at each other as if to say, "Who is this peon?"

"Well, how are you, Rock?" the general asked.

"Fine, sir, fine."

"How are you getting along?"

"Good, good."

The entourage was really pacing around him now, peering me up and down. One of them insisted, "We have to be moving along, sir." And they left.

Suddenly, the general turned on his heel . . . and with him, the whole group. He came back smiling, and put his hand on my shoulder.

"John Seymour, huh?" he asked.

"That's right, General."

"You realize I lost a five-dollar bet on that," he laughed. "But it's not your fault I can't remember all the great halfbacks from West Point. Well, good luck to you, Rock. We'll see you again some other time."

"Okay, sir."

Captured in that moment was my essential love-hate relationship with the Army. I hated the bullshit, the harassment, the meaningless duties, the inflexibility of some officers. What I loved in the Army, as in life, were the real people, the guys who didn't let regulations dehumanize them. The guys who took time to be genuine . . . like Hawaii, and Tom Murphy, and that selfless human being who carried me through the jungle on his shoulder. I thought about those men as I watched the entourage stalk off in finest military fashion. The captains, majors, and colonels were wondering why the little PFC was wasting the commanding general's time. The general, meanwhile, was unconcerned about it. He was too busy being human.

I got a thirty-day leave in October. I went home for a week, then to South Bend, where I stayed with Joe and Mary Hickey for Homecoming Weekend. Notre Dame was playing its biggest game of the season against Southern California.

I hobbled into Tom Pagna's office on Friday afternoon. He told me, "Rocky, when you went to Vietnam, I told my wife, 'He's the type of kid who might have something happen to him. Remember that saying about the truly good die young.' You son of a gun, you almost proved me right."

We didn't talk specifically about my football career, but I knew what Tom was thinking. Even then, he was one of the few people who never doubted I could play again . . . as long as *I* thought I could play again.

At the age of sixteen, Tom had had a deep hematoma in his thigh. It hemorrhaged, and blood hardened in the layers of the muscle. His mother made him promise he'd never play football again. Tom spent a year and a half in bed, practicing what he calls "ceiling philosophy." That's lying on your back and thinking hard. Eventually, he came back to football and became an honorable-mention All-America.

I guess I did some "ceiling philosophy" during my first three weeks at Fort Riley. I considered giving up football. I thought, "Why bust my ass, and then be hurt if I don't make it? I was a marginal player when I

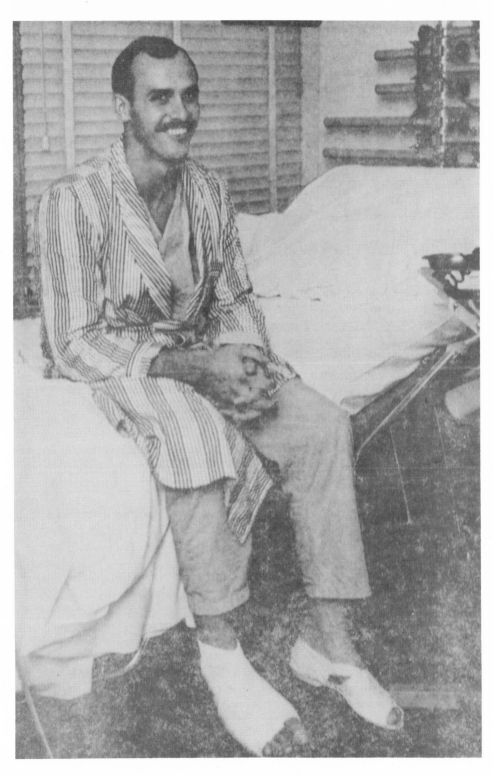

Recuperating at Irwin Army Hospital, Fort Riley (*U.S. Army Photograph*)

was healthy." But I had to try, at least. It all went back to freshman year at Notre Dame, when they gave me a questionnaire that asked, "Career Goals?"

I wrote, "Play pro football."

After leaving Tom Pagna, I went into Ara Parseghian's office and told him I was going to try to play again.

His secretary, Mrs. Barbara Nicholas, shook her head and told me straight out I couldn't. Ara didn't offer an opinion. That's not his way. But after I'd gone, he said to Mrs. Nicholas, "There's no chance. He's had half his foot shot away. Just to walk, you need your hip, knee, and ankle in perfect shape. Even with a little blister, you can't run. Here he's had all the ligaments, tendons, and muscles damaged. He'll need more surgery. I just hope he's able to walk normally again. Maybe he can restore himself enough to play a little golf or racquet ball."

On the way out of Ara's office, I ran into John Stephens, a retired Army colonel and Notre Dame's assistant athletic director. He asked me to speak that night at the big pregame pep rally. I said I didn't think so. I didn't want to intrude on the festive preparations for the game. But Colonel Stephens persisted. It was to be the last rally in the Fieldhouse, a grand old structure built in another century, whose walls were painted with tradition. I couldn't refuse.

Of all the emotional moments I've known, this was among the most intense. Start with seven thousand highly charged Irish fans jammed into this campus monument for what they thought would be the last time. Their team was at the crossroad of its season, desperately needing a win over USC. They chanted and hollered, built human pyramids, threw toilet paper, and sang the "Victory March" unceasingly.

I had nothing to add to their circus. I feared I would be out of place. Yet, somehow, I was not. As I moved to the speakers' balcony, to the same wooden benches where I'd sat as an undergraduate, I knew what would happen. Looking down, I saw some familiar faces in the crowd, and thought about what I would say to them. The mere act of composing the speech broke me. I started to cry.

Some of my listeners felt similar emotions. Antiwar sentiment was running high by the fall of 1969, even at conservative Notre Dame. Some of these people had known me as a big, strapping, fresh-faced kid. Now, seeing me so frail, with sunken cheeks, and limping against my cane . . . I guess it got to them. By the time I was finished talking, the whole building was crying.

It was hot and steamy in the Fieldhouse. I felt wilted. But I stood up to the microphone and gave it my best:

It's been two years since I stood before you. Much has happened in those two years, some good and some bad.

The good was that I met a group of men who gave me experiences I'll never forget, principles and ideals that will never leave me. They gave me guidelines to live my life by. Most of them didn't want to be in Vietnam. But they were willing to give their lives for others, whether or not they agreed with the policies that put them there.

So I ask you players not to win the game for me. Rather, win it for my friends—the men who are left on the battlefields and in the hospitals of Vietnam.

Saturday afternoon, I was to join Father Theodore Hesburgh, the university president, and Tom McKenna, the student body president, in a flag presentation on the field. Father Hesburgh rushed in from the airport, in typical fashion, and arrived on the field just before kickoff. He looked quizzically at me for a moment, then called McKenna to his side. I could almost read his lips, asking the oft-quoted question from the movie *Butch Cassidy and the Sundance Kid:* "Who *is* that guy?"

After McKenna told him, he said, "Hey, Rock, buddy, come on over here." He slapped me on the back a couple times. "How are you? How've you been?"

Was I so unrecognizable in my handlebar, and cane, and new svelte look? Or had the good padre become so busy with all his committee meetings that occasionally he slipped a gear? I've often wondered. As he stood at the 50-yard line, describing me as "a man whom we all know and admire," I had to chuckle.

I thought, "Father Hesburgh, you bullshitter. You've got us all fooled. You're beautiful."

The next weekend, I was in Pittsburgh for Steeler Alumni Day, an annual gathering of former players. I wasn't necessarily ready to be categorized that way, but I enjoyed their company, nevertheless.

The first man I went to see when I arrived was Art Rooney Sr., the team owner. You may know him as the most beloved man in sports, a designation he has earned by being the warmest, kindest, most human . . . suffice it to say this is a man for all superlatives.

I didn't know it at the time, but Mr. Rooney had serious reservations—as did others in the Steeler organization—about my ability to play again. I'd been writing him regularly, from Tokyo and Fort Riley, perhaps overstating the progress I'd seen in my foot. I didn't want to be forgotten.

When the first of those letters arrived in September, Art Jr. happened to be in his father's office. After Mr. Rooney read the letter, he flipped it into the air and said to his son, "Rocky says he got hit by a grenade, but he can still play." He paused a moment and looked off pensively. Then he said, "Yeah, he can still play." That last sentence was spoken with all his Irish sarcasm . . . kind of funny, and sad, and tragic, and sardonic, all at once, as Art Jr. later described it to me. As if to say, "Rocky's kidding himself."

But Mr. Rooney never showed that pessimism to me. He'd always been very encouraging while I was in the service. He sent me clippings and game programs in Vietnam, always with a cheerful note attached. In the preseason of 1969, when the Steelers played at Green Bay, he took a group of front-office people to Appleton for a fish dinner at Dad's bar. (Mr. Rooney likes to say my mother gave him a number and made him wait like everybody else, but she swears it's not true.) He told my parents he was sure I'd come back to the team.

That was a couple weeks before I was wounded. When he heard about my foot, he still never deviated from that outward optimism. Even seeing me on Alumni Weekend, pitifully underweight and limping, he maintained his exterior. Mr. Rooney simply told me to get in shape. He would take care of the rest.

Pittsburgh played Washington that weekend, and the game was memorable for several reasons, none of which referred to the caliber of football. Vince Lombardi was coaching the Redskins in his last football season before dying of cancer. Bill Austin was one of his assistants. Chuck Noll, meanwhile, was on his way to a 1–13 rookie year as the Pittsburgh coach. And this particular afternoon was one of the highlights.

It was the first time in anybody's memory that a home crowd had accorded the Steelers two standing ovations. One came during pregame ceremonies when I walked onto the field. The 46,557 fans shook old Pitt Stadium so hard, they brought a lump to my throat. They literally interrupted the Steelers' pregame meeting. The team sat silently for a second in the locker room, just listening.

The second standing ovation came during player introductions, when the PA announcer intoned, "Starting at quarterback for the first time as a professional, the rookie from Notre Dame, number five, Terry Hanratty." That's right, folks. The old golf cart racer himself had become a Steeler. Terry will argue, of course, that *his* standing ovation was louder, longer, and better deserved. I usually concede the last one, but not the other too. When reminded it was his interception that lost the game, I am forced to say he's wrong on all three counts.

After the Pittsburgh trip, I wasn't back at Fort Riley ten days when my uncle, Lieutenant Bill Marshall, arranged another leave for me. Since I couldn't do anything on post, the hospital staff was just as happy to get rid of me. Uncle Bill assigned me special duty . . . three weeks to help move his family to Texas, then drive to Los Angeles for my maternal grandparents' golden wedding anniversary. I accomplished both missions with time to spare . . . time for a week of relaxation.

L.A. had been good to me on my last visit. In the summer of 1966, I was driving with a friend on the Ventura Freeway when a man pulled alongside and motioned for us to pull over.

"I see the decal," he said. "You boys from Notre Dame?"

"Yes, sir."

"And the license plates. You live in Wisconsin?"

"Yes, sir."

"Well, I'm Scott Brady, and I'm fond of both places."

Of course, Scott Brady. He was one of my high school idols. He was "Shotgun Slade" on television at ten thirty every night after the news. Sometimes Mom would let me stay up and watch him. He loved it when I told him. Then he asked if we needed anything.

I said, "Well, Mr. Brady, there is one thing. We've been here on the Coast for a week now, and we don't have jobs yet. If we don't find something soon, we'll have to go back to Wisconsin. We don't have any more money."

The next week, through some Notre Dame contacts, we were working at Disneyland. My job was riding around in a bakery truck, watching the women, and eating myself sick on tarts, pies, and large sheets of chocolate brownies. Ah, such a summer.

The Coast was good to me again in '69. I met some friends from Notre Dame, who invited me down to the San Diego area for a couple days. No doubt, the top thrill of my stay was meeting Frank Stills.

Frank played every song I knew one night at the piano bar of the Seven Crown restaurant. Then he took us back to his apartment at 3:00 A.M., and amused us until dawn with the inside scoop on Martha Ray and Mae West. Frank was Ms. Ray's arranger-composer and Ms. West's confidant. I couldn't decide which was better.

By the time I left California and returned to Kansas, it was December. Time for Christmas leave, they told me. That was four weeks at home.

I showed up again January 6. The Army doctor examined me that day and said, "I think you need another operation. What we'll do is take those bone spurs off, cut some ligaments out of the scar tissue, and start giving you more flexibility in your foot."

I said, "Okay, Doc, you're the boss."

He turned to his nurse. "When can we get Bleier in?"

She said, "February twenty-eighth."

He looked back at me. "You want to stay around here?"

I said, "Gee, I haven't been around long enough to know."

He said, "The most I can give you is four weeks' leave. But you can call us and have it extended. See you next month."

So I turned around and went home again.

Of my first twenty-four weeks at Fort Riley, nineteen were spent on leave. Fort Riley, hell. "The Life of Riley" is more like it.

9] *Coming Back*

It is not true, as some people have said, that I am the only NFL football player ever to fight in Vietnam.

One NFL player was killed in Vietnam . . . Bob Kalsu, a guard with the Buffalo Bills in 1968. He came through the ROTC program at Oklahoma, was commissioned a second lieutenant, and died while leading a combat unit in 1969.

Roger Staubach, Dallas's quarterback, served with the Navy in Southeast Asia. Woody Campbell was a running back with Houston, and served in the Air Force. Remarkably, he did both at once. During the 1968 season, Woody took weekend leaves to play for the Oilers. He was a starter, and a rookie, and a serviceman, all at the same time. He went overseas and missed the 1969 season, just as I did. In fact, when the NFL–USO tour came through Vietnam, Woody renewed some old acquaintances.

Another player who went—and went reluctantly, as he did most everything else—was the legendary Joe Don Looney of Detroit, Washington, Baltimore, New Orleans, and several places in between. He was from the "Bill Saul School" of football players . . . crazy. The fact that the United States could not win with Joe Don Looney in its Army is a measure of the impossibility of the Vietnam War.

Not even Joe Don, however, had attempted so arduous a task as I: to play in the NFL with a body the Army had officially listed as 40 percent disabled.

My comeback began September 15, the day I entered Fort Riley. Fortunately, I had the sympathy and expertise of Dr. Peter Keblisch, a former guard, middle linebacker, and captain at Penn, and his associate, Dr. Phil Taylor, an ex-fullback from Cornell.

I asked Dr. Keblisch at the outset, "What do you think will be my biggest problem?"

He pinpointed it exactly. "Your start," he said. "Rocky, if you played another position, say, linebacker, where you didn't have to get into a three-point stance and explode out of it, you'd have a better chance. But as a running back, you have to start quickly. And you've injured the most important part of your anatomy for doing that . . . the toes of your right foot."

If you don't believe the good doctor, slip off your shoe and take a three-point stance. Now look at the first three toes on your back foot.

Nature's way, when healing broken bones, is to fill the cracks with calcium, also known as bone spurs. That makes the bone strong, but also less flexible. My second toe was broken in so many places, it healed as a mass of calcium. And as the tissue regenerated—"scar tissue" is the layman's term—it hardened around and constricted the extensor ligament. It was so bad around the bottom joint that I could not move my toe even slightly—either to curl it or to bend it back.

We had two surgical options: Remove the joint completely, thereby reducing the pain, but also leaving the toe to flop around uselessly in my sock. Or, leave the joint in, cut out the bone spurs around it, then go back to physical therapy to regain strength and flexibility. (I cannot resist the temptation to repeat my friend Tom Weyer's pertinent assessment of the situation. He used to look at my toes and say, "What's a joint like you doing in a nice boy like this?")

A doctor in Appleton argued for the first option, removing the joint. Drs. Keblisch and Taylor argued for the second. In the case of a football player, they said, there really was no alternative. I couldn't run effectively without the use of my second toe. I still thought of myself as a football player, so I went with Keblisch and Taylor.

Postsurgery, I began shock therapy. A medical technician would touch the bottom of my toe with an electrode, trying to induce movement in a mind-body reaction. No luck. Next, they constructed a slingshot-type device on the bottom of my walking cast. It had a rubber band which slipped over my toe and pulled it back at night. All that gave me was a lot of pain and sleeplessness. No added flexibility.

While I was struggling with it, I met two young men who were vital to my comeback . . . Steve Eller of Roland, Iowa (population 683), and Mike Curtis (no relation to the Baltimore Colts' linebacker) of Cleveland. With the skill and courage of two safecrackers, they ushered me out of the service of Uncle Sam and into the 1970 training camp of the Pittsburgh Steelers. I might also say the analogy with the safecrackers extends a bit farther. Their methods bordered on the illegal.

As personnel officer for the minimal-care patients, it was Steve's duty to find me a job. I knew they weren't supposed to be difficult jobs, but this was ridiculous. Begging your indulgence for the bad pun, I went to POT (Plans Operation and Training). Ostensibly, we were to maintain a center of continuing education for the hospital staff. In reality, all the work was done by our civilian secretary. We spent the day playing chess. All day, every day. From seven to five, Monday through Friday. Guys would stop in to watch us, or to challenge us. We were the best damn chess players on the post.

After a while, we diversified. The major in charge of us was a bachelor in his early thirties. He got tired of hitting the bars every night, so he decided he needed a hobby. Ceramics. He brought in all the ingredients, clay and molds, and taught us to make ceramic chess sets. We baked and painted them to a hard, glossy finish. Just like you'd buy at the store. Something to stave off the boredom.

It looked like the party was over in April, though. One Wednesday afternoon at the clinic, Dr. Taylor said, "Well, Rock, I'm afraid I'll have to send you back to duty. As far as I'm concerned, that's all I can do for your foot."

Catastrophe. I still had eight months remaining of my two years. If I could have stayed under hospital care until late June, *then* been declared fit, the Army would not have reassigned me. I would have had less than six months remaining, and been given the coveted "early-out" discharge. Without it, I'd miss another football season, and then I might never get back to the Steelers.

That night, I broke the bad news to Steve and Mike. "Leave it to us," they said, walking out of my room.

Next day, they were smiling.

"It's all been taken care of," Steve said.

"What has?" I asked.

"Your records. We just checked your records."

"Wh . . . wh . . ."

"There's nothing that says you have to go back to Dr. Taylor. All you have to do is not go to clinic on Wednesdays. We'll leave your records behind each week, and no one will ever miss you."

"I can't do that, Steve."

"Rock, why not? You've served your country. You got shot, almost killed. You shouldn't have to go back to that spit-and-shine bullshit. Besides, you have a good reason for wanting out. If you don't get an early-out, you won't be back in Pittsburgh until late November. Believe me, there's nothing illegal about this. I see guys do it all the time, with the consent of captains and majors. They *want* guys to get out, especially if they have something waiting in civilian life. It's an unwritten rule in the Army."

So I took Steve's advice and left the ranks of the minimal-care patients to become a category unto myself. I traded in my blue hospital gown for four sets of fatigues, which Mike issued from the supplies office. I still had my job. And Steve talked the captain into letting us off post, so we got an apartment in Manhattan, Kansas. "The Life of Riley" was back.

As soon as we moved, I was eager to begin working out again. I hadn't done anything physical in seven months. But the skin on my foot had healed pretty well, so I thought, "Well, it doesn't *look* bad, so it mustn't *be* too bad." I thought I'd run two miles or so along a road that first day, just to loosen up for the tough work ahead.

The first few steps were agony. I thought, "I'm probably just breaking down some adhesions." But it got worse. I felt like I had a sharp stone in my shoe. I wasn't even running flat-footed. I was running on the outside of my right foot, on the only two good toes I had left. And I was limping as I ran.

I felt like taking off my shoe and shaking it . . . shaking it, shaking it, *shaking* it . . . until that stone fell out. Except there *was* no stone.

I couldn't recall ever feeling like that. I had always been in reasonably good condition. But now I was wheezing and choking like an old man. I had the cardiovascular capacity of a sixty-year-old and the speed of a weekend jogger.

I thought, "Maybe I've *forgotten* how to run. In a minute, maybe I'll remember. Maybe my body will click into gear, and I'll run like before. Please, somebody, tell me this isn't so. I *can't* be this bad. I've never been *this* far out of shape."

Now I was staggering, dragging the right foot into place for each stride . . . hopping on it different ways. On the inside, on the outside, back on the heel . . . trying to find a spot that would bear my weight comfortably. There was none. I tried them all several times.

For the final few steps, I stumbled like a drunk, leaning forward with a crazed look on my face. My mind was racing in disbelief. After all those years as an athlete—my body skilled, strong, responsive—I was now a physical disaster.

I collapsed onto the grass, crying in deep, convulsive sobs as I gasped for air. My foot hurt, my heart was pounding, I couldn't breathe, and I lay there, with training camp three months away, wondering, "Will I ever play football again?"

I set up a Spartan-like schedule: Up at five thirty in the morning to run several miles around the apartment complex, shower, eat breakfast, be on post by seven, gulp dinner at five thirty in the afternoon, lift weights from six to eight, run sprints for an hour, be in bed by nine thirty. For three months, I did that, five days a week. Never missed a workout.

Steve was sometimes a hindrance. "Hey, Rock," he'd say. "Let's go chase some women tonight. There's a beer party at K-State." On weekends, I'd agree. We'd get a couple dates and a couple six-packs, and head for a pontoon on the river. It was relaxing and fun. But during the week, I resisted his temptations.

Other times, Steve was like a psychoanalyst, treating my periodic depressions. He was no perfect specimen at 6-feet-2, 270 pounds. Yet, he often beat me in the forty-yard dash. I'd find him lolling by the pool some evenings and say, "Son of a bitch, Steve, I quit. I'm gonna give up. My foot's not getting any better. I'm gonna start living like you. Look at this. All you do is eat pizza and drink beer. Here I am, supposed to be an athlete, running in cleats. And I can't even beat a big old farm boy like you, running in tennis shoes."

About then, Steve would put his beer can down, get up from his chaise longue, and say, "All right, asshole. That's enough. Let's get to work. And let me see you get up on your toes." Then he'd run sprints with me until darkness.

Once I began to progress, Steve built on what little confidence I had gathered. After a particularly good workout, I'd come back to the apartment, saying, "I'm gonna make it. Son of a bitch, I'm gonna make it. Everybody says I can't, but I'm going to."

Steve would say, "Well, you better make it, asshole. Anybody who works as hard as you do has to make it. Otherwise, you've been wasting valuable time that you could have used for drinking with me."

We'd run the steps at Kansas State's football stadium on weekends. I got to the point where I could run them five times, bottom to top, with ten-pound ankle weights. Then we'd run forties, and I might win a couple. It felt great.

In July, when I had less than six months remaining, Steve and Mike engineered my release. It took them exactly one day, which is surely an all-time record for the Army bureaucracy. They did it with such precision and blurring speed, Dr. Taylor was left agape.

A few weeks after I'd gone, Mike saw him at the post swimming pool. "Hey, Doc," he said, "you should have been at the hospital complex last night. We all sat around and watched Rock on television.

The Steelers were playing the Jets. It was just great to see him again. Did you happen to catch any of the game?"

"Yeah, yeah, I saw him," Dr. Taylor said softly, looking off toward the sky. "Tell me, Mike, who did Rock pay to get out of the service?"

Mike could barely contain himself. "Nobody, Doc," he laughed. "Nobody."

I went home to Appleton for a week, then to Pittsburgh in mid-July. This was the year of the first NFL player strike. I joined the other veterans in boycotting training camp. I called Hanratty, who told me to come on in. He was running a free hostel for guys who lived out of town.

For three weeks, I shared his living room with J. R. Wilburn, a wide receiver. We'd gather with the other players each day at a high school field, or wherever they'd let us toss a ball around.

While we were gone, Terry's wife, Rosemary, spent the afternoons worrying about me. Cleaning her living-room coffee table, she'd noticed the bottles of vitamins I had lined up . . . A, B_1, B_2, C, D, E, rose hips, wheat germ, protein, calf's-liver extract. She figured anybody who needed all of *that* shouldn't be playing anything more strenuous than old maids. She saw me come limping in the door every afternoon, a veritable cripple compared to her healthy husband. She asked Terry to speak to me for my own good.

He waited until we were both relaxed . . . sprawled across a couple easy chairs with beer in hand, one evening after dinner.

"Rock," he said, "you know the team's a lot different now than it was in 'sixty-eight."

"Yeah, I guess."

"Noll's really a hard-ass. He cleared out half the team last year."

"Yeah."

"What I'm saying is that it ain't gonna be that easy for you."

"I know. I didn't think it would be."

"Well, Rock, you know, I was just thinking. Maybe it would be better if you tried to get into law school. You can take the boards in October, and you might be able to get in somewhere in January. It'd be great for you. You'd make a helluva lawyer."

I wasn't mad. You can't get mad at Hanratty. He was just trying to help. "I don't think so," I said. "I'd just really like to give it a shot, and see what happens."

In early August, at a meeting of the veterans, I asked if I could be excused from the strike and be allowed to report, because of my special circumstances. Roy Jefferson, still our player representative, said, "I think we're all agreed that you've stayed out long enough. Go on in."

At camp, I found the press waiting for me. I was flattered by all the attention, but their line of questioning put me off a bit. Did I think the veterans were exploiting my plight by asking me to strike? I said no. Nobody asked me to strike. I did it because I support the Players Association. They asked about the Purple Heart, the Bronze Star with V-device (for valor), and several Vietnamese campaign ribbons that I'd been awarded a few months earlier. I went over the grenade story several times. We talked about everything except football. As Joe Gordon, the Steelers' publicist, later told me, writers were treating me as a human-interest story. After seeing me run, none of them thought I could make the team. Everybody wanted to do a Vietnam-related feature on me before I was cut.

Finally, one writer asked me how I regarded my chances, and what I'd do if I didn't make the team. I said, "I've been away from football for a year now. It's a whole new system here with Coach Noll. I don't know the plays yet. My goal certainly is to make the team. But realistically, when the veterans come in, I don't know. Coach may go with the guys he's seen in the past. If I don't make it, I think I can accept that. If I do get released, I'd try to hook on with another team. If I could make a taxi squad with somebody this season, I'd be happy. This year is important—not so much playing, but getting the offensive system down."

With the strike keeping the veterans out of camp, the rookies got great exposure to and teaching from the coaches. There were two rookie running backs that year . . . Danny Griffin, a seventh-round draft selection from Texas-Arlington, and Billy Main, a thirteenth-round pick from Oregon State. In the fourth round, the Steelers took Jim Evenson of Oregon, a really tough, slashing-type back who surely would have made the team. But instead, he went to the Canadian League and became a star, sparing me the additional competition in Pittsburgh.

When the strike ended and the veterans joined us, I began to recognize the enormity of my problem. Only two backs were left from the 1968 season . . . Dick Hoak and Earl Gros. Two had made the team as rookies while I was gone in 1969 . . . Warren Bankston of Tulane and Don McCall of Southern California. Then, in the off-season before 1970, the Steelers acquired two men who were to become the starters . . . John "Frenchy" Fuqua, who came from the New York Giants, and Preston Pearson, whom Noll had known from his days with the Baltimore Colts. Including me, there were seven veteran running backs, two rookies . . . and only five spots available on the roster.

At that point, there's an inaudible process that goes on within most players. Each man begins to count his position, saying to himself,

"Well, the coaches will keep me before they keep this guy or that guy." I'm sure the other running backs did that. Warren Bankston, for instance, who became my roommate and very close friend, later said he never felt threatened from the first moment he laid eyes on me.

It was in late October, 1969, on a cold and snowy Friday afternoon when I visited practice during that Steeler Alumni Weekend. As the team saw me hobbling toward them on my cane, they stopped in the middle of a drill and came over to me en masse. All except the rookies, who, of course, didn't know me.

Bankston said to Dick Hoak, "Who's that?"

Dick said, "That's Rocky Bleier."

"You mean that little-bitty guy is Rocky Bleier? He doesn't look to be more than a hundred and fifty pounds."

Dick said, "He never was very big."

By '70 training camp, I was back over 200 pounds, my normal weight. The problem, as always, was my speed. Those forty-yard dashes with Steve Eller had filled me with a false confidence. I hadn't timed them, but once I began to run with the veterans, I realized they couldn't have been faster than six seconds.

I was still trying to run kind of flat-footed, using the outside edge of my right shoe. I couldn't get up on my toes because it hurt so much to bend them back.

Tony Parisi tried putting a plastic bar on my shoe under the ball of the foot, hoping I could push off *that,* instead of my toes. Then he took the cleat under my right big toe and offset it toward the middle of the shoe, trying to relieve the pressure. None of it worked.

During two-a-days, when the ground was so hard, I wrapped the foot in extra socks and tape. Between practices, while the other guys slept, I had Ralph Berlin, our trainer, manipulate the toes and massage the foot. Nothing did any good, but I wouldn't admit it. Ralph would ask how it felt. I could have screamed, it hurt so bad, but I'd just say, "Oh, a little sore today, Ralph. It'll be all right."

At night, I'd lie on my bed, staring at the right foot, swollen almost a third larger than the left. I recall staring for long moments . . . transfixed by the ugly sight of it . . . sickened by the crease running down the bottom of it, where the doctors had laid it open in Da Nang. I began to think of the foot as a detached entity. I got mad at it, like it was a person. I cursed it silently. I vowed I'd punish it the next day. I asked it questions: When would it feel better? Why was it doing this to me? Didn't it know my football career was hanging in the balance? I sank back onto the pillow and thought I must be going crazy.

The Purple Heart, awarded to any member of the armed forces who has been wounded or killed in action (*U.S. Army photograph*)

The Bronze Star, awarded to any person who distinguishes himself by heroic or meritorious achievement (*U.S. Army photograph*)

Bankston would come into the room.

"Warren, are you doing anything?" I would ask.

"No, Rock, why?"

" 'Cause my toes are a little sore. Would you mind massaging them again tonight?"

"Hell, no, Rock. Be happy to."

"Thanks."

"Just one thing."

"What's that, Warren?"

"I better lock the door. If guys come in here and see me rubbin' your toes, they might start to talk."

"Warren, if people knew you were helping me, they'd say you're crazy. We're supposed to be competing for the same job."

"Forget it."

I didn't want to face the truth. As you must know by now, I have a certain self-discipline, an ability to persuade myself that reality is not what it seems. During that training camp, I convinced myself that I actually had a chance to make the ball club. I forced myself to ignore the fact that I still had a noticeable limp, especially late in the day when I was tired. Years later, in better times, players told me how they collectively shook their heads in 1970:

"Jesus, why's he doing this to himself?"

"I don't know. He's just wasting his time. He ought to get out and find something else to do."

"I don't know how he stays out there, the condition he's in. Christ, he's slow, he's not that well built. . . ."

Some of them actually feared for my safety. Art Rooney Jr. told his brother Dan, the Steelers' vice president: "The kid's going to get hurt. A back can't be *taking* all the blows. He's got to be *giving* them. Rocky can't protect himself. One of these afternoons when he's really tired, he's going to get killed on a sweep."

Later, there was a rather emotional meeting among Dan, Ralph Berlin, Tony Parisi, and Dr. John Best, the Steelers' orthopedic surgeon. Dr. Best opened the proceedings with his pet line about an injured player: "He can't go, Danny. He just can't go."

The conversational temperature was turned up by Parisi and Berlin, who were involved more personally. They had watched every day as I dragged my sagging body into the locker room. They had seen me wince during the massage treatment. Now they wanted it stopped.

"Dan, I dressed him up just like you asked," said Tony. "But I can't stand by and watch him go through any more."

"*You* have to stop it, Dan," Ralph said. "*You* do. Rocky won't quit on his own. You have to make him. It's not human for you to let him endure any more pain."

So Dan came to me in those early weeks of camp, suggesting I have another operation. Perhaps Dr. Best could give me some relief from the pain. Perhaps, with his special knowledge of a football player's needs, he could do more than the Army doctors had done.

I told him no, I'd like to try it awhile longer.

A few days later, Max Coley, the offensive-backfield coach, tried his rhetoric on me. He said, "Rock, it's not worth it. Football's not worth it, if you're going to be physically hurt, or injured, or handicapped for the rest of your life. I'm not saying that you shouldn't give it a try. I'm just saying you ought to weigh the consequences. There's a lot more to life than just this."

I appreciated Max's concern, but I knew there was only one man whose opinion meant something. That was Chuck Noll. In reality, I *was* having some self-doubt. I *was* thinking of retiring. If I could speak to Chuck, feel him out a little, find out what he was thinking . . . then I'd have a better idea what my chances were.

I didn't know Chuck. Even today, six years later, I must say I do not know him. He is an unusual man. An intellectual, I dare say. Perhaps even a "Renaissance man." He is a gourmet cook, a connoisseur of fine wines, a speed-reader of voracious appetite, a history buff, a scuba diver. During the off-season of 1975, he began taking flying lessons so that he might pilot his plane to his Florida condominium, both recently purchased.

He was a twenty-seven-year-old offensive guard when he retired from the Cleveland Browns at the apex of his playing career. His teammates called him "The Pope" because he spoke so knowledgeably and dogmatically about the game. O. J. Simpson, after playing one game under him, the 1973 Pro Bowl, began calling him "The Emperor."

The first time Chuck ever saw me was September 29, 1968. It was a beautiful, sunny afternoon in Pitt Stadium. The Baltimore Colts were beating us, 41–0. Late in the fourth quarter, we had third-and-long at our 39-yard line. Bill Austin sent me into the game with a double-wing pass play, one we'd rehearsed all week. Slotted on the right side, I was to check for a blitzing linebacker, then swing over the middle for a pass.

It was the first regular-season scrimmage play of my career. I was so excited, I forgot about the linebacker. And he blitzed . . . it was Mike Curtis, who was then playing on the left side for Baltimore. As I stepped five yards deep into the secondary, I remembered my assignment.

When I turned, all I could see was Curtis' broad back. The ball seemed to be launched from the middle of his "32." Dick Shiner, our quarterback, who had thrown it, was en route to a painful prone position, underneath Curtis. I caught the ball amidst open spaces. Our other receivers had occupied their secondary. I took it fifty-four yards to the 7-yard line, from where we scored our only touchdown of the day.

Chuck Noll coached the famous Baltimore defensive backfield that day . . . Leonard Lyles, Bobby Boyd, Rick Volk, Jerry Logan. They were playing the zone coverages which are prominent today but were barely known in 1968. Even though the Colts had the game well in hand, Chuck called his foursome together and explained, in detail, how their defense had been beaten. And he might even have flipped through his depth chart to see who the Steelers' lucky receiver was.

The first time Chuck and I ever met was in April, 1969, when I was on leave and he was settling into his new job as Pittsburgh's head coach. One important note: I was smashed. I'd had lunch with my '68 Steeler roommate, Dick Capp, and drunk three rusty nails in an hour. When I stepped out into the sunlight, I was destroyed. I hoped to stay only a minute at the Steeler offices, saying good-byes all around before I returned to Fort Gordon. But Ed Kiely, the public-relations director, insisted I say hello to Chuck.

That's all I wished it to be. To my alarm, however, Chuck asked me a question: What did I think of Brian Stenger, a linebacker and former teammate from Notre Dame? I suggested he call Ara Parseghian, and started for the door.

"The trouble with that," Chuck said, calling me back, "is that college coaches sometimes get down on certain players and don't give them a chance. Do you think Stenger is such a player?"

Pretty soon, he had me into a full-fledged discussion. I avoided his eyes and talked out of the side of my mouth, so he wouldn't smell my breath. I've always been a smiling, agreeable drunk . . . never loud or rowdy because, as you'll recall, I value my presentation so highly. This day, I was beaming all over Chuck's office. I've always wondered whether or not he knew. Chuck, did you?

Now I was in his office at St. Vincent's. I quickly learned he is not a man to be felt out. By nature, he does not reveal himself easily. Especially to his players. He is a pragmatic, unemotional man. He did not know me, or my football abilities. Nor did he care for any excuses. He wanted performance. He had no time for guys who couldn't play. He was trying to improve a 1–13 football team. His job depended on it.

COMING BACK [141

He told me to continue practicing, see how it went, see how it felt. If I couldn't do it, I couldn't do it.

He played me very little in the preseason games. But with one week remaining before the season opener, I walked into the locker room still thinking I had a chance. Ralph Berlin came up to me immediately and said, "Chuck wants to see you."

I went into Noll's office, and right away, he got up from behind his desk. He walked around to meet me, very cold. He said it straight out.

"Rock, I'm going to put you on waivers. You'll probably pass through waivers, so you'll be a free agent. If you still want to play football, I think you ought to go home and do what's necessary to get yourself back in shape. Then maybe you can come back next year."

Waivers is the procedure of offering a player to each club in the league for a nominal $100 before giving him his unconditional release. Of course, no team would want me if I wasn't good enough for the Steelers. Chuck was saying I was finished. I tried to argue with him, perhaps a bit emotionally.

"Why?" I asked. "Coach, my feeling is that I just want to be with this team, to do whatever I can to contribute. I don't think I did that bad. I feel pretty good, and I'd just like to really give it a try."

He looked me right in the eye and said, "No, I'm sorry."

As I turned to walk out, Chuck showed a crack in his impenetrable exterior for the first and only time in my experience. His voice softened a tone, and he said, "If you want, you can practice with us today."

I don't know why the hell I did—everybody on the team knew I'd been cut—but I did. Driving home that night, the tears blinded me. I could barely see the road. For the first time since fifth grade, I wasn't a football player anymore. It was over. I was finished.

The next morning, before I could get out of bed and face my future, I got a call from Dan Rooney. He said he'd talked things over with his father. The Steelers would put me on the injured reserve list, instead of waivers. Mr. Rooney wanted me to have another operation. Then I could rejoin the team later in the season. What did I think?

What did I think? Lord, thank you! That's what I thought. How soon did they want me in the hospital?

Dr. Best X-rayed and found another large piece of shrapnel had worked its way to the surface of my fourth toe. That was the sharp stone I had felt in my shoe.

He removed it, and while he had me under sedation, he physically ripped apart scar tissue in my other toes, in a brutal way that I could not have tolerated while conscious. When I awoke, my toes were sore as hell. But the adhesions had all been broken. Now, all I had to do was exercise, and keep them from reforming.

Recuperation meant another three weeks of "ceiling philosophy." This time, the man uppermost in my thoughts was Mr. Rooney. He only owed me thirty days' employment, according to the law for returning veterans. But Mr. Rooney is not a man who lives by minimums.

He bought the Steelers in the thirties, for $2,500. It was nothing more than a pittance to him, even during the Depression. In 1936, he had gotten very hot in two afternoons at a pair of New York racetracks, and returned to Pittsburgh with a quarter of a million dollars. "The Chief" once told me most of his public adulation comes from frustrated "railbirds" who admire his ability to beat the horses.

Mr. Rooney always felt he was lucky to gain the football team and five harness and flat tracks he now owns. So he worked hard at remaining the same guy he always was. He lives today in the same modest house where he was born on the North Side of Pittsburgh. The neighborhood is now a black ghetto. His is the only white family on the block. But every morning, as he walks to work, this spry, seventy-four-year-old gentleman can be seen "slapping five" with little kids.

His office is a gathering place for men who grew up as boxers and football players with him on the North Side . . . but never had it so lucky. Until Chuck Noll arrived, most of those men were also on the payroll. When Joe Paterno, the Penn State coach, came to be interviewed for the job Noll ultimately got in 1969, he found the largest administrative staff in football. As Mr. Rooney walked him past endless offices in the Steelers' Roosevelt Hotel suite, Paterno finally said, "Mr. Rooney, just one question: What do all these people *do?*"

Most workdays, The Chief spends the hours of ten to five entertaining those countless friends, sharing stories of the old North Side. He walks home for dinner, then returns to the office from 6:00 to 10:00 P.M. for some serious business. It was during those evening hours in the winter of '75 that he wrote a personal note on each of ten thousand letters, acknowledging congratulations for the Super Bowl victory.

Mr. Rooney always treated me like everybody else . . . which is to say, generously. During my visit to the offices in April, 1969, I asked Fran Fogarty, the business manager, if I could be paid for the last three games of the '68 season, which I'd missed. Mr. Rooney overheard, sitting on the other side of the office, and said, "Give him anything he wants."

"We can't do that, Art," Fogarty said. "There are league rules."

"Well, then, give him his bonus," Mr. Rooney said.

My contract stipulated a bonus of $1,500 only if 50 percent of my

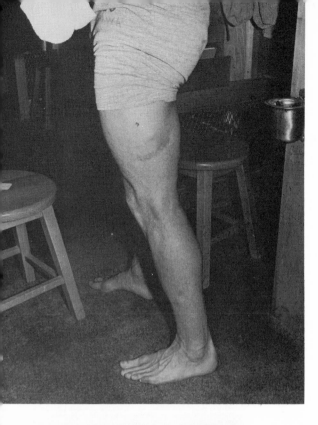

My left thigh scar; my un-curlable right toes; and an X ray showing the piece of shrapnel removed from my fourth toe in 1970 (*Divine Providence Hospital, Pittsburgh*)

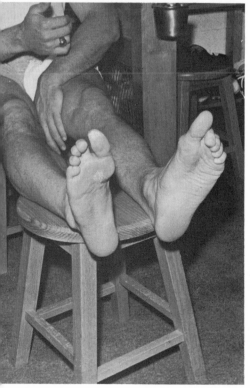

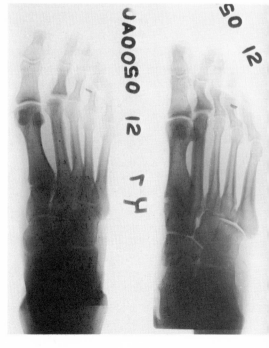

playing time was at running back. I hadn't earned it, but The Chief insisted I take it, anyway.

Now he was taking care of me again. Medically, I was the government's responsibility. I had been wounded in the Army, and treated in the Army. But instead of turning me out, Mr. Rooney absorbed the cost of my third operation, paid me a full year's salary, $19,000, and told his son Art Jr., "Get Rocky involved in scouting. He'll probably be good at it, and he might like it. In case his foot doesn't get better, let's see if we can find a place for him in the organization."

I was okay as a scout, I guess. Art Jr. sent me to Notre Dame several times. He said he could tell who my friends were. My reports made them sound like Heisman Trophy winners. I swore I was trying to be objective.

Artie was in the locker room before the final game of the '70 season. Two other running backs had been injured, and I was sufficiently rehabilitated that Chuck activated me for one game. I was so excited, I could scarcely get my uniform on. Artie came by and said, "I don't know why you're so happy. Anybody can be a player. It's the scouts that make this game go. You were doing okay for a rookie. Four or five years, who knows? You might make a *good* scout. Hell, anybody can *play*."

I laughed with him because he knew what I was thinking. I'd rather be a third-string special-teams player than the greatest scout in the world.

In the off-season, I became a field underwriter for Hinsdale (Illinois) Associates, outside Chicago, selling Mutual of New York life insurance. I lived in a broken-down first-floor flat in LaGrange, which is all I could afford. Actually, I didn't spend much time there. I'd get up at six o'clock in the morning to run a couple miles . . . along the streets during the winter, around the track at Lyons Township High once the snow cleared. I'd spend the hours of eight to one in the office. Afternoons, I'd lift weights at the YMCA or at health spas in Elmhurst and LaGrange. After dinner, I'd return to the office for a few hours, then head back to the track for a few sprints. I was normally in bed by ten. It was just like being back in the Army. I never missed a workout.

How can I tell you the agony and tedium of that routine? The sky passed from dark to leaden as the morning lengthened. The cold was constantly penetrating, the wind Chicago-ferocious. The world of 6:00 A.M. belonged to paperboys, milkmen, and occasional motorists, all of whom seemed intent on forcing me into ditches or splashing me with the heavy gray slush that collected along roadsides.

That scene always played in my mind as the alarm clock rattled me

Chuck Noll (left) and Art
Rooney, Sr.

to consciousness. The physical pain of those mornings—the creaking of my joints and the dull ache of my legs—was matched only by the mental anguish of knowing what lay in wait. Something in my head said, "Go back to sleep. Who's going to know if you miss this one lousy workout?"

I fumbled around in the darkness, searching for my sweat clothes. I'd find them rumpled in a ball, or hanging over a chair, still not completely dried from the day before. Putting them on shivered me.

I yawned and stretched. I groped for the bathroom light. I brushed my teeth and spat out the morning's taste. I walked circles around the apartment, looking for my jacket. Where had I left it after yesterday's workout?

I debated loosening up on the living-room floor. Should I stretch for a few minutes? Or should I just start running and break a sweat? What if I went out cold and pulled a muscle? Maybe that would give me an excuse to take a few days off. I looked outside. Would the track be clear today? Or should I run on the road again?

I grabbed my car keys and drove to the track. I turned on the radio to distract my mind. I crawled along slowly, begging the green lights to turn yellow, so I could stop. Anything . . . *anything* to delay the torture.

The track was muddy, dotted with puddles. The only footprints in the clay-and-cinder mixture were mine . . . from yesterday, and yesterday, and yesterday. Nobody else was in sight. The immense, rambling school sat mute. My car was the only one in the parking lot. Far off, I could hear a truck whining into third gear. But there was just one other sound . . . the squish and crunch of new footprints being made in the track. Footprints that would stare up at me tomorrow morning.

The frigid air snatched the warm breath out of me in short bursts and condensed it icily in front of my face. My windpipe seared like somebody had stuck a blowtorch down my throat. The morning taste returned. I coughed up mucus and phlegm, trying to bring it all out of my lungs with great, heaving *hakkkkfffs*. But still it came.

My legs loosened, as my lower back tightened. My heart drummed in syncopation . . . *bah-BOM, bah-BOM, bah-BOM*. My arms overworked, swinging furiously instead of easily and rhythmically. My running style was heavy and ponderous. I gouged out the steps, instead of floating them.

Near the end, I "tied up." My muscles fatigued and contracted. My stride shortened. My arm swing shortened. My breath shortened. I could not lift my knees. I could not stretch out with my feet. I looked like I was running in a phone booth.

Resting on the edge of the track, I crouched down with my head bowed. The beads of sweat froze inside my clothes and chilled me. I tried to rationalize the workout. "Ten laps, two and a half miles. That's all I can do." My right toes ached. I still couldn't push off them. I was still running cockeyed on the heel and the side of my foot. My toes had no strength, no endurance, no flexibility. "I can't do any more."

I thought of the other running backs—Bankston, Pearson, Fuqua. Plus the rookies who would be coming in. Ten laps would be nothing for them. Then I imagined myself . . . in super shape, running the football, breaking tackles, the crowd roaring. . . . I got up and ran some more.

I turned out to be a fairly proficient life insurance salesman in my first off-season. My biggest sale was to Joe Theismann, who was graduated from Notre Dame, got married, and signed a contract with Toronto of the Canadian League that spring. With all of that happening, I told him he *had* to have security . . . say, $200,000 worth. Joe agreed. What the hell did he know?

One afternoon in May, 1971, I was speaking by telephone to Dan Rooney, joking about my sudden emergence as a successful businessman. He said, "Rocky, we were just talking about you. If you've got something good going in Chicago, maybe it would be best if you didn't try to come back."

I pleaded. "Dan, my foot's coming along. I want to give it a try. I just asked Chuck if I could report with the rookies this year, and he said I should speak to you. That's why I'm calling."

Once I convinced him to let me try, I continued my training. It went pretty well until the last week before camp. On a hot July night, I was running sprints at eight thirty under a streetlight at the Lyons Township track. A gang of little children came by, playing tag or hide-and-go-seek. I'm sure they wondered why I was always there . . . and why I couldn't run gracefully like them.

Suddenly, a pain stabbed me in the back of the left thigh. I shot straight up in the air, the surest sign of a hamstring pull.

For two days, I did nothing, resting it. I heated and wrapped it. Then I began feeling guilty about the inactivity. I did a few light workouts, treating it tenderly. I said a prayer, and drove off to the Steelers' '71 training camp.

10] *Steelers '71–'73*

If I had been the coach in 1971, I'd have cut myself.

No kidding. I was that bad.

The only thing that saved me was lack of strong competition. Gros had been released. Hoak had retired. So the only returnees were Bankston, Fuqua, Pearson, and Terry Cole, another former Colt whom Chuck had acquired late in the '70 season.

That 1971 Steeler draft was one of the greatest in the history of the NFL. Pittsburgh selected six men who eventually became starters on the 1975 Super Bowl team ... Frank Lewis (first round), Jack Ham (second), Gerry Mullins (fourth), Dwight White (fourth), Larry Brown (fifth), and Ernie Holmes (eighth). In addition, the staff took Craig Hanneman (sixth), a top reserve along the defensive line for two years, and two men who were part-time starters in 1971–72 ... Ralph Anderson (fifth) and Al Young (twelfth). Just a sensational draft.

Fortunately for me, they picked only one running back in the high rounds ... Steve Davis (third) of Delaware State. He departed camp after one week, suffering a viral infection, and didn't return for a year. That was a godsend for me. There's no doubt in my mind that if Steve Davis had been in camp, I'd have been cut in 1971 ... and possibly never have played football again.

Larry Crowe (eighth) of Texas Southern and Dan Ehle (seventeenth) of Howard Payne were the other backs among that year's draft choices. Plus there were several free agents in camp, notably Jim Brumfield of Indiana State at Terre Haute.

So the battle lines were drawn again. Everyone felt Bankston, Fuqua, and Pearson were secure. That left one other spot, and maybe a place on the taxi squad, to be settled among Cole, Ehle, Brumfield, and Bleier. I didn't like my chances.

148

On the first day of practice, they all ran the forty-yard dash in 4.7 seconds or less, except Cole. He did 4.8, very creditable for a big, bruising back. I begged off, explaining that my tender hamstring would not allow an all-out dash.

That afternoon, we were loosening up with a short-pass drill. I reached a little too far for one ball, and . . . *boiiiing*. It was like somebody had stretched out a rubber band, then let go of the bottom end. I could feel the hamstring snapping all the way up my left thigh.

The only cure for that sort of injury, I was now convinced, was complete rest. So I took off two weeks, which, during double sessions, meant my competition had the extra benefit of twenty-four practices. Near the end of that second week, Chuck Noll, Ralph Berlin, and Dr. Best discussed my situation.

Ralph said, "This week, it's his hamstring. Next week, it'll be his groin. The week after that, it'll be his calf. Where does it all end?"

They agreed I did not have the body to play pro football. Chuck told Dr. Best to explain it to me in medical terms and persuade me to retire.

He found me in the locker room at Jeannette, Pennsylvania, just before the annual Steeler intrasquad game. He took down my pants and felt around the thigh for a few moments.

"Rocky, what do you do in the off-season?" he wanted to know.

"I sell life insurance, Doc. Why do you ask?"

"Well, I think you ought to consider it seriously as a profession. I think you ought to go back and see if you can get involved in the insurance business full time. I think you should give up football."

They're trying to retire me again, I thought. This time, the doctor was telling me. I didn't know that Noll had sent him as an emissary, but I wondered about it.

Dr. Best continued, "The muscles in your hamstrings are like rubber bands. You have two long ones and one short one. And the short one is only going to pull so far, until it snaps. The gunshot wound shortened it. The stitches you had, and all the scar tissue that built up while it was healing . . . Rocky, you'll always have trouble with it."

I thought it was bullshit, but I wasn't going to argue with the doctor about human anatomy.

The next week, as everybody else prepared for a game in Green Bay, I took daily treatment from Ralph. He asked me what I was going to do.

I had three options: First, wait until the hamstring healed completely, which might be near the end of the preseason and too late to make the team. Second, resume practice and hope it wouldn't pull again. If it did, my career was ended. Third, retire. I told Ralph, "I don't know, but I'm sure as hell not going to retire."

The next day, Chuck called me in. "How's it feeling?" he asked.

"I don't know," I said. "I think I need a little more time."

"I'm afraid we don't have much time. We have to start making some decisions about people."

"I understand."

"Look, Rock, why don't you follow up on your insurance business? I think you should retire and seek another career."

I told him I'd decide over the weekend. I asked if I could go to Green Bay with the team, even though I wouldn't play. I wanted to see my family and friends before making the decision. Chuck said that would be fine.

Friday night before the game, I took several teammates—Bankston, Dave Kalina, Bob Adams—and assistant trainer Bob Milie down to Appleton for dinner and a few drinks at Dad's place. I discussed the alternatives with my family. The next night, after the game, I poured it all out to Al Lison.

"Al, it really seems like the hand of God is directing my life. It's so obvious, I can't ignore it. He sent me to a great high school like Xavier and gave me Wisconsin state championships in football and basketball. I got a chance to go to Notre Dame, play on a National Championship team, and become captain. Then I got a chance to play professional ball. I got a taste of it, and it seemed like God said, 'Well, Rock, you should have some adversity in your life. Let's try another channel. Let's send you to the service. It's about time you paid some people back.' Now, I don't know what He's saying. It's like He's telling me to go in another direction. It's so cut-and-dried, like He's saying, 'What are you going to do with your life?' "

I figured, what the hell? I might as well go down trying. There were only four exhibition games to go. If I stayed out any longer, I had absolutely no chance. So I might as well wrap up the hamstring and give it a shot. I thought, "Rock, the next _boiiiiing_ you hear will be the end of your career."

I didn't play the next week at Cincinnati, but my competition did me a favor. Crowe ran seven times for seven yards, Cole three for four, Brumfield one for five. Ehle had been cut.

The next week, at home against Minnesota, Cole was nine for twenty-seven, Crowe three for ten, and Brumfield two for minus-one. Crowe was cut.

The next week, we could see the squad beginning to take shape. Among Cole, Brumfield, and Bleier, one would make the forty-man roster, one might make the taxi squad, and one would be cut. We played the Jets on a Saturday night, first game of the annual doubleheader in Cleveland. Cole played the entire second quarter and gained nineteen yards in five carries. He appeared to be the front-runner.

I finally saw my first action of the year with 7:50 remaining in the game. On first down, I bled four yards out of a dive play. A moment later, the line gave me a great hole at right tackle, and I popped it for sixteen yards.

The next series of downs tells you something about the kind of team we were. Our defense recovered a fumble, giving the offense first-and-goal at the Jets' 8-yard line. Brumfield lost two yards on his only carry of the evening. Then I caught a six-yard pass, but it was nullified by a penalty. We ended up with fourth-and-goal at the Jets' 31, and our holder fumbled the snap on a field-goal attempt.

Two days later, the coaches surprised me by cutting Cole. I guess they felt he was too slow. But hell, he was no slower than me. And he was twenty pounds heavier. I was in no position to question, however. It was now between Brumfield and me.

Neither of us played much in the final exhibition game against the Giants in Yankee Stadium. He ran the ball once for seven yards. I ran once for minus-two. After the game, I began feeling sick on the bus ride to the airport. My throat was raspy and sore. By ten o'clock, back in Pittsburgh, I had to leave my date and stagger home. An acute attack of tonsillitis had struck.

I was in bed Monday, practiced halfheartedly Tuesday. Wednesday was the day of final cuts. Ralph Berlin met me at the locker-room door. "Chuck wants to see you," he said balefully. It was nearly a year to the day since I'd flinched at the sound of those same words.

Chuck said, "Rock, we put you on waivers. Brumfield's going to start the season. We didn't know how your throat was going to be. We figure you'll pass through waivers, so you'll be on the taxi squad. In a few games, once you're healthy, we'll activate you."

Sure enough, after two games the Steelers restored me to the roster with one of those complicated front-office maneuvers that have since been outlawed by the NFL. It all started with a cornerback for the New England Patriots named Phil Clark. He was put on injured waivers September 22.

But Clark made a fast recovery, and the Patriots needed him for their third game. So Upton Bell, New England's general manager, called his friend Dan Rooney, to see what could be arranged. Dan wanted to activate me, so he put me on waivers again. (I had gone through waivers unclaimed, just as Chuck predicted, before the season opener.) This time, on September 29, Bell claimed me for the Patriots. That same day, Dan claimed Phil Clark for the Steelers.

Then, on October 1, according to their agreement, the general managers traded us. I went back to Pittsburgh, and Phil went back to New England. Of course, we'd never left our respective teams. The whole thing was paperwork. The only people who benefited were the telephone company stockholders.

Certainly the two football teams didn't benefit. Phil played only two games before he was released. I was injured in my first game and didn't return until December. My total output for the season was three games played, one kickoff return for twenty-one yards, one fair catch of a punt, and two tackles.

I was happy about sticking around for another year . . . but in a guarded sort of way. After trying to persuade me to retire, Chuck had kept me. But I wondered what he really thought of me. I still hadn't shown anything to convince him I was a football player.

There were rumors going around that Mr. Rooney had instructed Chuck to reserve a spot for me on the roster because he liked me, and I was Irish, and a Notre Dame graduate, and a war hero. I didn't know whether to believe it or not. I was actually afraid to ask. If it was true, was I taking advantage of his generosity? Nobody said anything to me directly, but the other players heard whispers. And I guess I grew paranoid. It seemed an unspoken part of my relationship with everybody in the organization.

Art Jr. told one of the scouts, "Last year, my father was the humanitarian and patriot. This year, it's Chuck. I guess he's just like the rest of us, after all. He's got a soft spot for Rocky, too."

You have to understand I was a pitiful-looking football player, limping around with that hamstring. Dick Haley, after several years away from the Steelers, rejoined them as director of player personnel in '71. He hadn't seen me play until that training camp. After final cuts were made, he said to another member of the organization, "Wait a second. I don't understand what we're doing with Bleier. Are we keeping him as a *player?* Does anyone actually think he can *play?* He can't run . . . he can't do anything."

Artie told someone else, "Last year, he was a cripple. This year, he's just bad."

Subsequently, Chuck and Dan told me I'd made the team in '71 on merit. They figured I could help once I got healthy. While it was more potential than actuality that kept me around, still it was not a favor. I didn't want a gift. Chuck, especially, with his vast personnel turnover, had acquired the reputation of a strict talent critic. He did not keep guys because of their nationality or their Purple Hearts. I took consolation in that.

I also learned that Max Coley had been firmly in my corner. He and Terry Cole had had a disagreement, Max finally telling Chuck that Terry couldn't do the job. Max, in fact, had argued to have me activated for the season opener in Chicago.

At the coaches' pregame meeting, he said, "Rocky's the only guy I have who will stick his nose in there and block that number fifty-one [Dick Butkus]." Sure I would have. Hell, that's all I *could* do.

Max lost his argument. I was not activated. But after Butkus caused several fumbles which lost the game for us, Max allowed himself to say, "I told you so."

Yet Max was wrong about me. I was still not ready in '71. It was another season of torment. Another season of hanging around, feeling alienated, being in limbo, not contributing. That's a trite phrase you've heard a million times. Every rookie ever interviewed has said, "I just want to make a contribution." But hear me out.

What that rookie is describing is the essential player-to-player relationship. When you're injured, you watch practice from the sideline, dressed in street clothes. You don't go to team meetings. You refer to the team as "they" instead of "we." When you see a "contributing player" in the hallway or the weight room, he seems to look at you like an interloper. As if to say, "What the hell are *you* doing here?"

It's not a conscious feeling . . . and most of it is probably caused by your own insecurity. But you feel so "out of it." You don't know what to say to "the contributors." You can't seem to make a joke that draws their laughter. You feel like the new kid who just moved onto the block. You want peer-group acceptance. You want to do anything for the team, no matter how insignificant. So the other guys will look at you while you're suiting up and think, "Yeah, he makes a contribution. He snaps for extra points," or "He plays in the wedge on kickoffs." *Anything* to make them look at you the right way.

On my way back to Chicago for the off-season, I stopped in South Bend to see Joe Hickey and Father James Burtchaell, a close friend and now provost at Notre Dame. We discussed my situation, and both men advised me to retire. Joe suggested I stay in insurance or think about going with his company. Father Burtchaell flattered me and said I probably had other talents. He didn't know why I was so infatuated with the one that developed first in life . . . the football talent. I thanked them both but left them with the correct impression that they hadn't changed my mind.

I also stopped at home, there to find my father in the lotus position. He had taken up yoga to counteract those middle-age aches and pains induced by a lifetime of standing behind the bar. He was sensational at it. He touched his head to the floor from a sitting position. I tried . . . but I couldn't do it! My father at the age of fifty was more flexible after a couple weeks of yoga lessons than I, a professional athlete at the age of twenty-six.

Maybe there's something to this, I thought. I bought a basic yoga book and picked out exercises to relieve tightness I'd been feeling in my lower back, hamstrings, and quadriceps. In addition, I rededicated myself to improved running speed. Instead of getting up at six o'clock, I got up at five thirty. I slipped an extra workout into the afternoons, which gave me three running sessions a day. I worked on the fire escape of my apartment building until I could run the eight stories, bottom to top, eight times in a row. I did the Steelers' suggested program every day . . . five consecutive 350-yard runs in sixty seconds apiece, with a twenty-five-second interval between them.

It all paid off on the first day of camp in 1972. "Frenchy" Fuqua ran the forty just ahead of me, and caused a big row with the scouts, who accused him of taking a "rolling start." He took off before they could click their stopwatches, and was marked down as a questionable 4.6.

The scouts insisted everybody else start from a three-point stance. I didn't mind. I didn't want there to be any question. I kicked away some dirt and rocked on my hands until I was absolutely comfortable. Then, with the normal twinge of pain from my toes, I burst across the grass.

When I circled back toward the scouts, I saw them huddled together, glancing quickly from one stopwatch to another. One read 4.55, another 4.6, the third 4.65.

Haley was screaming and jumping around. When I came over to him, he said, "Rocky, if I hadn't been holding the watch, I'd ask you to run it over again."

Artie Rooney said, "I've never seen anything like this before, and I don't expect to see it again. Rock, you're two seconds faster than you've ever been in your life!"

At the coaches' meeting that night, somebody joked, "We ought to check the slope of the ground out there. Are you sure he wasn't running downhill?"

Dick Hoak said, "If he was a kid nineteen or twenty years old and still maturing, I could see him improving his speed two-tenths. But he's twenty-six. People just don't *do* that."

Chuck talked about it all night, they told me, using words like "unbelievable," "phenomenal," "incredible."

Hoak, who is a sensational backfield coach and offensive strategist, but a better human being, told me the next day, "Rocky, I just thought you'd want to know this. Several times last night, Chuck just shook his head and said what a great job you've done with yourself."

That made me feel pretty good, but not as good as the first exhibition game. I played the second half and ran eight times for sixty-two yards. Most of it came on a third-and-six from the Steeler 9-yard line, late in the third quarter. Bruce Van Dyke, our right guard, escorted me around end for forty-seven yards.

Despite the improvement, I felt I was on a treadmill. For the third straight year, I was in danger of not making the team. We had everybody back from 1971, plus a healthy Steve Davis, plus four outstanding rookie runners . . . Franco Harris of Penn State, Tommy Durance of Florida, Stahle Vincent of Rice, and Ron Linehan of Idaho.

I was nervous in preseason, expecting Chuck to carry five running backs. But he kept six . . . Fuqua, Pearson, Harris, Davis, Bankston, and Bleier. I was last once again. Chuck eventually put me on waivers, but only because he knew I'd pass through unclaimed. The rest of the league didn't know I was for real, "a live one," as Artie chuckled. The Steelers weren't advertising my 4.6 forty. Before the first game, they activated me and taxied a player who would not have passed waivers.

In the thirteenth game of the season, I got my one and only chance to run from scrimmage in the three years 1970, 1971, and 1972. We were thrashing Cleveland 27–0, so I was allowed to play the last two minutes.

I went seventeen yards on a draw play up the middle. Nobody seemed to care very much. Most of the fans were on their way home. But I felt great . . . that is, until I got into the locker room. I caught Hanratty pasting a sign above my stall: "983 yards or bust." Far from the Thousand Yard Club, I finished as the ninetieth-ranked rusher in the American Football Conference. But for the first time in three years, I was listed.

Just as Rocky Bleier turned the corner in 1972, so did the Steelers. From 1–13 in 1969, to 5–9 in 1970, to 6–8 in 1971 . . . now, in 1972, we went 11–3 and won our division, the team's first title of any kind in forty years. It was exciting for us. Winning was new. We were cohesive. We discovered our potential gradually, game by game . . . like a newborn baby who looks down and sees he has legs, then feet, then toes. Franco was Rookie of the Year. Terry Bradshaw established himself as our quarterback. And the city of Pittsburgh loved us all.

Our first play-off game was against Oakland. We seemed to have victory in hand until late in the fourth quarter. On a third-and-long, Ken Stabler scrambled thirty yards for the go-ahead touchdown.

Silently, I cussed our defense. Why couldn't somebody pick him up?

Where were the linebackers? That play cost me a $5,000 playoff bonus and another game check. Damn it. I started thinking about where I'd go for Christmas . . . home to Appleton, or should I stay in Pittsburgh?

There was less than a minute to go. Our offense had to move seventy yards. Bradshaw threw three straight incompletions. On fourth down, he chucked it up the middle toward Fuqua, who was flat-nailed by Jack Tatum, the Raiders' safety.

I lowered my head. Damn. Suddenly, I heard this roar . . . and there was Franco, running into the end zone.

Tatum, though to this day he denies it, had knocked the ball into the hands of Harris, who crossed the goal line to complete a play known in Pittsburgh as the "Immaculate Reception." The clock showed five seconds. We won, 13–7.

The next week, we played Miami in a game that positively spooked me. During our film study of the Dolphins' special teams, I noticed that their guard on the kickoff receiving team always blocked the coverage team's L-1 (first man to the left of the kicker). As L-1 with the Steelers, I was a "wedge buster," one who hurried downfield to make the tackle. Preston Pearson, our R-1, was the safetyman.

About midweek, I suggested to Chuck, "Since their guard always blocks L-1 and ignores R-1, let's have Preston 'force' this week. He should have a clear shot at the ball carrier. I'll lay back and play safety." Chuck agreed.

We could hardly wait for our first kickoff. Roy Gerela booted it, I took a few steps and pulled up, Preston took off at top speed . . . and the guard blocked him! The Dolphins were psychic. We had changed our coverage for the first time all year . . . and they had compensated with a change in their blocking pattern, also for the first time all year.

They outfoxed us on special teams in the second quarter, and this time, it cost us the game. We were receiving a punt, and called a return-right. We double-teamed the end on that side, and each Steeler did a great job shielding his man away from the right sideline. Too great, in fact. Larry Seiple, the Dolphin punter, ran the other way and slipped our "contain man," who was recently activated and new to that position. While we were setting up a beautiful return on the right sideline, Seiple ran left end for thirty-seven yards to our 12-yard line. To the fans, it looked like we were running interference for him. Miami then punched it in, a cheap score and their margin of victory in a 14–7 game.

I returned to Chicago for one last off-season, probably the bleakest period of my life. I only pulled through it with the help of Tom and

Mary Weyer, friends from Notre Dame who housed me in their game room and supplied lots of understanding for a young man who was confused in several different ways.

First, my interest in insurance was dying. My commissions fell from $11,000 in 1971, to $5,000 in 1972, to $2,500 in 1973. That wasn't enough to cover my business expenses, let alone my living expenses. In '73 I went to the office for just two hours a day . . . shuffled a few papers around, tried to act busy, made a couple phone calls, then left for another workout.

I simply didn't have the mental picture that is so necessary to me for self-motivation. I couldn't tell myself, "Now, Rock, after you're done playing football, you're going to live the rest of your life in a little house in Hinsdale, go to the office every day, and write insurance in this area."

One morning at eight o'clock, Tom and I caught a good look at each other . . . dressed up in business suits, carrying briefcases, ready to fight the rush-hour traffic, dedicated practitioners of the nine-to-five routine. It was so incongruous with our memories of the carefree days at Notre Dame . . . blue jeans, T-shirts, no socks, late for class. We sat down at Tom's kitchen table and laughed for ten minutes. I knew I wasn't ready for that life-style.

Second, I broke an engagement in February, 1973, two weeks before the wedding. For several months I'd been sure I didn't want to marry this girl. But I procrastinated, fearful of upsetting all the plans. When I finally called the wedding off, I was relieved. Still, I had guilt feelings about the embarrassment and inconvenience I'd caused.

Third, I was about to quit playing football. My career was going nowhere. The coming season would be my fifth, enough to qualify me for the NFL pension. That's all I wanted. When I went into Dan Rooney's office to negotiate my 1973 contract, I really thought it would be my last. He offered me a $5,000 bonus, raising my salary to $25,000, and I jumped at it. There were some future considerations, as well, but I didn't even think about them. I wanted the cash immediately, before I retired.

After I signed the contract, I raised another matter. "Dan, I don't know what your policy is, or whether you'd even want me . . . but I've been thinking about retiring, and I'm wondering if you might consider me for a position here in the front office."

He said, "We'd love to have you, Rocky. Everybody here likes you. But we have a policy of not hiring former players until they've worked a year or so elsewhere . . . for instance, at BLESTO-V. Besides, I don't understand why you're considering retirement. There's no reason why you can't play ten years in this league."

Dan's words heartened me, but they were not enough to fulfill me. Yes, I would play another season of football, because that's the only goal I had. But what a hollow goal. There's so much more to life . . . and I had none of it. Only football!.

I would return to the Weyers' apartment at night, feeling empty and drawn from the day of workouts. There would be Tom, having worked three times as many hours, sold ten times more insurance, and he would be so vibrant. He and Mary were so happy together. Their two-year-old son, John Joseph, was such a joy to them.

I would say goodnight and retire to the game room, retreat into my self-imposed exile, thinking what a weak and lonely person I was. I had nobody to share my ups and downs. But there were so few ups, who would want to share all the downs?

I was being absolutely spineless about my insurance career. I had talked myself into liking the business, then recognized my lie. Now I was masquerading as an agent. Yet I did nothing to correct the situation. Why didn't I get in or get out? I was gutless and indecisive. What was I going to do with my life? I was twenty-seven years old—pretending to be a football player, pretending to be an insurance salesman—and what did I have to show for it? A car and a couple thousand dollars in the bank. No furniture, no stocks, no real estate. Not that material goods were important . . . but what did I have to show for my twenty-seven years on earth? Virtually nothing. Certainly none of the important things . . . the kindness, love, and affection of another person. And no prospect of things improving. *What was I going to do with my life?*

I had some rambling philosophical discussions with Jerry Urbik, my very sympathetic boss at Hinsdale Associates. I stayed with Jerry's family for a few months after the 1970 season, and he became a surrogate father for me. Jerry convinced me I still had one constant in my life . . . the desire to play football, no matter how discouraging the past few years had been. Thus, he argued, I should toss myself headlong into off-season workouts.

That was one endeavor where I could see improvement . . . and forget the shortcomings of my personal and professional life. I ran and lifted as much as ten hours a day. It was only a diversion, an escape from my real difficulties, but it was effective. It gave me some sense of pride. Several times, I told Tom Weyer, "I can *see* myself getting bigger."

If 1972 was the off-season of added flexibility and running speed, 1973 was the year of muscle. Strength and bulk. I wanted to compensate for my lack of height, eradicate the inferiority complex. Instead of a five-day program, I undertook a heavier schedule . . . six days a week, three hours a day. I stepped up my intake of vitamins and diet supplements. People were always staring as I poured some strange concoction into my milk shakes. I devoured protein and calf's-liver extract by the handfuls. I met some serious body-builders, who shared technique with me.

I incorporated their theories with a system designed by Lou Riecke, the first "strength coach" in the NFL. Lou came to the Steelers in 1970 with a year-round program to make us more powerful football players, especially in the legs, back, and shoulders. If you saw the 1975 Super Bowl, I think you'll agree he's done a good job. Our guys manhandled the Vikings. Ara Parseghian later told me, "That was the most awesome *physical* display I've ever seen on a football field."

Lou's primary difficulty was overcoming that old wives' tale about becoming "muscle-bound." He says there is no such thing. In addition to the expected benefits—strength, better conditioning, resistance to injury—Lou says weight training actually enables a player to run faster, jump higher, and be *more* flexible.

The Steelers were taking no chances, though. They also hired a "flexibility coach," Paul Uram. Right now, we are the only team in the league that has both strength and flex coaches, though I fear the others will soon follow suit if we keep winning.

Uram, by coincidence, was an assistant coach to Terry Hanratty and Bill Saul at Butler High in the sixties. He taught Hanratty passing accuracy by tossing footballs the length of a basketball floor, into the hoop at the opposite end. Paul says he almost always won their daily contest by sinking four of five shots. Hanratty doesn't deny it, so you know it must be true.

Paul was also a fine gymnastics coach, which is how he developed a unique set of stretching exercises for the legs and back. When he introduced them to the Steelers, our number of muscle pulls and serious leg injuries was cut by more than half.

Uram's program was backgrounded, for me, in scientific terms by Dr. Robert Kurucz, a physiologist at West Virginia University. I spent an afternoon with him in Morgantown, discussing red corpuscles, ligament fibers, and the like. He showed me a basic three-step process for improving musculature ... first, stretch the muscle; second, strengthen it; third, ingrain it with a motion pattern, a kind of "muscle memory," so it will respond properly when needed.

For running in the open field, he taught me to roll all the way up to my toes, instead of planting and lifting the balls of my feet. He suggested I kick higher and extend farther, to produce a longer leg arc, and thus, more speed. He tried to induce the bouncy, graceful stride that

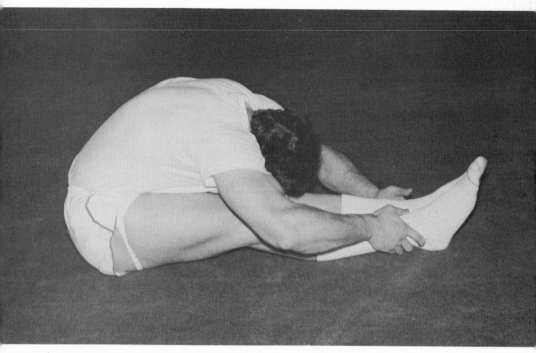

Flexibility exercises with Paul Uram

Workouts in the Steeler weight room, and the Bleier body at age 17

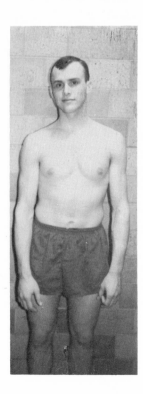

comes so naturally to athletes like Ron Shanklin, our wide receiver . . . but not to me.

By the '73 off-season, I had accumulated some pretty extensive knowledge about kinesiology. Hanging around those health spas and YMCAs, I met all kinds of self-styled experts. A black belt in karate, for instance, told me that hip and lower-back rotation is the mobility a man loses earliest in life, perhaps as early as age thirty. To retain it, he devised a series of exercises which helped him to spin and kick karate opponents . . . and helped me to cut on a power sweep. He also showed me ways I never imagined to untighten my groin and quads.

Putting all that knowledge into practice was the difficult part. The body can be tricked into doing almost anything, but the head keeps saying, "Rock, let's take a day off. Training camp is four months away!"

Running workouts, particularly, were still tedious, mindless, laborious, and just a pain in the ass for a guy like me, who isn't built to be a long-distance runner. I knew they had to be done, though. And when you get the head talking positively to the body, wondrous things are possible.

Weight lifting I didn't mind as much, but it was still drudgery. It always started with stretching exercises, then an analgesic rub on my arms and shoulders. That, of course, lied to my muscles . . . making them feel warm and supple, when, in reality, they were sore and stiff.

All weight rooms feel the same. They are dank with the mixture of analgesic, body odor, and a kind of "gym smell." They are always windowless. The walls are normally cinder block, painted a color that is not white, so much as it is a bland, blank cream shade. The ceiling is a network of heating ducts and water pipes, running at every which angle, with cobwebs and dust globs at the corners. Doing bench presses, there's lots of time to study the ceiling.

There is very little writing to be seen in weight rooms. The men who inhabit these rooms do not live by linear expression. Writing is bullshit to them. There are no graffiti on the walls. A sign may say: "Lifters Only." But that is a given. A program may be scrawled on the blackboard, but it is written in shorthand that only they can understand:

3×10 row

curl

french

mil.

squats

rev. curl

calfs

The weights themselves are usually inscribed with the word "York." That is the brand name, but I like to think of it as the simplistic process of lifting, itself. You grab the bar, and you *y-y-york* it.

The weights are black, ominous-looking, inscribed with their poundage. They are scratched, and rounded at the edges from years of being kicked around . . . but they are indestructible. This is *their* room. *We* are the intruders. They allow themselves to be used. But none of us can endure more than a few hours. Ultimately, we leave, exhausted. They stay, the victors in our battle . . . always potent, always capable of exerting the same force.

The actual lifting is done mostly in the mind. There, a conviction can be assembled that is so strong, so fiercely held, that the body cannot refuse it. The mind can dictate, "Full squats, five hundred pounds, three sets, ten reps each." And the body will respond.

The neck will shift and wiggle, conforming itself to the shape of the bar. The shoulder will droop under the weight. The back will arch itself straight, belying the tension that reverberates down the spinal column. Then the process begins. The knees bend full, dropping the barbell two feet. The back of the calf meets the back of the thigh, the muscles in full contraction. They push away from each other, straightening the leg. The quadriceps quivers. The knee locks again. Nine reps, two sets to go.

Sometimes, you look at your face. Your cheeks are puffing, like after a running workout. The sweat is forming little rivulets on your neck. Blood vessels are standing out at your temples. Little strands of hair are matted against your forehad. Your eyes are lidded and not focusing very well.

But the progress is there to see. The muscles look larger, better-defined. Only some of that appearance is real. But to the mind, it does not matter. The illusion of strength is just as helpful in hefting the bar. Remember: *Weight is lifted in the mind.*

There's a certain satisfaction involved that borders on narcissism. You work in front of mirrors to watch technique . . . and to encourage the mind by displaying progress through the eye. It's a very inner-directed pursuit that leaves you feeling guilty about the selfishness of spending three hours a day on your body. But how it benefited me in 1973.

I had gotten as high as 225 pounds in the off-season, all of it good weight. By training camp, I was down to 216 . . . still quick, and strong as an Appleton millwright.

At the first-night meeting, Chuck welcomed us back and said a few words of caution: "I got the results of your weigh-in this afternoon, and some guys are having trouble with their weight. Joe Greene, you're a little heavy. Be careful of your diet in the next couple weeks. 'Fats' Holmes, we'd like to get you down to a lighter playing weight. And you too, Rocky, we don't want you to get any heavier."

The room burst out in laughter. I was in the absolute best shape of my life. The players were astounded at what I'd done to myself. Even Rosemary Hanratty said, "Rocky, you look like you put an air hose in your mouth." I was that pumped up.

Tony Parisi changed my shoulder pads and told me I was two sizes larger than I'd been as a rookie, something unprecedented in his experience. He recorded my measurements . . . chest normal 45, chest expanded 49, waist 36, biceps 18, thigh 26, neck 17.

There were only two guys on the team stronger than me . . . Jon Kolb and Jim Clack, a pair of offensive linemen. Kolb is just a damn bull at 6-feet-2, 262, a dedicated lifter. He does a bench press of 550 pounds. You read it right—more than a quarter of a ton. Jon benches *twice* as much as Joe Greene, a huge specimen at 6-feet-4, 275 pounds . . . but a nonlifter.

Clack's story is akin to mine. He was 215 pounds during his senior year at Wake Forest. He was twice cut by the Steelers, but he stayed with it . . . pumping weights and playing in the Continental Football League. Today, he's 6-feet-3, 250, and a lovely sight to be running behind.

Besides my newfound strength, I was also among the fastest men on the team, according to the scouts' timings. Ahead of me were Frank Lewis and Steve Davis. Frank is a wide receiver and what the scouts call a "straight 4.5." You can tell him to run the forty any time of the day or night, in heat or cold, wet or dry . . . and he'll give you a 4.5. Not 4.45 or 4.55. Frank gives you a 4.5 every time. Steve Davis is the running back whose body I'd most like to have. He's 6-feet-1, 218, which is just right. He runs an honest 4.55, and it's no wonder with thighs like he's got.

Being third-fastest and third-strongest on the team was useless, however, unless I could impress it on Chuck. So I undertook certain tricks to catch his attention.

In practice, I'd anticipate the snap of the ball by just a fraction. It's a maneuver I learned by watching the Cleveland Browns, especially Leroy Kelly. Everybody always remarked how quick he was. Hell, Kelly and his entire line were often in motion a split second before the snap.

I one-upped Leroy a bit. I'd pop the hole quicker than the quarterback could hand me the ball. I was using the sprinter's technique of bursting straight out of the blocks, instead of "duck-waddling" side to side with my first few steps, as most football players do. I was already into the secondary when the quarterback turned to look for me. On the way back to the huddle, I'd suppress a smile and mutter something about the missed handoff being my fault. I'd hear the coaches say to each other, "Jesus, Rock looks quick. The extra size hasn't hurt his speed at all."

The next step was locker-room talk. Each year, rookie linemen whispered to us in a quiet corner, "Is it true Kolb can *really* bench five-fifty?"

Now rookie running backs were asking if Bleier could really bench four-forty. One assistant coach told a rookie he'd never seen a guy my height built any better.

Then a couple reporters began hearing conversations, and they mentioned these things in the newspaper. Pretty soon, a consciousness—indeed, an aura—surrounded me. The coaches were touched by it. They heard the talk and read the papers like everybody else. Finally, Chuck said, "Hey, this guy is quicker and stronger. We gotta play him more."

You see, coaching is a subjective science at its essence. Any time one man judges the capabilities of forty-seven other men, and determines which twenty-two are the best . . . that's subjective. But his decisions are based on objective criteria, such as forty-speed, strength, and past performance. If you think those things aren't important, consider the fact that a scout once timed a prospect's forty down the concourse of an airport. He promised the kid two-tenths for poor running conditions.

Sometimes the objective criteria lead the coach's subjective judgment astray. Of a running back, I've heard it said, "He looks good and quick, but shit, he's a 4.9." That's too slow in an objective sense. Backs should be faster. Nobody thinks that the back might have stepped into a hole or pulled a muscle the day he ran 4.9. Nobody cares that he might be as quick laterally as he is straight ahead. None of that. He's a 4.9, so he can't play. Dick Hoak once told me coaches make mental notes to cut certain guys during their first hours in camp . . . after weigh-in and the running of forties.

Other times, the objective criteria will keep a guy in the lineup who shouldn't be there. A coach's subjective inclination may be to bench the guy because he isn't doing the job. But then he thinks, "Well, he *is* 6-1, 220, he *is* 4.7, he *was* good for us last year, and there's nothing physically wrong with him. What the hell, I'll stay with him."

What I did in 1973 was give my coach the objective reasons—the "excuses," if you will, or the "rationalization" for his critics—to play me. I had the requisite numbers. And Chuck reponded like any coach would. He played me.

I was the team's leading ground gainer in preseason. I carried thirty-two times for 220 yards, a seven-yard average.

But in the last exhibition game, against Atlanta, I bruised my knee. By the time it healed, Franco Harris was also coming back from knee problems. Chuck decided Franco needed all the work he could get, so it was back on the bench for me.

Hoak argued, "Bleier needs just as much playing time to get back in shape." But Chuck said no.

If I couldn't get any recognition as a back, I decided to pick up where I left off in '72 and get some notice as the best special-teams player in the NFL. Nobody can evaluate that accurately, of course, but I knew I was among the best. I don't say that with any arrogance. Nor do I say it with any false pride. It's simply a statement of fact.

I played all four teams—kickoff and punt coverage, kickoff and punt return. I was consistently the first man downfield, and made a larger percentage of the tackles than anyone else. As one of our three wedge-busters on kickoff coverage, I threw my body around recklessly. TV directors loved me. They trained their isolated cameras on me, and I hit or got hit nearly every time.

Warren Bankston, who was traded to Oakland that year, told me the Raiders' special-teams coach, Joe Scanella, warned his players, "Rocky Bleier is the man to stop on every one of the four special teams. He's their best. We have to be aware of him on every punt and every kickoff."

Warren, who consistently grades out as Oakland's best special-teams player, once told an interviewer, "I want to become the Rocky Bleier of the Raiders."

There is a little theory involved in special-teams play. Oakland and Pittsburgh, for instance, believe the coverage unit should stay on its feet at all times. If you're on the ground, you're not a football player. Also, never take a one-for-one trade-off. If you have to fall, make sure you take two or three opposing blockers with you. Other teams, like Kansas City, have one man who intentionally dives in front of the kickoff wedge, giving himself up so his teammates can make the tackle.

Mostly, however, special-teams play is a lot of desire. If you're a return man, you have to see that crack and hit it right now . . . knowing it will close from all sides and everything in your mind will go stark *white* for a second. If you're a coverage man, you have to run full tilt, because 95 percent of the time, blockers can get only a piece of a man running top speed. The other 5 percent are those high-speed, head-on collisions you see on the pregame television shows each Sunday afternoon. After those ones, you spend the day shaking your head . . . blinking your eyes and sniffing ammonia capsules. But still it won't clear.

I made some big plays on special teams in '73 . . . a blocked punt that preserved victory in the second Cincinnati game after both our quarterbacks had been hurt . . . a fumble recovery in the victory over Houston that broke a three-game losing streak and put us into the playoffs.

I made some bad plays, too. In the first Bengals game, which we lost, I drew Chuck's iciest stare by fumbling a punt. In the first Oilers game, I made a fair catch with tacklers twenty yards away, prompting him to scream, "*Run* with the ball. Put two arms around it and *run!*"

Running punts is kind of like being in the middle of a Fellini movie. It's a montage of conflicting scenes and images, jump cuts that disorient and bewilder, pictures and sounds flashing for milliseconds.

Your eyes scan frantically from the onrushing Bengal linemen to Dave Lewis' left-footed, wickedly twisting, curveball punt. In one ear, you hear the official stage-whispering, "Now, get that hand up high for a fair catch. Let everybody see it." Your teammate, the other returner, is screaming, "You take it, Rock. You take it." In your memory, Noll is screaming, "*Run* with the ball." The ball is dipping . . . the tacklers are charging . . . the voices are louder. . . .

Once, I raised my hand to ear level (kind of a semi-fair-catch signal), then jerked it down, caught the ball, and ran. The official threw a fifteen-yard penalty. As Chuck glared at me, I thought, "I must really be tight and nervous. I'm not loose or fluid in my thinking or my movement. I'm more conscious of avoiding mistakes than running effectively. I wouldn't do that if I had a reasonable amount of playing time."

I didn't like being judged, for an entire season, on two kickoff returns, three rushes, and two fair catches. That's all I did in 1973. My every play was magnified fifty times beyond its actual importance. One insignificant tackle was cause for elation. One missed block wrought despair.

For four games near the end of the season, I was inserted into the regular lineup on third-down-and-short-yardage situations. I replaced Preston Pearson, whom Chuck did not regard as a strong enough blocker. I was uncomfortable in that role. I told Preston, "You can do a better job, having the feel and tempo of the game, than I can coming off the bench cold." But Chuck did not believe that sort of theory. He thought I should do the job . . . no matter when I was asked. Or however seldom.

Somehow, I could not inspire him to have confidence in me. One game, when a starting back was injured, Chuck wheeled to find a replacement. I was standing next to him along the sideline. He looked right at me . . . and called for Steve Davis. Despite his raves about my "suicide-squad" play—Chuck, himself, coached special teams—I had not convinced him I was a player. He called the backs together at practice one day by saying, "Harris, Pearson, Fuqua, Davis, and . . . uh . . . uh . . . you know . . . Rocky. Come on over here."

We made the playoffs in '73 as the wild-card team with a 10–4 record. But Oakland blew us out, 33–14.

11] *Super '74*

Staying in Pittsburgh for the '74 off-season gave me time to continue fulfilling the pact I'd made with God behind that hedgerow in Hiep Douc. He'd done His part . . . getting me out of there alive. Now I was going to do my share.

As early as 1970, I resumed my work with handicapped children. I affiliated with the Pennsylvania Association for Retarded Children and served as honorary chairman of the state convention. Later, I was appointed to the steering committee of the National Association for Retarded Children—YOUTH.

I welcomed the bureaucratic involvement because dealing with the children on a personal level had become very difficult for me. I'd spend a full day playing with one of the most severely retarded . . . then, the next morning, he wouldn't even recognize me. All he knew were the physical sensations of affection. He wanted only to be hugged and loved. Everything else was beyond his comprehension. I didn't have the personal qualities to deal with that very effectively. So I was glad to contribute as a public representative.

I also made myself the most available free-of-charge speaker around town. In those early years, I recruited Warren Bankston and Bob Adams to share engagements with me. We must have talked to every Boy Scout troop and high school assembly in western Pennsylvania. One group, in fact, invited us three straight years before they got tired of our act. Warren and Bob were always great about agreeing not to take money from nonprofit organizations.

I also became active with a committee called the President's Jobs for Veterans. Vietnam veterans need education, drug rehabilitation, but mostly jobs. A 1974 government study showed that one-third of our Vietnam vets were unemployed that year. The national rate for youth in the same age bracket, with high school–level education, was 17 percent . . . only half as great.

Education might be the veteran's road to a good job, except that the GI Bill is no longer adequate. Thirty years ago, when first introduced, it was used by eight million veterans of World War II. But today, with college expenses soaring, the Vietnam veteran cannot educate himself on $1,980 per year, the GI Bill's maximum allowance.

Especially handicapped are the five million vets who must support a family while going to school. Only 13.5 percent of them are using the GI Bill. Less than 25 percent of black veterans are using it. Less than 30 percent of educationally disadvantaged veterans are using it. GI benefits are adequate only for the single, white veteran who wants a four-year college education at a low-cost public school and can gain admission without remedial study. And he is the veteran who least *needs* help.

I felt the system was clearly discriminatory. And it's especially tragic for veterans of Vietnam because the national sentiment toward that war was highly ambivalent, to begin with. These veterans neither expected nor received the hero's welcome their fathers got after World War II. I wish we could do a better job of receiving them back into American society.

On an organizational level, I didn't think our Jobs for Veterans committee accomplished much toward the goal. We couldn't seem to muster much support in Congress for a revision of the GI Bill and other legislation we advocated.

But on a more personal level, I enjoyed talking to veterans' groups in Pittsburgh. Hanratty always said, "If Rocky's not speaking tonight at the VFW, he'll be at the American Legion or the Daughters of the American Revolution."

That kind of work, far from being an act of charity, was my source of good vibrations. Without it, the 1974 off-season in particular might have been my "winter of discontent." My life was still without direction or purpose.

I was dating different girls, but nobody I really cared about. My professional life was totally confused. I was finished with insurance . . . that much I knew. Night law school at Pitt had been an alternative, but I barely missed the cutoff score on an entrance exam. It was just as well . . . I knew I wasn't the lawyer type, anyway. And, of course, my football career was still going nowhere.

I have to laugh sometimes when I read these stories about "gutty, courageous Rocky Bleier, who kept his goal in mind without ever wavering." That's such fiction.

I had plenty of self-doubt. Every year I played, I considered retirement. Bankston and I used to sit on the bench and tell each other, "I can't take this anymore. I'm not going to play special teams till I'm thirty-five. I'm going to get five years in, qualify for the pension, and get the hell out of here. This is for the birds."

When Warren was traded to Oakland, a cornerback named John Dockery became my bellyaching pal on the bench. John is a Harvard graduate, and a deep thinker among football players. Our typical bench conversation might go like this:

"John, look out there on the field. What the hell are we doing?"

"What do you mean, Rock?"

"Running around like a bunch of maniacs . . . grown men playing a boys' game."

"That's all it is, Rock. I'm glad you finally realized it."

"And I don't even get to play."

"Stop feeling sorry for yourself. Neither do I."

"Yeah, well, I can't take it anymore. After this year, I'll be gone."

"No you won't, Rocky. *I'm* the one who'll be gone."

"I'm serious, John. I'm quitting."

"Okay, okay. You're quitting. Now, in the meantime, where are you going after the game?"

"I don't know. You have any ideas?"

"Yeah, let's get 'Ratso' [Hanratty's nickname, from "Ratso Rizzo" in the movie *Midnight Cowboy*] and go for a couple drinks."

"Okay, John, but I'm still quitting."

In spite of my oaths to Bankston and Dockery, I decided to try it again in 1974. Dan Rooney's encouragement stuck with me, and besides, what else was I going to do? I still wanted to be a football player more than anything else in life.

So once the normal off-season period of self-pity expired, I determined to give it another shot. But this time, by God, I was going to give *150* percent. If I was coming back, I was going to do it all the way. I told myself, "Rocky, pretend every play, in practice or in games, is the last play of the Super Bowl. Carry out your assignments *desperately* . . . as if your life depended on every one of them."

First, however, I embarked on the annual off-season rite of masochism. I went back to the Midwest to see one of my weight-lifting colleagues, Bob Guida, a former "Mr. Chicago." Bob had fantastic development and muscle control. His body just rippled. You could say, "Bob, flex your deltoid muscle," and he flexed his deltoid muscle, while the rest of his body stayed motionless.

He was also very good at devising a program for specific needs. I told him I wanted a routine to maintain my strength and increase endurance. He gave me both endurance and "pre-exhaust" programs, which were horrors-come-to-life.

The endurance schedule involved a series of five unrelated exercises, done ten reps for three sets apiece. Phase one was bench presses, quad lifts, calf raises, squat thrusts, and reverse curls. Phase two was military press, upward rows, flies, jumping from squat position, and functional "good morning," a hip-thrusting exercise. The weight I used wasn't much . . . perhaps 100 pounds for the benches, fifty pounds for the curls. But I did the whole series without stopping. In case you're counting, that's 150 consecutive exercises without a rest. Try that sometime if you want to find out where your pain barrier is.

The pre-exhaust program burned me out just as completely. The upper-body series employed benches and flies (hold dumbbells at the middle of your chest, fling arms out to the side, return to starting position). It was a quick program: ten benches, ten flies, rest one minute, ten benches, ten flies, ten benches, ten flies, rest thirty seconds, ten benches, ten flies, ten benches, ten flies, ten benches, ten flies. In peak condition, I used three hundred pounds for the bench and sixty-five-pound dumbbells. My pectoral muscles have never forgiven me.

In addition to the lifting, I played paddleball in Pittsburgh's health spas with Jack Ham and Gerry Mullins, two of my teammates. Ham, in fact, once told a reporter I spend more time in spas than I do in my apartment.

I also joined linebacker Andy Russell a couple times each week to "run the ramps." Andy devised a twelve-minute workout which took us once around the stadium . . . running all the way up, then all the way down the fans' walking ramps at each of the four main entrances. Even at my most convincing, I was not able to persuade my legs to make more than three and a half trips around the stadium that way.

By July, I was in pretty fair shape. One night, at Joe Namath's Football Camp in Dudley, Massachusetts, where I'm a part-time instructor, I had my shirt off, striking a few poses for the boys. Joe Gilliam, a Steeler quarterback and the skinniest pro football player you ever saw, and Pete Athas, a slender safety for the New York Giants, were moved to bestow a new nickname on me.

Joe said, "With all this weight lifting, we decided you've gotten too big to be a 'Rock.' From now on, you're 'Bo-o-o-o-o-oulder.' " Joe would insist that you say it with the elongated "o-o-o-o-o-o" for effect.

Tom Pagna was also at the camp. He hadn't seen me in person since that afternoon in 1969 when I limped into his office, a frail 170-pounder. I think he was about semi-amazed at the transformation I'd undergone in five years.

"Rocky," he said, "you look great. You've got all the speed, all the quickness, and more strength than you ever had. Why the hell aren't you playing?"

I said, "Tom, I don't know. But this year I'm going to find out. I am just going to play my ass off for Chuck Noll. Maybe he doesn't believe a guy can go from invalid to NFL running back in five years. Maybe the Rooneys really *did* keep me around back in 'seventy and 'seventy-one, and Chuck resents their intervention. Or maybe he just has me categorized as a special-teams player. I don't know what the hell it is. But I tell you this: I'm going to play like a man possessed for him this exhibition season."

For a while, it seemed I wouldn't have a chance to employ my newly adopted monomaniacal style. The NFL Players Association called another strike against the owners and asked all players, rookies and veterans, to boycott training camp. I became directly involved when Andy Russell sensed a strike coming and resigned as our player representative. That left all the burden on Preston Pearson, so I agreed to help him.

My active participation was not well received around town. In Pittsburgh's mills and bars, where the real fans are found, the question was often asked: "How can Bleier turn on the Rooneys after they carried him in 1970 and 1971?" Even my mother said to me, "Rocky, how could you get involved with this thing?"

Well, the answers were pretty simple. First, I wasn't attacking the Rooneys. I was disagreeing with inequities in the pro football establishment. Secondly, my beliefs were strong enough that I was compelled to take a stand. The issue was put to me, and I made a decision. If implementing that decision meant a strike, I was prepared for it.

Such reasoning was not sufficient for some Pittsburghers. Twice in one week, a gentleman phoned "Myron Cope on Sports," a WTAE radio talk show, to discuss my behavior. In a scholarly, almost lawyer-like way, he ripped my ass from one end to the other. Mr. Rooney happened to hear this man's second dissertation while driving to training camp in Latrobe.

By coincidence, he also heard, that day, of some work I'd done with children at St. Leo's School in town. A friend of Mr. Rooney's had asked me to visit, and I spent a very enjoyable day with the kids, playing games and talking about football.

When he arrived in Latrobe, Mr. Rooney called the talk show with a rebuttal in mind. But the line was busy. Next best, he thought, would be to call me. I wasn't home, however. I was having dinner with friends when my roommate reached me at the restaurant.

"Rock," he said, " 'The Old Man' just called. I don't know what he wanted, but he didn't sound too happy. I told him you'd be home later. He said he'd try again about eleven o'clock."

I excused myself and went home to wait for his call, imagining all kinds of horrible things. It was foolish of me. Mr. Rooney is not like "The Godfather," granting favors in order to gain lifelong obedience. He's not that kind of man. His eleven o'clock news was gracious, thoughtful, and sincere.

He said, "Rock, I was in the car this evening, listening to the radio. Somebody called in and questioned your allegiance to the Rooneys. He said you owed us more loyalty than you're showing during this strike, because we supposedly 'carried' you after your Vietnam experience.

"I just want to tell you that's not true. You've been an asset to us, both on and off the field. We don't want you ever to think you owe us anything. Whatever debt you feel you might have had . . . you've paid it.

"All I have to say is this: If you feel that what you're doing is right, that's fine with me. Carry on."

I thanked him for his understanding. I recalled that old stereotype about people becoming less tolerant of opposing viewpoints as they grow older. But here was a seventy-four-year-old man who accepted the players' right to free speech, while men half his age inflamed the situation, shouting about "the destruction of pro football."

Some owners contended we were striking at the foundation, the very underpinning of the football business. I didn't think our remedies were quite that drastic. Nevertheless, it's a business which had engaged Mr. Rooney for forty-two years, and he might have been excused for being somewhat emotional about it. Instead, he calmly discussed the issues with me, and said he respected my opinion. I told him the strike was nothing personal, but I was committed.

The Players Association began by presenting a list of fifty-seven demands, and yes, I'll admit some of them were extreme. But don't forget, we were in a negotiating posture. Our prime issue was the so-called Rozelle Rule, which prevents us from moving freely in the marketplace . . . a right enjoyed by steelworkers, plumbers, secretaries, attorneys, and everybody else I can think of, except professional athletes.

To win his freedom in the NFL, a player must fulfill his contract, then play one more year—his option year—at a salary as much as 10 percent below his contract salary. At that point, he is free to deal with the other twenty-five club owners. But those men are reluctant to sign him, because they must make compensation to the player's former team. That compensation is set by Pete Rozelle, the league commissioner.

In the very first case under his jurisdiction, Rozelle ruled that New Orleans had to pay *two* first-round draft choices for tight end Dave Parks, who played out his option in San Francisco and signed with the Saints. *Two* first-round choices. That was absurd.

His first decision set an inflationary standard far beyond anything we're now experiencing in the American economy. It also intimidated movement of players within the league. No owner would dare sign a top player, for fear Rozelle would raid his team in compensation. Therefore, while NFL spokesmen correctly maintained that a procedure existed to gain freedom from one's contract, in practical terms, no freedom existed at all. We failed to negotiate away the Rozelle Rule, but I'm confident it will be ruled unconstitutional in the legal suits of Joe Kapp and John Mackey, two former players.

Looking back on it, I guess one of our major problems was failing to marshal public support. The molders of fan opinion, the sportswriters and broadcasters, were 90 percent in favor of the owners, I would estimate. And it was our fault for not presenting our case to the press. Until April, 1975, we never even *had* a public-relations man. Can you imagine how naive we were? For instance, it was only *after* the strike ended that the public learned, in a *Washington Post* article, of Kevin Hardy's tragic story.

Kevin and I came out of Notre Dame together in 1968. While I was a sixteenth-round draft pick, he, ironically, became one of those No. 1 draft choices swapped for Dave Parks in the first of the Rozelle rulings. Kevin played five years and had four knee operations. One year, he played with his knee bent and taped at a 15-degree angle. Today he needs still another operation, but it looks like he'll have to pay for it himself. The San Diego Chargers cut him in 1973, saying he couldn't perform. Kevin said the Chargers owed him another operation and his '73 salary as part of a three-year contract. The Chargers said he had signed three one-year deals, and they owed him nothing. The case is in arbitration.

Meanwhile, Kevin works for a liquor company near San Francisco. He built a one-level ranch house because he can't climb steps with his bad knees. They pain him constantly. Arthritis has already set in . . . and this is a man twenty-nine years old. He can't play tennis, or ski, or ride a bike, or do anything that involves running. The doctors let him swim a little and play golf, if he rides a cart. Kevin Hardy literally gave his body to pro football. I think pro football should, at the very least, give him proper medical attention in return.

Consider also the case of Dick Butkus. "Mr. Chicago Bear." Maybe the fiercest middle linebacker who ever played. He also had knee problems. The Bears told Butkus in 1973 he did not need another operation. Dick was limping. He could barely walk, let alone run. He consulted several of his own doctors, who said, positively, he needed more surgery. Still, the Bears said no. Butkus was past his prime, virtually useless to the team. His salary and medical bills weighed heavily on the Bears' cost-control sheets. They forced him to retire. Butkus sued, and the case is still in litigation.

Those are the kinds of stories we should have explained to the public. We players question the objectivity of a doctor who is employed by, and therefore beholden to, a club. Especially when outside medical opinion contradicts the team physician. The game is hazardous enough, especially when played on artificial surfaces. We'd like to have confidence that medical decisions are being made on the basis of what's healthy for the player, not what's cheapest for the club accountant or most productive for the team.

With the Steelers, I have such confidence. But that's not true of everybody. A player from another team told me he dislocated his shoulder in a game, then suffered this insult from his coach three days later: "What the hell are you doing here, always in the training room? You're chicken. You're a pussy. Always faking it. Get your ass out there and hit the goddam blocking sled."

That kind of harassment must be stopped. It's not a practice in any other profession I know. Yet, on some football teams, it's a way of life. When an Altanta Falcon came to the sideline last year after an unsuccessful play, Norm Van Brocklin, the coach, greeted him with, "You no-good, chickenshit motherfucker. You got no guts. You're worthless. Worthless! Get away from me."

Once, when Art Malone, a Falcon running back, missed his assignment, Van Brocklin replayed it for twenty minutes in a Tuesday film session, before Malone burst out of the room in anger.

George Kunz, a Falcon tackle and another teammate from ND, told Hanratty before the '74 season, "Terry, you know me. You know I'm as competitive as anybody. I want to win as much as anybody else in this league. But this year, I hope we lose every goddam game . . . just so Van Brocklin gets fired." George got his wish, and then some. Van Brocklin was fired, and he was traded to Baltimore.

Those kinds of stories might have swung the public in our favor. Still, it wouldn't have been enough, because the Players Association wasn't sufficiently unified.

Take our team, for example. At a players-only meeting in December, 1973, our punter, Bobby Walden, stood up and said, "Yeah, let's strike. Let's get our money. We'll stay out till they give us everything we want."

If anybody could strike without fear, it was this man. The Steelers had no other punter in camp to challenge him. And he needed only a football to get into shape. Hell, he could have kicked in his backyard. He didn't need training camp.

Yet Bobby Walden was among the first veterans to defect. He reported on the very day he was due in Latrobe.

Mike Wagner, our safety, was just the opposite. He disagreed with the strike on rational grounds, but he stayed with us for the sake of team unity. So did Hanratty, even though the strike cost him a promised chance to bid for the No. 1 quarterback job.

Another quarterback, Joe Gilliam, broke ranks, however. The first day he came to Pittsburgh, he promised to stay with us. But that night he called his father in Nashville, Tennessee, and was convinced to grab the opportunity. He reported the next day as the only veteran quarterback in camp.

A week later, Terry Bradshaw traveled from his home in Shreveport, Louisiana, to Latrobe. He passed through Pittsburgh but never stopped to tell us why he had decided to report. To this day, I don't know.

Except for Walden, Gilliam, and Bradshaw, it was mostly marginal players who were frightened into leaving the strike. Dick Haley called several of them, suggesting their places might be taken by good-looking rookies. By singing the praises of Lynn Swann and John Stallworth, rookie wide receivers, he forced the incumbents—Barry Pearson, Glen Scolnik, and Chuck Dicus—to go in.

Pearson was motivated in one other way. Noll had seen him carrying a placard one day and said to someone, "What's that son of a bitch doing on the picket line? He should be here in camp with us. His job's not secure. He needs to work out." Word got back to Barry, and he obliged.

Eventually, Pearson, Scolnik, and Dicus were all cut or traded. Being in camp early didn't help them. Three rookies made the team as wide receivers. That proved our summer-long argument: Noll is going to keep the best players, regardless of when they come to camp. Going in early won't help you, if a rookie is better. Going in late won't hurt, if a rookie is worse.

For the guys who understood and believed that rationale, I have huge admiration. Ray Mansfield is one. At the age of thirty-three, he was "in the twilight," the second-oldest man on the roster. In 1973, he split playing time at center with Jim Clack. Clack went to camp early, joining a rookie named Mike Webster, whom the coaches extolled as talented, hardworking, and can't-miss. While those two guys fought for his position, Mansfield fidgeted. But he stayed with us. On Super Sunday, he was our center.

During the darkest days of the strike, however, it seemed there would be no Super Sunday for us. Haley, acting as a communications vehicle between the club and the players, pleaded with us, "This is our year. This is the year we could go to the Super Bowl. And we're blowing it with this strike. Cincinnati, the biggest competition in our own division, has more veterans in camp than anybody else in the league. Every day, another one or two go in."

"Yeah," we argued, "but they have problems. Their team is split. Half of them are sticking behind Pat Matson [the player rep], and half are taking bonuses to report. I heard they doubled [tight end] Bob Trumpy's contract to get him into camp."

"No, no," Haley countered. "They won't have problems as long as Paul Brown is coaching them. He'll get those guys under his thumb."

Thankfully, Cincinnati had a 7–7 season, and we won the world championship. If the records had been reversed, I'm afraid we strike leaders might have been blamed for the team's failure.

As it was, there were never any personal recriminations by Noll. I'll never forget him, sitting in the back of a meeting room one night as we asked the rookies to walk out of camp with us. His grim, steely demeanor intimidated them from discussing it, much less taking a vote. Later, after our union had been broken, Chuck called Hanratty aside after the first quarterback meeting and said, "All right, now, tell me what this strike was *really* about." That's just like Chuck, always wanting to be fully informed. But he never took a stand on the issues involved.

He resented the strike because it impeded the development of his football team. Once it was over, he said, "We have a lot of catching up to do. Let's get to work." And that was it. Nobody made the team or didn't make the team because of his views on the strike.

Among the players, there were occasional comments for several weeks. Guys called each other "scab" or "strikebreaker." But striving toward a common goal soon made us forget our animosities. And winning has a way of making people friends again.

We started by blitzing Baltimore, 30–0. Joe Gilliam threw for 257 yards and two touchdowns. He had won the starting position when Bradshaw came up with a sore arm and Hanratty fell behind on the picket line.

The next week, Joe was super again, completing thirty-one of fifty passes for 348 yards, as we tied Denver, 35–35. Unhappily, we suffered a couple of serious injuries in that game. Lynn Swann had four teeth punched out of his mouth by John Rowser, a rather aggressive cornerback who had played for us from 1970 to 1973 and didn't appreciate being traded to the Broncos. Why he took it out on Lynn, I didn't know. Franco Harris also left the game. He suffered a leg injury in the fourth quarter.

That left the running-back situation a bit scrambled. At the start of the season, it had been obvious that Franco and Steve Davis would be the starters. The coaches had been high on Steve for a long time. Remember, he had the computer's favorite numbers for a running back . . . 6-feet-2, 218 pounds, 4.55 speed. He was literally given the job.

Sadly for him, Steve didn't hold on to the job, because he developed a certain inability to hold on to the ball. That happens to a back occasionally. He fumbles, maybe drops a couple passes . . . the fans boo, the press gets on him. Pretty soon, it's a mental thing. When it gets to that point, only the player can help himself. Nobody else can extricate him from that hell. He must work through it in his own way. In 1974, at least, Steve was not able to escape.

And it all began in that Denver game, when he fumbled twice. With Franco injured, however, Steve stayed in the lineup, joined the following week for the Oakland game by Frenchy Fuqua. The Raiders beat us, 17-0. But the game was even more lopsided than that. They had their final margin at halftime. They played the last half conservatively, as if to mock our futile offense. Gilliam hit only eight of thirty-one passes. The next week, he was off target again, as we barely beat the lowly Houston Oilers, 13-7.

Now the commentators attacked *him*. "Gilliam's throwing too much," they said. I thought it was unfair. Joe loves to throw. He has supreme confidence in his arm . . . bordering on cockiness. Besides, that's all he had going. Our running game was barely discernible. Our new offensive line coach, Don Radakovich, was making changes, literally every quarter of every game. So our line didn't have a chance to settle down and work itself into a groove. Over the first couple weeks, only one position was stable. Our depth chart was interchangeable for the first month of the season:

LT—Jon Kolb

LG—Sam Davis, Jim Clack, Mike Webster

C—Ray Mansfield, Clack, Webster

RG—Gerry Mullins, Clack, Webster

RT—Mullins, Gordy Gravelle

TE—Larry Brown, Randy Grossman

A back likes his line to come off the ball all together and win the line charge . . . that "battle of the yard," that "warfare in the pits." Bring out your pet clichés. This is what football is all about. I said it before the Super Bowl, and I'll say it before every game I play. The team whose line executes instantly, without hesitating to think, and controls the scrimmage area . . . that team wins football games.

With all the different positions our guys were playing, they couldn't possibly be instinctive or dominating. Imagine the immensity of Webster's burden, for instance. First he's a rookie, so he has to learn all the blocking techniques . . . pulling, cut blocking, X-blocking, pass protecting, and all the rest. Now the quarterback calls a play in the huddle: "Full, right, split, thirty-eight-sweep on one. Ready, break."

He comes up to the line, thinking, "Okay, what position am I playing? Right guard. Okay, what's 'thirty-eight-sweep'? Three-back around end. What front is the defense in . . . even or odd? If it's odd, is it over or under? Do we have a line call for that defense? If so, who makes the call?"

By the time he has all that established in his mind, the quarterback might come to the line and scream, "Brown-thirty-four, Brown-thirty-four." That's an audible, a play called just before the snap to exploit a particular defense. Now the lineman must reassess. "Jesus Christ, what's thirty-four?" he's thinking.

Brown-34 changes from week to week. One week it might be 34-toss. Another week, it might be 34-power. Another week, it might be 34-dive. The lineman must determine which 34 it is, then recall his assignment.

The guard is thinking, "Do I pull, or do I block back?"

The center is thinking, "Do I reach for the onside tackle, or go get the middle linebacker?"

The tackle is thinking, "Do I block the man over me, or block down, or do I have the outside linebacker on this play?"

Each must make a decision in the time it takes the quarterback to scream, "Ready, set. Hut-one. Hut-two."

Our linemen did not reach the same conclusion on one particular play against Kansas City in the fourth week of the season.

Gilliam called, "Brown-thirty-four." And we ran three different plays at the same time. Joe and I ran 34-power. Some of the linemen blocked 34-toss. The others blocked 34-dive. Nobody blocked 34-power, and needless to say, I got nailed.

But it really wasn't too painful, because at least I was playing. That's right, folks. Ol' No. 20. Robert Patrick Bleier was actually running the pigskin in the National Football League. Can you believe it?

My first opportunity came at Houston. Frenchy and Steve started, but we fell behind and couldn't move the ball. With 1:51 remaining in the first half, Noll sent Preston and me into the game. Immediately, the team seemed to pick up. We marched thirty-nine yards in less than a minute, and kicked a field goal.

At halftime, Dick Hoak came up to me, rather unceremoniously, considering the occasion, and said, "You and Preston will start the second half." And did we ever. Preston gained 117 yards. I gained thirty-seven, and had one of my greatest days blocking.

Two days later, in our film critique of the game, Hanratty began a campaign on my behalf. If I made anything resembling a half-decent block, Terry would holler, "Attaboy, Rock. Great block. Way to hit him."

That made it quite impossible for Noll to say, "Keep your feet moving, Rocky," or anything of the sort. Respected as Hanratty is for complete knowledge of the game, his appraisal was taken as dogma. If he said I made a good block, everybody believed . . . whether they'd seen it or not.

He campaigned me right into the first start of my pro career, against Kansas City. I also scored my first regular-season pro touchdown, against the Chiefs, triggering us to a 34-24 victory. The following Sunday, Preston and I started again in a 20-16 triumph over Cleveland.

The next week, Franco was due to return for a Monday night game against Atlanta. His leg was healed. Since I'd been playing fullback, which is also his position, it looked like I'd have to step aside. Franco is our biggest, most powerful runner. When he's ready, he plays.

To my surprise, however, Hoak approached me at the team meal, just hours before kickoff. Again in his reticent, low-key style, he said, "You and Franco are starting tonight."

I was going to play halfback! I hadn't practiced so much as one play at halfback all season. I rushed off to study my playbook. Monday nights are no time to make a mistake . . . not with Frank, Howard, Alex, and all the rest of the world watching.

As it turned out, I didn't make many mistakes. None that was detectable, anyway. Franco and I each had career highs rushing. He gained 141 yards, and I had seventy-eight. I knew my blocking was excellent, because Claude Humphrey, the Falcons' All-Pro defensive end, was cursing me all night. I was cutting him nearly every time, hitting him at the knees. Defensive linemen don't like that. With all their bulk, a knee injury can be incapacitating. As I hustled back to the huddle, I could hear Humphrey yelling, "You motherfucker. You better watch it. If I catch your ass, I'll break it in half." I don't think he even knew my name.

That victory over Atlanta was truly a turning point for our offense. In retrospect, I guess I was in the right place, with the right skills, at the right time. Coach Radakovich finally had his line working as a unit. I enjoyed and profited from their newly developed cohesiveness.

And as Dan later told me, the feeling was mutual. "The linemen like your style," he said. "You get your ass turned north-and-south and bust straight ahead. There's nothing more frustrating than opening a hole for somebody, then watching him veer off toward the sideline, hoping to break a long one, and get caught from the side by an end or an outside linebacker."

Behind their backs (no pun intended), those kinds of runners are called a lot of things by linemen . . . pickers, lookers, hunters, sliders, tiptoers, and some names a whole lot worse. Backs like that *can* be useful, depending on your team philosophy. They can pop the long run occasionally with their gambling style. But nine times out of ten, they only piss off the linemen.

Our guys didn't need to worry about me. As a runner, I suffer from an inferiority complex, or a weak self-image. I don't think I'm very good at cutting in the open field, so I don't do much of it. In fact, I don't even like to watch myself run. In film sessions my jerky, choppy stride contrasts so vividly with the graceful, fluid gait of the other backs that I sometimes turn my head and refuse to look at myself. But jerkiness and choppiness were acceptable to the coaches, I guess, as long as they were done straight ahead.

Clearly, though, the biggest factor that won me the starting half-back job was my blocking. For that skill, I am indebted, among others, to Tom Pagna, who watched me hit a blocking sled fifteen minutes every practice for four years. He forced good techniques on me, made them belong to me. That, Tom says, is the definition of coaching.

He used to explain, "Gentlemen, it's all timing and explosion. Blocking, after all is said and done, is tackling without using your arms. And that's just a lot of wanting to."

In the pros, I certainly wanted to. And I had a few other advantages. I was shorter than most everybody, which gave me better leverage. All the years of weight training made me denser than most guys . . . a lot of mass packed into a small area for better explosion potential. Also, the Steelers adopted a fullback-oriented system to exploit Franco Harris' great talent, which meant that the halfback's blocking was just as important as his running and receiving. Finally, Noll thought I had good blocking instinct.

One of Chuck's more unusual theories involves running backs' "radar." He says we're all born with either an "elusive radar" or a

Cutting on my right foot—the doctors thought I'd never do it.

"homing radar," but not both. The two are diametrically opposed. Therefore, the greatest runners—the O. J. Simpsons and Gayle Sayerses, who escape tacklers with all those open-field moves—are the worst blockers. Conversely, the guys who can pinpoint their assigned defender, and deliver him a sharp, solid blow ... these superior blockers are normally not elusive runners. Chuck actually speaks of these "radar" skills in terms of frequencies. Against Atlanta, I guess I was operating on the proper wavelength. Chuck called me the team's "third guard," and Radakovich began using film of my blocks as instructional material for his linemen.

Two weeks later, during another very important game, I executed the most devastating block of my career at Cincinnati. On a play called lead-15, I ripped through the center, with Franco carrying the ball behind me. I caught Ken Avery, the Bengals' middle linebacker, right in the stomach and drove him seven yards back ... just like he was on roller skates. Then, for a finishing touch, I flipped him over on his back. Our film session erupted with a cheer for that block ... Hanratty leading, or course. Nobody mentioned that Avery was really an outside linebacker, playing out of position. He's too small to plug up the middle. Somehow, I also neglected to bring it up.

Later in that game, I stretched the Achilles tendon behind my ankle. I didn't want to take myself out. I was afraid I might never get another chance. Still, I didn't want to hurt the team. At halftime, I told Hoak about it. He insisted I hang in there.

In the third quarter, Avery tackled me and rolled up on the ankle with his full weight. Goddam, it hurt. The next play was a swing pass to me, in front of our bench. I went for the ball with a semi-limp, and missed it badly.

On the sideline, Dr. Best said, "You can't go. You can't play out there. That ankle's bothering you too much."

"Well, yeah," I said.

"I'll go tell Chuck."

During practice for Cincinnati, I had acquired some negative thought patterns. My body was tired and bruised, crying out for a rest. After all, this was the most playing time I'd had since 1967.

For some reason, I had begun to back off mentally. Something in my subconscious was saying, "I hope Noll takes me out. I've played well so far. I hope he takes me out before I screw up. I don't want to tarnish what I've done. I've had enough."

Can you imagine that? After all the years I had hungered to play, I was getting these negative vibrations. I also had begun to fear the possibility of injury.

Before the Bengals game, I had tried to shut out these thoughts, because they can make a back less reckless than he needs to be. Still, they churned in the back of my mind. A player who thinks he might be injured, often is. I was. It left me wondering how frequently the meta-physical is translated to the physical, the preconceived to the actual.

For the next three weeks, we continued to search for offensive continuity. Hanratty started in a 26–16 win over Cleveland. But he suffered leg cramps near the end of the game and was replaced by Gilliam. You remember Gilliam. He was replaced after six games by Bradshaw . . . who was replaced, for no announced reason, by Hanratty.

Behind the quarterbacks, the running-back situation was no less confused. With two of us injured against Cincinnati (Preston had a severe hamstring pull), Frenchy and Franco started against Cleveland. Frenchy dislocated his wrist.

The next game, another Monday night affair, in New Orleans, we seemed to put it all together. Bradshaw was sensational at QB. Franco and Steve Davis each had good games running the ball. It was our most impressive offensive performance to date, a 28–7 romp.

I was happy for the team, but I couldn't help feeling a twinge of personal disappointment. "Damn it," I thought. "When will my luck change? I had the job . . . so close to the end of the season . . . and then an injury. Now the offense is moving. Steve is playing well. I'll probably never get another shot."

My fears proved unfounded. Our offense was as bad the next week against Houston as it had been good against New Orleans. Two plays from the end of the first period, Davis dropped a pass and Chuck was livid. "Bleier," he barked on the sideline. "Get in there."

We lost to Houston, 13–10. But it was the last time we would lose all season. And it was the last time I would be out of the lineup. We stopped New England, 21–17, in a game that clinched the division, and finished the season with a 27–3 bombing of Cincinnati. Stand by for the playoffs.

Buffalo came to Pittsburgh for the first round. Leading 7–3 in the second quarter, we moved to the Bills' 27-yard line. Bradshaw called a fly pattern to Frank Lewis, but he was well covered. Likewise, Franco's pass route was blanketed over the middle. My assignment was to occupy Dave Washington, the outside linebacker, on a wide flare.

I wasn't supposed to be a possible receiver. But Washington didn't come to me. Nobody did. When Jim Cheyunski, the middle linebacker, noticed me, a panicked look came across his face. He started chasing, and I figured somebody screwed up. I turned up the sideline as Bradshaw lofted a beautiful pass. All I could think was, "Don't drop it. Don't lose it in the sun. Don't fall. Don't do anything. Just catch it."

I did, for a touchdown. In fact, we scored three more TDs in that period, and won going away, 32–14. I had ninety-nine yards rushing and receiving, which is thirteen more yards than O. J. Simpson gained, I'll have you know.

For all our offensive exploits, though, the best player on the field was a Buffalo defender, Rex Kern. He's the former Ohio State quarterback who now plays safety. He's a lot like me . . . too small and too slow.

Sure. He led the Bills this day with thirteen tackles and recovered one fumble. When a safety makes that many tackles, you know his team's in trouble. Most of his stops, in fact, saved touchdowns. They were made on Franco or me in the open field, after we'd popped for eight to ten yards and gathered a full head of steam. Poor little Rex was having his body kicked all over the place.

But he hung tough. In the second half, he dislocated his finger on a play near our bench. In agony, he jumped up squealing, with his finger bent back at a grotesque angle. Any football player recognizes that injury immediately. One of our guys grabbed his hand and jerked the finger back into place. Rex thanked him, went right back to his huddle, and never said another word. The guys on his team never even knew about it.

A little later, he was hurt again in a freak accident. An official threw his penalty marker, which is weighted with iron or brass so it flies true toward the spot of the foul. This time, unfortunately, he hit Rex in the ankle with it. That was all he needed to top off a lousy day.

"Jesus Chrust, ref," he railed. "You hit me in the ankle. Goddam it, watch where you're throwing that thing."

I don't often feel sorry for an opponent, but I felt sorry for Rex. Everybody was picking on him. The Bills hadn't even decided to start him until the Thursday before the game. All he did was play his ass off. And for his trouble, he got the physical beating of his life.

That same weekend, contrary to Steeler wishes, Oakland beat Miami in the other American Conference playoff game. Some of our guys had bluffed, "Oh, I don't care who we play. We'll kick their asses." But I sensed a deep concern. If Miami had won, we'd have played the AFC title game at home. As it was, we had to travel to Oakland and play a team which was, clearly, better than the Dolphins. The Raiders had the best record in football. And they'd squashed us, 17–0, in the second game of the year, we all remembered.

Oakland also has the reputation of being the "dirty-tricks" capital of pro football. In previous years, they had slightly deflated the footballs our offense used, written obscenities on the balls, and smeared their linemen with grease so our guys couldn't hold them.

Noll was so paranoid about Raiders' spies at our last practice in Oakland that he ordered us to run several plays from an unbalanced line. If the Raiders' secret agents were watching, he reasoned, it would give them something to think about. Our game plan, of course, included nothing from an unbalanced line.

We ran everything else, though . . . dives, specials, traps, reverses. We even gained six yards on a busted play. Franco rambled for 111 yards, and I—get this now—I ran for ninety-eight. Just two yards short of my first hundred-yard-game since high school. I wasn't even mad, though. How can you be mad after beating Oakland, 24–13?

Despite the good running, my biggest play was a fumble recovery. We were only leading by four points, with half the fourth period to play, when Bradshaw kicked the ball out of his own hand on a bootleg. Dan Conners, the Raiders' middle linebacker, seemed to have it for sure. I was racing across the field to tackle him. But the ball took a crazy hop into my arms. We ran down the clock, and added one more score for good measure.

After the game, I shook hands with every member of our team and thanked each of them. It was a great mutual feeling of accomplishment. I kept waiting for it to sink in: The Pittsburgh Steelers were going to the Super Bowl, and I was going with them. As a starter, no less. A real, live, sure-enough starter in the Super Bowl.

I couldn't help thinking how closely the Steelers' collective pattern had paralleled my own individual pattern in the past three years. In 1972, we *arrrived* together . . . the team with its first division title ever, Rocky Bleier with a return to physical capability. In 1973, we each began the season with great expectations, suffered injury, and finished in dismay. In 1974, we staggered together in the early going, each of us groping for consistency. We found the right combination for a while, before losing it to injury. Finally, when we regained our health late in the season, we began a slow, steady climb toward a Super Bowl peak.

12] *New Orleans*

I began the day, as I do some Sundays, by hearing Mass. My religious habits are not what they used to be.

I grew up with blind faith in the Catholic Church. At St. Joe's grade school, attendance was mandatory at eight o'clock Mass each morning before classes. There was also biweekly confession, Stations of the Cross during Lent, abstinence from candy and other pleasures during Lent and Advent, First Communion, confirmation, Easter vigil services, and a host of other Catholic ceremonies. For some of them, through high school, I served as an altar boy. I did it automatically, unthinkingly.

Blind faith was a comfortable, no-risk experience for me. But it was also not very rewarding. Whie the Lord may have smiled on the appearance of devotion during my grade-school years, He certainly realized I was following the nuns' orders. That wasn't faith. That was obedience to authority.

The Sisters could even tell us how to comb our hair. I recall a day in fifth grade that was perhaps the most embarrassing day of my life. I had switched hairstyles from the standard combed-over fashion with a little pompadour in front—the kind all "Bobs" wear—to a new, very "in" look ... sides combed up, ducktails in back, and a little strip in the middle combed straight down to my forehead. Oooo, it was "tough."

Until Sister Hilaire saw it, that is. She called me out into the hall and harangued me with a lecture about what did I represent, didn't I know I was a leader of the class, did my parents know I was combing my hair like that, and why didn't I just march into the boys' room and comb it back to the "right" way? So I did. And then I had to walk back into class, and everybody knew what had happened as soon as they saw my pompadour was back.

That authoritarian religious climate of my youth did not leave me easily. In fact, it stayed through my Army years. Then, gradually, I began to discover the mixed joy and pain of religious doubt. Why Mass? Why confession? Why Church rules? Why? Why? Why?

It was refreshing to put religion on something of a rational basis. But the questions were so new to me, so profound, so basic, so incongruous with my lifetime of religious training . . . and the answers were so hard to crystallize. Eventually, Father Burtchaell helped direct my thinking during several visits to Notre Dame.

I came to a kind of compromise between my background and my newly arisen doubts. Simply put, it is this: I am a believer in the works and essential teachings of Jesus Christ. Among those are the Ten Commandments, and several virtues he urges us to nurture within ourselves . . . charity, patience, kindness, love. I try my best—again in accordance with my "hedgerow pact"—to be a "Christian," in the truest sense of that word. A Christian is a follower of Christ.

I have trouble, though, putting that into the context of the Catholic Church. For generations, the Church insisted we must abstain from eating meat on Fridays. Violation of that decree was a mortal sin. Finally, in the sixties, the ban was lifted. Yet some of the staunchest Catholics still observe it. My parents, for instance, continued serving their fish luncheon in the bar. No meat was available on their Friday menu, even for non-Catholic or Catholics who wished to take advantage of the new guidelines.

It left me wondering: How could eating meat be a mortal sin on one Friday, and an acceptable practice the next? And did God really care what we ate? How important was Friday's diet, compared, say, to visiting a friend in the hospital? Which one would God rather see me do? Which does more to alleviate human suffering?

Similarly, which is the better way to spend Sunday morning . . . going to Mass, or playing with a group of retarded children?

The bottom line is that I haven't been to confession in several years. A good confession requires that I promise not to miss Sunday Mass again. I can't do that. I won't be a hypocrite. Perhaps I'll change again someday. I don't know. I'm still working my way through it. I try to worship God in my everyday actions. I try to find Christ in other people, and treat them accordingly. I might be wrong, but I think that's more important than observing Church rules.

I must say, however—and I'm somewhat ashamed of it—I revert to form when the situation is tight or I need a favor from the Lord. The Sunday prior to the Super Bowl, I went to Mass.

Afterward, I went to the airport for our team flight to New Orleans. Pittsburgh was really hyped up about us, and despite a police request to stay away, lots of 'Burghers were there to see us off. It was nothing like the fifteen thousand fanatics who greeted us at 1:30 A.M. after the victory in Oakland, but their warmth was genuine. The city that had been told so often it wasn't New York, it wasn't LA, it wasn't Chicago, now yearned to rank above them all . . . at least on the football field. A man-in-the-street interviewer asked what a Super Bowl victory might mean to Pittsburgh, and one millworker responded, "In a working-man's town, it means a helluva lot."

As the photographers clicked away and some of the United Airlines personnel cheered me, I began to feel a little bashful about all the attention I'd been getting. But another part of me said, "Enjoy it while you can."

After our arrival in New Orleans, I had a quiet evening with Terry Hanratty, Preston Pearson, and Joey Diven. Apparently, the perform-ance of the evening was rendered by Messrs. Mansfield and Ham at a place called Pancho Sanchez in the Fat City section of town.

If I had any fears about our guys being too tight for the big game, they were rudely dispelled this night . . . continuing into Monday morning . . . continuing into Monday daybreak.

It seems Ray and Jack were feeling a little disappointed with the entertainment provided at Pancho Sanchez. Feeling certain they could do better—indeed, being convinced of it, deep within the alcohol-cleansed recesses of their brains—they took to the dance floor. Ham, I understood, performed admirably, but he was reserved compared to Mansfield. "The Old Ranger"—so named for his look-alike on the "Death Valley Days" TV series—saw fit to remove his shirt, bare his ample belly, and dance away until 6:00 A.M. The crowd, I was told, merely loved it.

The Ranger's little escapade typified our team attitude. We were supremely relaxed. Even I felt calm . . . maybe too calm. I was still in a dream world. I couldn't imagine reaching the Super Bowl. And I sensed a lack of comprehension among the other guys, too. Was that just a facade? Were they really tight? Would the anxiety and anticipation tighten within us during the week? Or was this just another game?

Sure, it was blown up by the press. But would our team be sucked into that fabricated buildup? Or would we continue to emulate The Ranger's loose attitude, and regard this as merely another Sunday football game?

MONDAY, JANUARY 6

In the morning, we went to Tulane Stadium for pictures. In the afternoon, I did some shopping and took a nap. About nine o'clock,

Preston, Terry and I headed out for Pancho Sanchez to see if Mansfield had left the place standing.

We met Joe Namath there. He and Hanratty immediately launched into a debate over the recent Beaver Falls–Butler high school football game. Namath smugly pointed out that his alma mater, Beaver Falls, had won. Hanratty countered with some kind of specious argument about "technicalities."

It was incredible to observe the Namath charisma in action. In those terms, he is probably the all-time "football hero." But he's very smooth about it. He knows who he is and where he's at. He seems to know why strange women have that look in their eyes, why they're clamoring to touch him, and why their men are trying to buy him drinks.

Even among the players, he's held in awe. Later, back at the hotel, I noted into the tape recorder I was using to pull my thoughts together, "Tonight was a big thrill in Terry Hanratty's life. He came face to face once again with his boyhood idol, Joe Willie Namath."

Overhearing this, Hanratty sat straight up in bed and said, "That's bullshit. It was a big thrill in Joe Willie's life." He protested so vigorously, I knew he wasn't serious. Meeting Namath is a big deal for all of us. *He's* the man who forced the merger of the pro football leagues. He's the only factor that makes the Jets a representative team. He's still the consummate passer and field general. Yet he's bigger than football. He's an entertainer, a personality. If he quit football tomorrow, his career would continue to ascend. I think all football players envy that.

Also among the crowd were several of the Vikings . . . Fran Tarkenton, Doug Sutherland, Ed White, Bob Lurtsema, and Ed Marinaro. As far as I knew, it was the first meeting between the Steelers and the Vikings.

Marinaro remined me of a St. Patrick's Day when he persuaded the bouncer at a New York City nightclub to admit my brother and me, improperly dressed. Later, he took us to a private club, where we continued the celebration. I thanked him again.

White, the Vikings' player rep, told us about the pitiful support his team had given the strike. Minnesota was supposed to be a union stronghold. But when Ed took a vote, only fourteen men vowed they'd strike. Of those fourteen, ten went into camp early, and eight hadn't paid their dues to the Players Association. No wonder the owners broke us.

Our evening with the Vikings was interesting and congenial, contrary to the popular myth. Some people think pro football players seethe with hatred for each other before a big game. Not so. I have lots of friends on other teams. We play the game, and whoever wins, wins . . . whoever loses, loses. There's very little genuine animosity.

As we fraternized, though, it was peculiar to hear us talking all around the edges of a subject uppermost in everybody's mind . . . the Super Bowl. I was afraid of leaking some vital information. Then one of them let it slip that Jim Marshall had played all year with "walking pneumonia." Could this be a weakness in their defense? Or was it a psyching maneuver? Was Marshall really healthy as ever?

I couldn't resist the urge to size up Lurtsema and Sutherland, two defensive tackles, knowing I'd be running and blocking against them on Sunday. They didn't look too big, certainly not overpowering. But it was hard to tell. I wondered if they were thinking the same things about me. As we laughed at each other's jokes and small talk, I imagined myself breaking free of their tackles. They probably imagined themselves stuffing me and causing a fumble.

I was supposed to be relaxing, but already my thoughts were gravitating toward the game. I wanted the tension to start building. I was eager for the holidays to be over. I didn't want to spend any more leisurely nights. Except for practice and meals, I wanted to stay in my room and concentrate on the matter at hand.

More than team challenge, the Super Bowl had tremendous personal significance for me. I knew I'd be highly visible and have a chance to establish my worth as a ball player. I wanted to *prove* I'd always had the ability . . . if only I'd been given some playing time.

I began to think of it in terms of next season. I hoped a good Super Bowl would secure my positon as a starter in '75. Already I was planning another off-season of heavy weight training, running, and stretching. I was setting new goals. My dream of becoming a starter was realized. But the fall from the top is quick and straight, I knew, because pro football is not a business that deals in security. Getting there had been too long and hard a grind to let it slip away. A good Super Bowl would solidify my grip, I was certain. I wanted it badly.

I thought about those things as I smiled at the Vikings.

TUESDAY, JANUARY 7

Dick Hoak once told me, "During the sixties, we had so many guys come through training camp, I couldn't even count them all, let alone remember their names. A guy came up to me in 1971, when I was coaching high school ball in Steubenville, Ohio, and said, 'Hey, Dick, remember me?' I swore I'd never met him. He said, 'I was your roommate for two weeks with the Steelers a couple years ago.' "

In a peculiar way, the glory of this Super Bowl appearance belonged to guys like Hoak, who had suffered through the horrible years. Guys who poured out their guts every Sunday without reward. Guys like John Reger, George Tarasovic, Tom Tracy, Ernie Stautner, Clendon Thomas, Dale Dodrill. Great old Steeler names, never illuminated by the spotlight.

Among the players, Mansfield and Russell were our only links with those days. Mansfield . . . picked up for the $100 waiver price from Philadelphia in 1963 and hadn't missed a game since; imagine the torment he'd known in 168 consecutive games. And Russell, like me a sixteenth-round draft choice who wasn't given much chance; he'd never missed a game for the Steelers, either. I ate breakfast with them this day, and wondered about their thoughts.

An hour later, at the first of three daily press conferences, I watched with delight as they told the story of the old Steelers. In his rookie year, Andy said, he addressed a group of one hundred steel foremen. After a few minutes of perfunctory bullshit, one guy in the crowd yelled out, "You bums are disgraceful." Then another yelled, "You're a punk."

What the hell did Andy know? He was a rookie. So he yelled right back at them, "I don't care what our record is. We'll hit you! See . . . we'll hit you . . . we're tough!"

Mansfield went him one better. He told about a speech he gave to a Little League group back in the sixties. Outside the banquet hall, a couple kids approached and asked if he was Ray Mansfield. Ranger figured they wanted his autograph, so he said, "Yes, boys, I'm Ray Mansfield." They took rocks out of their pockets and nearly stoned him to death.

Poor Ranger. He said the Forbes Field fans were so accurate with their snowballs in those days that standing on the sideline was more dangerous than playing the game. Unless, of course, you picked a fight. He started a hey-rube in front of the Minnesota bench one time, and the Steelers ran like an army in retreat, leaving Ranger to fight forty Vikings by himself.

"There are no good *old* days for me," he said. "I'm afraid somebody in power is gonna check the starting lineups for Sunday and say, 'Hey, Mansfield is on this Pittsburgh team. We can't have a guy like Mansfield in the Super Bowl. He played on nothing but losers.' Then I'll disappear through a trapdoor."

Somebody asked him how long he'd been waiting for this chance to stand on top of the mountain. Ranger said, "Put it this way. I taught English to Bruce Kison, who's pitched four seasons for the Pittsburgh Pirates. This summer, when we played the Cowboys in an exhibition game, one of their rookies came up to me and said, 'Mr. Mansfield, remember me? I'm Ron Howard. You taught me in high school.' "

Ranger figured a Super Bowl ring would make his long career complete. "At least I won't have to wear my helmet to any more Little League banquets," he said.

I attracted a crowd of reporters, as well. Mostly they asked about my comeback. Some wanted to know about Vietnam. How did combat on the battlefield compare with combat on the football field? I didn't want to be melodramatic in my response, but I wanted to be understood clearly.

"There is no comparison," I said. "A parallel has been drawn in our society on the basis of semantics. People talk of football in terms of hitting, fighting, bravery, courage, valor. Some say it's an honorable conflict between opponents, like war.

"Actually, some of the terminology we use in football is taken directly from war. The word 'flank,' for instance. And there's a similarity in some of the defensive maneuvers . . . two sides using strategy to compete for a piece of turf. But the emotional feeling is the difference.

"There is no combat on the football field. Combat is life-and-death. War is a matter of survival. A fighting man in Vietnam is only concerned with one thing . . . how to keep himself alive. With football, there will always be a Monday. Win or lose, we'll all go to sleep after the Super Bowl and wake up the next day. There is no life-or-death pressure in football . . . only opportunity to do well. Real pressure is deciding whether to jump forward or backward when a grenade is rolling toward you."

Mansfield, Russell, and I combined, however, did not give as many interviews as Mr. Rooney, the unquestioned No. 1 celebrity of Super Week. This is a man who deserved all the fawning, all the flattery, all the compliments he modestly accepted. Patiently he did suffer the forty-two-year wait for this week. Silently did he endure the pain of constant defeat.

He never told the story, for instance, of losing Johnny Unitas. The full story would have blamed Mr. Rooney's coach, Walt Kiesling, and he didn't want to do that.

Mr. Rooney's sons had played pickup games with Unitas on Mount Washington, across the river from their North Side home, and returned with reports of a splendid quarterback prospect. On that recommendation, Mr. Rooney insisted Unitas be given a tryout in the preseason of 1955.

But Kiesling didn't like him. Said he was slow and gangly. The Rooney boys argued in Johnny's behalf. The Chief asked Kiesling if he was sure the kid couldn't make it. Kiesling said yes, and he was cut.

Ultimately, John Unitas became one of the league's all-time quarterbacks, winning four NFL titles. For eighteen years his distinctive high-topped shoes and the familiar No. 19 were as much a symbol of Steeler futility as they were of Colt greatness. In Pittsburgh newspapers, the stories of Baltimore triumphs were told thus: "Johnny Unitas, Steeler castoff, led. . . ." Still, Mr. Rooney kept his cool.

As a matter of fact, only once in forty-two years did he raise his voice to one of the coaches. Kiesling was the provocateur, and coincidentally, it happened later in that '55 season.

Walt had a distressingly conservative habit of starting every game with a line plunge to fullback Fran Rogel. Defenses stacked for the play. It became a joke around the league. Ten minutes before the opening kickoff, Forbes Field fans were heard to chant, "Hi-diddle-diddle. Rogel up the middle."

That melodic ridicule drifted through Mr. Rooney's box Sunday after Sunday, until he could bear it no longer. Finally, against his grain, he issued an order to Kiesling: Call a long pass on the first play of the next game.

The coach, of course, complied. As the opposing defense bunched for a run, Quarterback Jim Finks faded back and arched a long toss to "Goose" McClairen, who caught it and raced into the end zone for an apparent touchdown. But the Steelers were ruled offside. On the next play, first-and-fifteen, Rogel butted into the line for no gain.

After the game, another loss, Kiesling told his boss, with disarming accuracy, "See, Mr. Rooney, I told you your play wouldn't work." The Chief never interfered with another of his coaches. He took the public heat for their failures without uttering a word in self-defense.

After the press conference, we took to the puddles. Tulane's rain-soaked practice field reminded us of our respective college days. Pampered as we pros are, playing on our antiseptic artificial turf, there is scarcely a chance to get muddy as a bunch of five-year-olds. This afternoon, we recaptured that sloppy feeling . . . and it was fun. It made for a good practice.

Waiting in the locker room after practice were two shoe company representatives. First, I saw John Bragg, who had provided me with Adidas for the past two years. He now gave me a pair of tennis shoes, two pairs of turf shoes for the game, two T-shirts, and a leather carryall bag. Then Bill Mathis, the Puma representative and former New York Jet, took me off to the side. "I know you've been wearing Adidas all year," he said. "I'd like to have you try our Pumas. If you wear them during the game, we'll give you a nineteen-inch color television set or a cassette stereo, whichever you prefer."

The shoe companies are gluttons for the kind of TV exposure a Super Bowl can give. An athlete wearing their shoes amounts to a free advertisement. In the 1968 Summer Olympics, Adidas and Puma bid as much as $25,000 apiece to the top track stars . . . under the table. In the 1970 soccer World Cup, seen by about 600 million people on television around the world, Puma paid $250,000 to Pele, the Brazilian legend. Ironically, he didn't even wear their shoes. He simply cut off the Adidas three stripes, sewed on the Puma flying wing, and collected his payment.

American football players have not yet emerged into that sort of high finance. We're still struggling along with offers of televisions and stereos. I didn't accept the Puma deal, however, because it wasn't extended to everyone, and John Bragg had been very good to me. He supplied all the Adidas I ever needed in 10½ lefts and 10 rights. The gift would have been nice, but it wasn't that important. Besides, the Puma shoe didn't seem to give me as much traction.

Chuck had warned us, "Don't sell your soul for a couple hundred dollars. Let's not slip all over the field and lose this game for a lousy television or stereo. Wear what you've been wearing all year."

Only a few guys switched . . . Hanratty among them. He took the stereo. With six televison sets in his house and one in his car—Terry sometimes watches the test pattern, I think—he didn't need another. On the question of slipping in the Pumas, Terry reasoned, quite correctly, "What the hell? For all I'm going to play, I'll go out there in my stocking feet if they want me to."

WEDNESDAY, JANUARY 8

As late as this day, I still had the idea we were too loose. Guys were still going out on the town, having a good time, in spite of curfew. That was expected. I didn't begrudge them a few laughs. But I didn't want them to be lulled into a state of complacency by all of New Orleans' diversions. Nobody seemed to be taking the game as seriously as I was.

Even Coach Noll, who can be grim and unsmiling for weeks at a time, was carefree as we ran through Tuesday's light workout. Still, I was sure he sensed the atmosphere. The game meant a great deal to him, as well. He'd come too far to let this one get away. He'd clamp down on us, I felt certain. He felt like me. He wanted to get it over with . . . and win it.

We weren't the kind of team that always had good, sharp practices. One day of each week, it seemed, we had a sloppy one . . . guys not concentrating, missing assignments, lumbering through the motions without intensity.

This was the day during Super Week. We had practiced for four days in Pittsburgh before coming to New Orleans. Now, with four more days to go before the game, we were bored with routine, tired of studying the game plan, not yet charged up for the Vikings. A simple midweek case of the blahs. Noll seized on it.

He called us together, very disappointed, and said, "If we're not going to get anything out of these drills, we might as well take it in and get off the field. Maybe we can get our heads together and come back for a good practice tomorrow."

That was it. He screamed a little, and then ended it. Just enough to shake us up, but not too much to make us uptight.

Chuck continued to be relaxed for the rest of the week. His meetings with the quarterbacks were twenty to thirty minutes, instead of the normal sixty to ninety. Reporters told him at the morning press conference they'd never seen a team so loose for its first Super Bowl appearance. Chuck responded, "We're here to have a good time, *and* win the game."

Meanwhile, in team meetings, he was saying to us, "This is a business trip. We're only here for one reason . . . to win the Super Bowl. It's not enough just to be in the game." He was treading that middle ground, keeping us loose, but not too loose.

My view of Noll had changed in 1974. It's remarkable how a little playing time can change your perspective. Previous to this year, our relationship was neatly summarized by a scene in San Diego in 1972, moments after we'd clinched the division title.

Several players crowded around Chuck as the clock ticked down. At the final gun, Mansfield, Clack, and Kolb hoisted him into the air. I wanted to be involved somehow, but the only thing left for me was Chuck's ass, sagging down among their shoulders. So I pushed up on it as the others carried him off the field. They, of course, got their pictures in the paper, while I was hidden in the back, doing all the work. I believe that one moment, suspended over four seasons, typified my position with the Steelers. I was an ass-wipe for Chuck Noll.

Rarely did he show any personality to me. Sometimes, passing me in the hallway, he'd say nothing at all. After games, he'd go from locker to locker with brief congratulations. But if I was bent over, unlacing my shoes, not standing up to accept his handshake, he'd pass right by. To marginal players like me, he barely said ten words in a given week. He spoke at length only to a select few, such as Russell, Greene, Harris, and the quarterbacks.

During my recovery period, I often saw him in the weight room or the training room. He said nothing. Under similar circumstances, Ara Parseghian would have grabbed my arm, testing it like a piece of meat, and said, "C'mon, hurry up, get well. We need you." It was a nice sentiment. But pep talks were bullshit in Chuck's view.

In 1972, just before the playoffs, a group of veterans went to him, asking that he say a few inspirational words to pump up the rookies. Chuck said a flat no.

By '74, I had determined to deal with the man on his own terms. His was the calculated, intellectual approach, and I began to see virtue in it. For instance, after our game with Kansas City, he wondered aloud how their linemen, the most prized specimens in pro football, could be physically blown off the field.

A lot of coaches would have said, "Ah, we just kicked their asses." But Chuck analyzed it and came up with a theory.

"Their offensive line has bigger people than anybody we play," he said, "but their defense also has big people. I guess when the offense is blocking every day in practice against Buck Buchanan and Curly Culp, they try to stay away from the solid, one-on-one contact. So they allow themselves shortcuts, hop-around techniques to position-block the defense."

Noll didn't need to spend time critiquing the Chiefs. We didn't have to play them again that year. But he took the time, and he was right. Not only that, his analysis was understandable and demonstrable. There it was on film. Kansas City *was* trying to position-block, and our defensive line was blowing right through them.

In summary, there are two words that describe Chuck Noll . . . knowledgeable and aloof. Only once have I engaged him in anything resembling a casual, personal conversation. That happened one afternoon in training camp. He wandered into a room where Warren Bankston and I were strumming a guitar. We offered it to him, and Chuck began playing . . . fairly well, in fact. The conversation turned to sound systems, and he gave us a few well-considered thoughts on that topic. He'd just read a book on sound systems, before assembling a stereo unit in his home.

THURSDAY, JANUARY 9

Stripped of its press buildup, the Super Bowl is nothing more than another football game. I know I've said that before, but I was never more convinced than this morning. Hundred of reporters had been waiting all week for a story, a morsel of news . . . *anything*. Finally, Mel Blount, our cornerback, gave it to them. As the recorders turned and the pencils scribbled, Mel criticized Bud Carson, our defensive coordinator, for removing him from the Oakland game after he gave up a touchdown pass to Cliff Branch. Most of our team, incidentally, agreed with Mel.

Carson replaced him with a rookie, Jimmy Allen. Blount called that a "stupid" move. "I don't think smart coaches would have done something like that," he said.

He indirectly accused Bud of angling for a head coaching job, with the observation, "Once you've been a head coach [as Bud was at Georgia Tech], it's hard to be an assistant."

And while Mel had a forum, he broached a few other subjects. He said he didn't get enough publicity in Pittsburgh. He said he was on his way to Hollywood to start an acting career. And he defied Fran Tarkenton—whose arm he rated worse than four AFC quarterbacks'—to challenge him Sunday.

It seems every Super Bowl has a principal pregame news source. Before the first game, it was Fred "The Hammer" Williamson, daring Green Bay to throw into his area. The Packers dared, all right. On the way to victory, they knocked The Hammer cold. In 1969, it was Joe Namath, "guaranteeing" the Jets' win over the Colts. Joe was as good as his word. A year later, Lenny Dawson was linked to a betting ring during Super Week. He survived the false charges and beat Minnesota. Now we had a media star of our very own in Mel Blount. How would he turn out?

Our team meeting after the press conference was more like a pep rally. Cheers, whistles, and catcalls greeted Dwight White, our defensive end who arrived from the hospital after four days of treatment for back spasms/pleurisy/pneumonia, depending on where you got your information. Dwight returned to the hospital later that night, but checked out again Sunday morning . . . just in time to play a helluva game for us.

White's projected substitute was Steve Furness. He had been practicing with the first unit all week, and hearing conjecture that the Vikings would try to exploit him as the weak link in our defense. He'd had his hopes and anticipation built up, then punctured when Dwight returned this day. Steve seemed to be venting his frustrations in the afternoon at practice.

During a goal-line drill, he hit me a little late, and I hit him right back. I'm sure he felt his shot was legal, and mine was cheap. I thought the opposite. It made for a little animosity.

That was friendly, however, compared to a conversation, or nonconversation, I had with Terry Bradshaw after practice. A Louisiana boy, Terry was coming home a conquering hero, so the local people treated him royally. But the national press was all over him about his reputation as a "dumb" quarterback. One reporter even asked what his college board scores had been.

A television sportscaster asked me about it, and I said, "Terry's really come into his own this season. He used to get very excited and uptight, sometimes even stuttering in the huddle. We'd have to settle him down. But this year, he's very cool and calm. He seems to have everything under control. Now he calls the plays with full command. Against Oakland, for instance, he called about thirty percent audibles."

One of Terry's friends or family saw the interview and told him about it. I guess it lost something in the translation, because he confronted me in a highly agitated humor. "What right have you to criticize me?" he asked. "You ran the ball five times in your first five years. You haven't even been *in* the huddle until this season."

For the past few years, there had been two major debates in Pittsburgh . . . a mass-transit proposal called "Skybus," and "TGQC," otherwise known as The Great Quarterback Controversy. Who should play? Bradshaw, Hanratty, or Gilliam?

It was easy for the fans to choose a favorite, because each quarterback had a distinctive style. In 1972, they displayed their different personalities through their chinstraps. Bradshaw, in a show of bravado, wore none at all. He had his helmet knocked off several times, even lost a tooth. But he never wore a chin strap until an NFL rule compelled him. Gilliam fastened his strap on one side only, letting it dangle in a cocky, defiant manner that said to the defense: "Come pull it off, if you can." Hanratty buckled up properly. His confidence was equal to the others', but it was inner-directed.

There were differences, as well, in the huddle. That's where a player looks for something extra in his quarterback. Call it leadership or inspiration, if you like those words. By the nature of his function, a quarterback cannot help but reveal himself to the ten men surrounding him.

Take James Street, for example. He played quarterback at the University of Texas in the late sixties. Beat Notre Dame in their first Cotton Bowl, in fact. He was a nonstop talker in the huddle, always rallying, "C'mon gang, dig down now. Suck it up. Gimme your best." While the plays were being shuttled from the bench, Street knelt in the huddle, predicting, "Well, it's about time for fifty-seven again." He correctly guessed his coach's play selection about three-quarters of the time. Can you imagine what confidence that gave his teammates? They called him "Slick."

At Auburn about the same time, Pat Sullivan did the job another way . . . by keeping his voice low and his team calm. Terry Beasley, his

The NFL's top rushing backfield in 1974: Franco Harris, Rocky Bleier, Terry Bradshaw (*Al Herrmann Jr., The Pittsburgh Press*)

The quarterbacks three: Joe Gilliam, Terry Hanratty, Terry Bradshaw

top receiver, once told me about a drive Sullivan directed against Tennessee. Playing before national television and seventy thousand partisans in Knoxville, Auburn was down, 6–0. They hadn't moved the ball all day, and now, with less than two minutes to play, they had to go eighty yards for the winning touchdown. Sullivan did it with six straight pass completions. Through the whole frenzied drive, battling the clock and all the odds, he was the only man who said a word in the huddle. And all he did was call the plays. Pat Sullivan won the Heisman Trophy that year.

In the pros, I encountered various styles. Dick Shiner was always berating us: "Why didn't you catch the ball?" or "Who missed his block?" Bobby Layne was like that, they told me. He literally kicked guys off the field if they weren't playing well for him. Only once in his life was he at a loss for words in the huddle. At the 1959 Pro Bowl, he was so hung over from a night out, he couldn't remember the plays. Frank Gifford, a halfback, called signals for the Eastern Conference.

Andy Russell has spent a career observing quarterbacks, and he tells some great stories. In *the* critical moment of our '74 playoff game at Oakland—the Raiders behind by four points with a few minutes left —Ken Stabler caught Andy's eye during a time-out and winked at him. Actually winked! As if to say, "Andy, you *know* I'm going to put this ball into the end zone."

Another afternoon, Fran Tarkenton called time-out for a sideline conference, his team trailing by less than a touchdown with thirty seconds to play. When he returned to the huddle, he was smiling broadly, almost laughing about the brilliant play he had conceived. Neither Stabler nor Tarkenton pulled those games out, but Russell said it blew his mind to see such confidence.

Of our three quarterbacks, Hanratty was the one most likely to inspire that feeling. Terry's the most popular player on our team. When he got into the game, I always had a feeling everybody played a little harder for him. He came into the huddle with a glint in his eye and a series of plays in his mind.

If Hanratty's forte was cerebral, Bradshaw's was physical. At 6-feet-3, 230 pounds, he's bigger than some linebackers. In the Super Bowl, Wally Hilgenberg came though untouched on a blitz and hit Bradshaw a vicious shot. Terry just shook him off and turned the play into a five-yard gain.

Juggling their diverse skills was a problem. After one game in which neither played particularly well, Preston Pearson said to me, "If Hanratty had Brad's body, or Brad had Hanratty's head, we'd have one helluva quarterback."

Gilliam, the latest arrival, was most inclined to throw. He loved nothing more than to rush into the huddle and call a fly pattern: "Full, right, split, sixty, maximum, takeoff." Just saying the words brought a grin to his face. I didn't blame him for passing thirty times a game. That was his only weapon before the running attack jelled. But Noll decided we couldn't win consistently with a passing offense. So Joe went to the bench, having lost just one of six games.

Of the three, he was least content on the sideline. He sulked and refused to chart plays. By contrast, Hanratty made a game of "riding the oak." When he handled the telephone and Bradshaw the clipboard, he nicknamed their duet "Chart and Chat." Every Sunday, his opening line to our spotter in the press box, Dan Radakovich, was, "Earth to Rad, Earth to Rad. Come in, Rad."

Bradshaw performed his sideline duty with a false show of indifference. He tried to cover his disappointment with a big, wide smile and occasional comments like: "I don't care. Let Joe play awhile." In reality, though, it was killing him. After all, he was the NFL's No. 1 draft selection in 1970. He came to Pittsburgh billed as the messiah who would lead the Steelers out of their football desert. That was a huge responsibility for a twenty-two-year-old kid, and Terry always bore it heavily.

Somehow, during his six weeks of inactivity, though, Bradshaw shed his burden. When he got back into the lineup, his presence in the huddle was dramatically different. And in the locker room, he was suddenly friendlier, more down-to-earth, feeling less pressured to do it all himself. Paul Martha, from the perspective of a retired former player, explained it this way to me: "Bradshaw had just been divorced, he was going bald, everybody was saying he was dumb. He looked the situation over and said, 'The hell with it. I'm just gonna play football. That's all I have left.' "

Hanratty, meanwhile, probably got the biggest shaft of the three. After a sensational 1973–with two broken ribs, he beat Cincinnati, Washington, and Oakland, and played brilliantly in a loss to Denver–he threatened to jump to the World Football League. The Steelers lured him back with a big contract and a promised shot at the starting job. That chance was snuffed out by the player strike, but to his immortal credit, Terry held fast with the union.

He says Noll never gave him an equal chance at the job . . . that Bradshaw was always his quarterback. He says Noll had a personality conflict with him from the first day they met. Lately, Terry had taken to feeding that conflict. Sometimes he'd purposely wait until Thursday before suggesting a play for Sunday's game. Then he'd watch with concealed delight as Chuck exploded: "Goddam it, it's too late for a new play. We've been working on this game plan all week!"

Whatever his personal feelings, Chuck holds immense respect—as we all do—for Terry's knowledge of the game. When we formed a new "Chart and Chat" team at midseason—Gilliam having declined the assignment, and I being available with my ankle injury—I was amazed how frequently Terry actually called the play during sideline conferences. If his play failed, Chuck often wheeled on him and scolded through gritting teeth, "Goddam it, I *knew* we shouldn't have thrown that." But Terry only turned away, chuckling.

Very few players on our team speak to Noll the way Hanratty does. He is the only man in the quarterback meetings who will say, flat out, "Chuck, that play won't work against this team."

On a more personal level, he found Noll surprisingly defensive about his hometown, Cleveland. Hanratty went for the jugular. Every time we screened a film of the Browns, he cried out in the darkness, "Well, another great day in Cleveland." The words fairly dripped with sarcasm.

Ironically, his only start of '74 was in Cleveland. All week, Terry droned on so mercilessly about the dreary weather and depressing urban blight that Noll was moved to offer a truce: "If you don't say any more about Cleveland, I won't say any more about Butler."

Hanratty refused to accept, and renewed his attack. "Chuck, the only reason W. C. Fields bad-mouthed Philadelphia," he said, "is that he never visited Cleveland."

That sort of attitude usually gets a player traded . . . and that's exactly what Terry wants. But I don't think it will happen. The club knows he's an ideal No. 2 quarterback . . . knowledgeable and gracious in helping the starter; competent as hell when he plays; patient, despite his occasional zings at Noll; and, very importantly, a lovable Irish rogue who fills the locker room with laughs and good cheer.

He is our acknowledged master, for instance, in the art of turning a rookie's shower cold while he has a face full of soap. For rookie starters, he has other tricks. In those tensest weeks near the end of the season, he fractured us almost daily by hiding cups of water under Jack Lambert's shoulder pads. It was the highlight of getting dressed every day. The locker room poised, fifty pairs of eyes sneaking sidelong glances, as Lambert grabbed his pads, pulled them from the shelf above his locker . . . and *splash* . . . soaked himself for the umpteenth consecutive day. Hanratty shook with glee.

On the field, he'd wait until Lambert, by nature a deadly serious young man, was snorting and snarling with full intensity. Then Hanratty would come up to the line of scrimmage, look over at Jack, the middle linebacker, scowling not three feet away, and pucker up his lips with a little kiss.

Only once do I recall catching Hanratty with hook, line, and sinker in his mouth. It was 1973. Not having visited the laundry in several weeks, I was down to my last pair of underwear . . . a frayed, faded green pair of Army-issue, left over from Fort Riley. When Hanratty saw them, he bellowed, loud enough for the whole locker room to hear, "Hey, Audie, nice underpants." Terry calls me "Audie" (for Audie Murphy) when he wants to hear a war story.

As the room snickered at my sartorial disarray, I put on a most pious face and said quietly to Hanratty, "I'll have you know these are the undershorts I wore the day I was shot. I've kept them for sentimental reasons. This is the actual bullet hole." I pointed to a ragged edge near my thigh.

Hanratty bit. "Ah, gees, Rock, I'm sorry," he apologized completely convinced by my act. "I'm really sorry. I didn't know. . . ."

I allowed him to plead for forgiveness another minute before roaring, "You asshole. You'd believe anything, wouldn't you?"

It took him several months, but Hanratty got even with me one afternoon during the past off-season. We were leaving the stadium's Allegheny Club one day after lunch, passing a wall covered with pictures of Pittsburgh sports heroes. Terry noted the irony of having his picture close to Noll's. He also mentioned something about being better-looking.

At that moment, the club manager happened to walk by, and Hanratty stopped him. "Mr. DiCroce," he said, "Rock's been too modest to ask himself, but he'd like to know why *his* picture isn't up here."

Of course, I'd never said anything of the kind. But Alex DiCroce and I spent the next five minutes verbally falling all over each other, he apologizing, I denying . . . and Hanratty laughing himself sick.

Despite Terry's solid consistency as a practical joker, I humbly submit that the finest single effort of the past few years was rendered by one R. Bleier, in a rare fit of revenge, against Joe Gilliam. Even Hanratty agrees it was pretty good.

Joe and I are pretty close. We locker next to each other, so we've had some long and highly introspective talks. Many times, I could see the fire in his eyes as he told me, "Rocky, I can *play*. I know I can play. I can take this team to a title." We were both part-timers who yearned for an opportunity, so I could empathize with him. Joe and I formed a strong friendship . . . but, alas, a friendship which might suffer when he reads the following passage.

One day in October, we were returning from Carnegie-Mellon

University, our practice site when Pirate baseball playoffs occupy Three Rivers. It was warm, and the early-afternoon traffic was thick. Our bus crawled through the city streets, seeming to catch every red light. Some of the boys grew restive, and began throwing wadded-up balls of tape. Gilliam threw one which accidentally hit me in the head. I said nothing at the time, but vowed to get him back.

The next day, I conceived a brilliant adaptation of an old locker-room trick . . . filling a foe's underwear with hot, burning liniment while he's taking a shower. In Joe's case, there was no underwear, because he doesn't wear any. Instead, I rubbed liniment through a towel and lightly wiped inside the crotch of his slacks with it. I didn't want to ruin his slacks. More important, I didn't want to cause an instant reaction. I wanted the burning to begin later, when he was in the quarterback meeting with Noll.

Joe is always very quiet in quarterback meetings. Normally, the only words he ever says are, "Gimme one, Biggie." That is Hanratty's cue to give Joe a cigarette. (Terry is also known as "Biggie," or "Biggie Rat," the cartoon character.)

At this particular meeting, Joe began squirming in his chair after fifteen minutes. Like he had ants in his pants. Noll and the other quarterbacks looked at him quizzically, but said nothing. The meeting proceeded. Several cigarettes were requested. Finally, Joe could take it no longer. With Noll in midsentence, discussing some kind of zone defense, he shot straight up from his chair—like a Saturn rocket, as Hanratty later described it—and announced, "Damn! I gotta get out of here."

Noll searched Hanratty's and Bradshaw's faces, as if to ask, "What the hell's wrong with him?"

Joe came running into the locker room like he was . . . well, like he was burning. He said. "Rock, you see anybody messing around in my locker?"

I said, "No, Joe. Why?"

He whipped off his slacks. "Man, I got a *flame* in my pants."

FRIDAY, JANUARY 10

We practiced in Tulane Stadium for the first time, thanks to Chuck's petition of the NFL. Minnesota used the field under clear skies in the morning. We had it in the afternoon, amidst another deluge. Once again, it was not a sharp practice. I had the feeling that we'd been in New Orleans too long, that we'd been working on the game plan too long. This was our seventh day of practice, with one more to go.

Our kickers had their first "legal" workout in New Orleans. Paranoid as they are, the kickers refused to practice on grass, since the game was to be played on artificial turf. Tuesday, Wednesday, and Thursday, they sneaked into the stadium for quick workouts. They told us the Vikings were probably doing the same thing.

This afternoon, I really began to put my "game face" on. I must do serious mental preparation for every practice, and especially, for every game. I'm not one of those gifted athletes . . . like Bradshaw, for instance. He can play eighteen holes of golf in the morning, have a leisurely lunch with friends, then go to practice and perform flawlessly. I can't do that. I have to concentrate, block out all distractions.

Don Barley, a Pittsburgh attorney and great friend who shared an apartment with me for four years, says he can tell, by my disposition, what day of the week it is. Monday and Tuesday, I'm fine. Wednesday, I start to get edgy. Thursday, I'm about semi-rude. Friday and Saturday, I'm downright surly. Sunday, all the emotion runs out of me.

Don tells a great story about a Friday afternoon when I came ripping into the apartment, cussing the world and all its denizens. I finished my tirade by shouting, "And Duke is just a pain in the ass." Duke is his dog.

The next morning, I apologized to Don for being so irritable. He said, "That's fine with me, Rock. But if you want to square yourself with Duke, I'm afraid you'll have to speak to him directly."

So I took Duke for a ride in the car, had him trimmed at the canine shop, and bought him a huge, succulent bone at the butchers'. After that, Duke wanted me to put my game face on every week.

This day, I allowed my concentration to be broken only once . . . and it was highly enjoyable. The first planeload of Steeler family and friends had arrived, so I enjoyed a rib dinner with Terry and Rosemary Hanratty, Preston and Linda Pearson, my brother Dan, and my fiancée, Aleta Giacobine.

SATURDAY, JANUARY 11

Aleta will soon be my wife, I'm delighted to say. I met her and she was beautiful. We had that instant meeting-of-the-minds which I'd come to think was impossible with anybody. She understood me. She knew what I was thinking before I said it . . . and she did it so frequently it actually scared me.

Aleta immediately perceived my state of depression over not playing regularly, and not having a career outside football, and not having someone to care about me. She took care of the last problem right away.

Then she forced me to overcome the other two. She would not tolerate self-pity.

She brought out the strong points of my character. She acted as a catalyst for the personality changes I wanted and needed so badly. In return, she introduced me to new ideas and new interests . . . good literature, classical music, fine antiques, and a lot of life's other joys that I'd never known.

The amazing irony, of course, was that I should find her at the precise moment when I most needed her. Just as my football career was finally brightening, I found the lady who filled my soul with light. What a happy coincidence! She made the years of searching—both for her and for professional success—so worthwhile. If I'd attained only the football goals, my happiness might have been hollow. Having someone to share it made the fulfillment deeper and richer. It would have been nice to know Aleta during the comeback years, but I actually needed her more as the struggle ended. Now she and daughter Samantha Aspen are the focus of my life.

I never believed those people who said, "When you find the right girl, you'll know it. You'll hear bells ringing and sirens blowing . . . just like you read about in storybooks." Now I had to amend my beliefs. After missing Aleta all week, Friday was full of bells and sirens.

I saw her again Saturday, and sent her off to enjoy a day in the French Quarter with my family. They were all in town by now . . . my parents from Appleton, Patty and Paul from Elgin, Dan from New York, Pam from San Francisco . . . and a whole flock of relatives from everywhere else. The Bleier clan numbered more than twenty.

Our last practice was mostly a tune-up for the special teams. Once again, we weren't sharp. The week seemed terribly long. Several guys dropped remarks like: "I wish we could have played the game Tuesday or Wednesday." Were we past our peak?

We were like little kids losing interest in a new toy. Our attention span had expired, leaving us unenthusiastic for any more practice. I could only hope we'd find some inspiration within ourselves for tomorrow's game.

Dinner was a family affair at Brennan's, a famous New Orleans restaurant. It was great to see my parents enjoying themselves so thoroughly. They had suffered with me through the bad times. Now I was happy to see them enjoying the good.

I left the group and returned to the hotel, there to find a lobby full of well-wishers who were demanding, rude, and mostly drunk. "Rocky, do this. . . . Rocky, do that. . . . Rocky, sign here. . . . Rocky, pose for a picture."

Aleta, Samantha and Rocky (*Ronald L. Betush*)

I'm normally pretty accommodating in that situation. Hanratty, in fact, thinks I'm too accommodating. One night before a game, about eleven forty-five, a fan called our room and asked me to come down to the lobby to meet his son. I said okay and started getting dressed. Terry said, "Rock, don't let these people take advantage of you. Tell the guy you'll see him tomorrow." But I couldn't . . . I went downstairs. This night, however, Hanratty would have been proud of me.

I endured the pictures and autographs as long as I could. Then I simply turned and marched to the elevator. It was the first time in my memory that I had been uncooperative with a group of fans. I hoped they'd understand that my game face was screwed on securely. I was edgy, wanting the hassle to be over, so I could return to a normal life-style.

Up in my room, I lay on the bed, thinking pregame thoughts. I recalled seeing television cameras in the locker room. I imagined those cameras capturing a wild Steeler celebration after our victory.

I also thought about losing. I imagined how unsatisfying it would be to come this far . . . and then fail. Especially, I shuddered at the prospect of beating ourselves. If Minnesota played better and beat us, I thought I could live with that. But if we beat ourselves through mistakes, carelessness, lack of concentration, fumbles, interceptions, missed assignments . . . that would destroy me.

All week, I kept thinking, "If we play the game we're capable of playing . . . If we run effectively and control the ball . . . If we continue on this upswing that began four victories ago . . . If our line handles them like we did Buffalo and Oakland . . . If we play *our* game, we'll win."

Carefully, I ran our offensive plays in my head. I didn't want to program myself too specifically, because that eliminates flexibility. I simply wanted to remind myself where the blocks were, so I could read them tomorrow.

In the stadium of my mind, I rattled Hilgenberg and crushed Marshall. I burst through mammoth holes and juked safeties off their feet. Our offense flowed down the field like maple syrup over a stack of pancakes. The thoughts heightened my tension.

I took a sleeping pill and drifted off.

13] The Game

In the flesh, the Vikings look no different than they did on film. They're playing us exactly as we expected. On our second possession, they come with an "underdefense." Alan Page, the Viking right tackle, plays opposite our center instead of the left guard, as he normally would. When Terry Bradshaw sees it, he screams, "Brown-ninety-three, Brown-ninety-three." Brown is the "live" color for an audible today. Ninety-three is the new play, a tackle-trap to exploit Page.

From studying film, we know his first move will be to his right . . . "going home" toward his regular position. Bradshaw fakes a toss that way, just to encourage him a little more. Page chases a few steps, and Gordy Gravelle, our right tackle, rides him out of the play. Bradshaw pivots and hands the ball back to me. I blow through the vacated space for eighteen yards.

I get up, thinking, "Boy, I wish I had more speed. A chasm like that, I should have made more of it. I should have cut. If I was a halfway decent runner, I would have cut after I popped into the secondary. Damn."

Next play, they're in an "over defense." Instead of Page opposite our center, it's Doug Sutherland, the left tackle. Bradshaw sees it and goes immediately to the audible, just as he's been instructed. "Brown-ninety-two, Brown-ninety-two."

That's the mirrored play to the opposite side. Fake the toss to me, then hand back to Franco Harris. Sutherland is trapped, and Franco gets four yards. Isn't this easy?

Our game plan is working. Minnesota's line is jumpy, overreacting to our every fake. If we twitch an eyebrow, they're chasing. We can run traps all day. We've got them pursuing false movement. Even if they take only one step in the wrong direction, that's enough to give our linemen a good blocking angle.

In the first quarter, we dominate with sixty-four yards on twelve running plays. All but two of them are traps. Three times, we're in Minnesota territory. Yet we can't score. The first time, a clipping penalty stops us. The second time, our kicker hooks a field-goal attempt. The third time, our holder bobbles the snap on another field goal try. First-quarter score: 0–0.

On the sideline, we're telling each other: "Don't worry about it." "Let's keep moving." "We'll get some more chances." Still, we're all a little anxious. Over the course of the season, we can rely on the law of averages. The team that moves the ball will eventually score points and win its share. But in a single game like this . . . well, we could end up with all the statistics, and no Super Bowl trophy. It has us concerned.

We start the second quarter with "statue-right," an adaptation of the old Statue of Liberty play. Bradshaw fakes a pass and gives to Harris, who runs right end for five yards. This is about the closest thing we have to a sweep, though it's surely not the old Green Bay Packer sweep with two guards pulling and a back leading. That kind of play says, "Here we come. See if you can stop us." We don't do anything that obvious.

O. J. Simpson once told me, "I wish we had your offense. Everything you do is quick and deceptive." At Buffalo, O.J. lines up seven yards behind the line of scrimmage as an I-formation tailback. That gives him time to read his blocks, but it also gives the defense a similar advantage. We don't run anything that develops slowly. We want to be into the secondary before the defense recognizes our play.

After Franco's run, Bradshaw tries a bomb to John Stallworth, but Jackie Wallace has great coverage for the Vikings. On third down, our other rookie wide receiver, Lynn Swann, makes a fine catch, but he's called for pass interference. So it's third-and-fifteen at our 10-yard line.

The play is 52-straight. They're in a five-man line, preparing a big rush, expecting a pass. We outguess them again. Our line smashes a big hole at right tackle, and I explode through it.

Out of the corner of my eye, I see Jeff Wright, their tight safety. He has me man-to-man. He's coming . . . but I should be able to carry him a few steps to get the fifteen yards and a first down. I let go of the ball with my left hand, reaching out to stiff-arm him.

He flings his right arm around my back and . . . goddam it. He punches the ball out. I see it bouncing. I have a shot at it. If only it will bounce sideways or backward . . . No, it bounces forward. Randy Poltl falls on it, a Viking recovery at our 24-yard line.

I feel lousy as I get up. I'm putting our defense into a pressure situation. They've been sensational to this point, keeping Minnesota to

Into the secondary with Carl Eller and Jeff Wright pursuing

a net of minus one yard rushing. They'd just gotten off the field for a little breather. Now I'm making them come back.

On the sideline, there's a funny little game you play with yourself and your teammates after a mistake like that. Okay, so I fumbled. We had all the momentum, I probably had the first down made . . . and I dropped the damn ball. Noll glares at me in silent admonition: "Look what a spot you put the defense in!"

Guys come around with all the clichés: "Shake it off." "Get 'em next time." "Don't let it bother you."

Well, I *don't*. Maybe I used to, but not anymore. Not even in a game as big as this one. But I have to act out this football ritual . . . keep my head down and put on a contrite face. That's what Noll and my teammates expect. I think it makes *them* feel better. And, of course, I know it looks good for national television. I see the hand-held camera creeping around for a close-up of me. I can almost hear the announcer saying, "Rocky Bleier seems dejected after his fumble." But all the while, I'm thinking what a charade this is. Sure, I feel sorry. But fumbles happen. So what?

And I know what my teammates really think. They're just like me. When somebody else fumbles, I'm screaming, "Son of a bitch, what the hell's he doing out there?" Until he gets within earshot, that is. Then *I* start to recite the clichés: "Shake it off," and "Don't feel bad." Yeah, I know these guys. I fumbled, so right now, they hate my guts.

Minnesota saves me by moving only two yards in three downs. We have them absolutely stymied. Next time the Vikings have the ball, they botch a handoff and our defense swarms on Fran Tarkenton for a safety.

For the rest of the period on offense, our traps and inside running game are suddenly ineffective. Jeff Siemon, their middle linebacker, apparently has gotten an adjustment from the coaches in the press box. He's filling the holes quickly. Near the end of the first half, he makes the tackle on four of five trap plays . . . all of them for two yards' gain or less.

In the locker room, with a 2–0 halftime lead, our coaches discuss Siemon. If he's going to fill the traps, we decide to run partner plays known as "specials." To him, they'll look like traps. He'll be plugging an inside gap. Then, when it's too late, he'll realize we've blocked the end and we're running outside. Hopefully.

Our second-half kickoff is a squibber. Minnesota's Bill Brown handles it, then drops it. He's reaching for it, trying to pick it up . . . when our coverage team obliterates him. Marv Kellum dives on the ball for us. First down at the Viking 30.

Instead of the deceptive trap plays, we come at them with straight power. First dive-34 to me, then 19-straight to Franco. They stop me for no gain, but Franco shakes loose on a diagram-come-to-life. Siemon jumps into the line, and Ray Mansfield cuts him. I kick out Wally Hilgenberg, who is playing very wide in another of the "guesses" that can make him look very good or very bad. And Franco is just Franco, slamming his 235 pounds into high gear at the point of attack. He goes twenty-four yards to Minnesota's 6.

Two plays later, the call is counter-15 special. Three times in the first half, the Vikings' right end, Jim Marshall, saw me run past him to block Hilgenberg on 15-trap. Counter-15 special looks identical to him for the first split second. But this time, as Marshall stands there . . . hesitating, reading, waiting for the inside trap play . . . I bury him. Hit him in the thighs with my head and shoulders, as if I were going to run through him. Which, incidentally, is what the coaches always tell you to do.

The helmet jams down on the bridge of my nose. The shoulder pads whack against his legs. My back arches and my head raises, knowing they cannot drive up through his massive weight, but trying nonetheless. The first impact stuns my upper body, sending shock waves from one vertebra to another, down my spine. Then the burden lightens as I feel him off balance. My legs keep driving, convinced they can support my weight and his, too. He teeters on one foot. Momentarily, I have him in the air . . . before the damn 275-pound monster lands on top of me with a thud. But oh, it feels good.

Nothing is as much fun as lying under Jim Marshall, looking over at Gerry Mullins, our right guard, who has blasted Hilgenberg . . . then looking up at Franco, who is easing into the end zone. Incidentally, the man chasing him, four steps away, is Siemon. He jumped into the line again, as if to fill a trap, and couldn't recover to the outside. Our halftime counteradjustment is paying off. Pittsburgh 9, Minnesota 0.

On the next series, the Vikings pay me back. In their gambling, stunting style, the Minnesota tackles slant to the left on a third-down play. They make a huge hole, and I think, "Big yardage." Suddenly, in the corner of my vision, a large purple figure is coming . . . unimpeded. It's Carl Eller, their end, looping behind the tackles for a clear shot. I flinch, try to cut away. He waffles me, bending my left foot back and turning the ankle sharply. He drives me *down*, adding his force to mine until the ankle collapses with a twist. It hurts like hell. As we get up, Eller has a slightly astonished look on his face. I sense that our violet chance meeting surprised him as much as it surprised me. But it surely did not hurt him as much.

At the bench, I say to Ralph Berlin, "I need some tape."

"What's the matter with you?"

"Nothing, nothing. I just want to tighten my ankle a little."

"You sure there's nothing wrong with you?"

"Sure, I'm sure. Just wrap it a couple times, please."

It feels stiff and sore as I run behind the bench. I can't seem to push off it. I can't get a drive. I hope Ralph won't tell Chuck. And I hope nobody sees me limping around back here. If I keep moving, maybe it'll work itself out.

Meanwhile, our defense is giving a fantastic imitation of the Strategic Air Command. Impregnable. Through forty-eight minutes of the game, they force two fumbles and two interceptions, while holding Minnesota scoreless. The Viking running game will finish the day with twenty-one yards in twenty carries. For the longest time, it seems we can let our defense win it.

Then, a fluke. Somehow, Minnesota's Matt Blair breaks through and blocks a punt. The ball bounces perfectly to Terry Brown, who skips into the end zone for a Viking touchdown. Cox misses the point. Pittsburgh 9, Minnesota 6.

Now our offense has to play football. There's 10:18 remaining. Plenty of time for them to score again. We have to move the ball. We need a solid drive to eat the clock and reestablish our control of the game.

We start at our 34-yard line. Franco gets nothing on 34-trap. Second down, he gets eight yards behind some improvised blocking. The play is 35-trap. I'm supposed to take Hilgenberg. But before I can get him, Marshall penetrates, so I block him. Gerry Mullins takes Hilgenberg on the "read," and Franco makes a helluva run.

Third-and-two. Bradshaw throws over the middle to Larry Brown, our tight end. It's a thirty-yard gain . . . but as he's tackled, the ball pops loose. Jackie Wallace falls on it. The two officials nearest the play signal: "Minnesota ball." At this, the Vikings begin rushing off the field.

A moment later, they're in confusion. The head linesman, Ed Marion, runs up to them, signaling: "Pittsburgh ball." The officials confer a few seconds before giving it to us on a no-fumble ruling.

The Minnesota players are screaming at Marion, "Jesus Christ, you were back on the line of scrimmage. It's not your call. How could you see it better than these two guys?"

They're still arguing as we huddle. First down at the Viking 28. I make five yards behind Franco's block on dive-34, but the gain is nullified by a motion penalty. First-and-fifteen. We try the tackle-trap on Page, but Marshall closes it hard. He's looking for it now, we've run so many, and stops me with no gain.

Second-and-fifteen. For the third time in the game, we run a "sucker play" at Doug Sutherland. Twice, we've gotten good yardage on the sucker, which is simply a trap play without the blocking.

Sutherland is taught to "key" or follow Mullins, who plays opposite him. So we pull Mullins, as if to run a wide play, and fake to Harris, just to make it look convincing. Our linemen leave Sutherland alone as he chases Mullins and Franco. The next sound he hears is *woosh*, as I go zipping through the hole he's just created.

When Tom Landry was with the New York Giants, he coined the phrase "false keying" for what we do to Sutherland. A couple months later, as we laugh at his lurching and groping in our film room, we will say—a bit more graphically—he was "suckered" for the third straight time.

I make seventeen yards on the play, but I don't do it with the expected *woosh*. My ankle is really hurting. My takeoff is very poor. But I still am not going to leave this game.

Now Franco makes five yards in two tries. So it's third-and-five at the Viking 11-yard line. We have to pass. As I circle out of the backfield, I notice Siemon has dropped very deep. I hook up at the 5-yard line, just in front of Paul Krause, their free safety, and Bradshaw drills me. First-and-goal at the 5.

Again, the Vikings jam the middle on Franco. He gets one yard in two attempts. Another big third down coming up. Third-and-goal at the 4.

My pass route is into the right corner. Larry Brown curls behind me, deep in the end zone. Bradshaw rolls toward us. Franco devastates somebody with a block. Bradshaw might run . . . he might pass. Siemon can't decide. He comes up to play the run, and Bradshaw rifles the ball past him to Brown. As Dick Hoak would say later, "It was embedded in his stomach."

I get to Larry first, hugging him thankfully as the others rush to join our celebration.

Back near the line of scrimmage, Alan Page takes off his elbow pad and flips it at Jim Clack, who has blocked him to a Mexican standoff all afternoon.

"Hell, Clack, I'm all through," he says.

Alan was a college teammate of mine. He's a man of intense pride. Stung by the realization of another Super Bowl loss, he takes himself out of the game. He did the same frustrated thing last year against Miami after picking a fight with Bob Kuechenberg, another of our Notre Dame colleagues.

The scoreboard reads, "Pittsburgh 16, Minnesota 6." With victory

A prayer of thanks for the Super victory (*Wide World Photos*)

in hand, our huddle is raucous on the following series. Bradshaw giggles, "Okay, okay, what play you guys want to run?"

In chorus, the linemen respond, "Sucker. Sucker. We've got some new meat in there. Let's try sucker again."

"Sucker, it is," says Bradshaw.

Page's replacement at tackle is Gary Larsen. Like Sutherland, he dutifully follows his key, the pulling guard, and makes a hole for me. I hobble through for six yards. That play would normally succeed just once a game, but we've worked it four times.

Our linemen are laughing and pounding each other's shoulder pads. Less than a minute remains. Back in the huddle, Mansfield says to Clack, "I'll bet the 'Burgh is in ashes by now."

Running off the field, I can already imagine the victory scene. The locker room will be about knee-deep in self-satisfaction. People will be coming around, asking, "How does it feel? How does it feel?" I'll only be able to shake my head and give them a big smile.

One thing I'll want to do for certain: go from player to player, slowly, around the room, shaking hands and exchanging those big smiles. To the other running backs, in particular, I want to deliver an empathetic sentiment. I know what they'll be thinking. They'll be feeling a little bit "out of it." Each was a starter at one time during the season. But this day, they were all special-teams players. Each knows the euphoria I feel now. And I know their condition, too. The forced grins . . . the bittersweet emotions . . . the limited fulfillment . . . the wanting, the craving to revel in it all, but somehow the inability to feel it's *yours*. I know that emptiness. I endured it in a lot of postgame locker rooms. I'll try to tell Frenchy and Preston and Steve. I hope it comes off well.

Just inside the locker room, I spot Mr. Rooney, standing strangely alone against the wall, while the latecomers celebrate his long-awaited victory. Look at this man. Do any of us really know what it's like to hunger forty-two years for something?

I want to tell him that. Mostly, I want to thank him from the bottom of my heart. Actually, from the bottom of my scarred feet. With everything in my non–NFL–caliber body.

So I hug him and say, "Thanks for everything."

I look through the thick tinted glasses he wears. There are tears welling up in his eyes. He doesn't seem capable of saying anything. Now I feel like crying. But instead, I walk away. I know I can be more eloquent another time. Besides, I've done enough crying in the last six years.

Index

Adams, Bob, 150, 169
Allan, Denny, 37
Allen, Jimmy, 199
Anderson, Ralph, 148
Appleton, Wisconsin, 17–18, 25
Asbury, Willie, 56
Athas, Pete, 172
Atlanta Falcons, 29, 176, 181–82, 184
Austin, Bill, 59–60, 61, 62, 126, 139
Avery, Ken, 184
Azzaro, Joe, 41

Baltimore Colts, 139–40, 195
Bankston, Warren, 135, 136–38, 147, 148, 150, 155, 166, 169, 170–71
Barley, Don, 207
Barz, Bill, 37
Baughman, Dr. John, 116, 118
Beasley, Terry, 200–02
Beban, Gary, 29
Bell, Upton, 151
Berlin, Ralph, 136, 138–39, 141, 149, 151, 215–16
Berry, Raymond, 54
Besh, John, 26
Best, Art, 37
Best, Dr. John, 138, 139, 141, 149, 184
Blair, Matt, 216
Bleier, Bob (Robert, Sr.), 18, 20, 22–25, 26, 35, 77–78, 116, 118, 126, 153–54, 208
Bleier, Dan, 21, 22, 76, 208
Bleier, Ellen, 18, 20, 22–25, 35, 77, 116–17, 118, 126, 208
Bleier, Pam, 21–22, 92–93, 94, 208
Bleier, Rocky (Robert Patrick, Jr.)
    army draft, 68–71
    background, 17–29
    childhood athletics, 25–26
    college football, 35–47
    family of, 18, 20–25, 208,
    feelings about the war, 75–77, 100

high school athletics, 26–29, 34, 37
insurance work, 144, 147, 157, 158
nicknames, 20, 172
nonfootball college activities, 47–48
off-season training, 144–47, 154, 158–63, 171–72
physical size, 15, 136, 163, 172
and religion, 16, 76–77, 93, 102–03, 150, 188–89
war experiences, 13, 79–111
work with handicapped children, 47–48, 169
BLESTO-V, 51, 52
Blocking, 182–84
Blount, Mel, 198–99
Blue Ghost, 106–07
Boland, Joe, 65
Boston College, 32, 33, 35
Bowers, Joe, 26
Boyd, Bobby, 140
Bradshaw, Terry, 54, 155, 156, 177, 185, 200, 203–04
    Super Bowl IX (1975), 15, 16, 199–200, 202, 211, 212, 216, 217, 219
Brady, Scott, 127
Bragg, John, 195, 196
Branch, Cliff, 199
Brennan, Terry, 36
Britton, Jim, 79, 90, 99
Brown, Bill, 214
Brown, Ed, 58–59
Brown, Larry, 54, 148, 179, 216, 217
Brown, Paul, 178
Brown, Terry, 216
Brown, Tommy, 104–06
Bruhn, Milt, 34–35
Brumfield, Jim, 148, 150, 151
Buchanan, Buck, 198
Buffalo Bills, 185–86
Bullock, Wayne, 37
Burtchaell, Father James, 153, 189
Butkus, Dick, 153, 175–76
Butler, Jim "Cannonball," 60

Calabrese, Jay, 56
Campbell, Earl, 49
Campbell, Woody, 129
Capp, Dick, 140
Carr, Fred, 29
Carson, Bud, 198–99
Cheyunski, Jim, 185
Cieszkowski, John, 37
Cincinnati Bengals, 167, 178, 184
Clack, Jim, 54, 164, 177, 179, 197, 217, 219
Clark, Gene "Torchy," 27, 28, 33, 38
Clark, Phil, 151–52
Cleveland Browns, 204
Coaching football, 165–66
Cole, Terry, 148, 149, 150, 151, 153
Coley, Max, 139, 153
College athletics, conditions of, 48–49
Conjar, Larry, 37, 38, 41, 51
Conn, Billy, 64
Conners, Dan, 187
Cook, Carroll "Beano," 64
Cope, Myron, 173
Cordileone, Lou, 58
Crowe, Larry, 148, 150
Culp, Curly, 198
Curtis, Mike (Baltimore linebacker), 139–40
Curtis, Mike (Fort Riley), 130, 131, 132, 133–34

Davis, Sam, 179
Davis, Steve, 148, 155, 164, 168, 179, 181, 185, 219
Dawson, Lenny, 199
Denver Broncos, 178–79
DeRosa, Tom, 69
Devore, Hugh, 32
Dial, Buddy, 59
DiCroce, Alex, 205
Dicus, Chuck, 177
Diven, Joey "Big Face," 64–65, 190
Dockery, John, 171
Dodrill, Dale, 193
Durance, Tommy, 155
Duranko, Pete, 44
Dushney, Ron, 37

Eddy, Nick, 37, 38, 39, 40, 41, 51
Edwards, Glen, 12
Ehle, Dan, 148, 150
Eller, Carl, 215
Eller, Steve, 130, 131, 132, 133, 136
Evenson, Jim, 135

Farrell, Joe, 37
Finks, Jim, 195
Fogarty, Fran, 142
Fort Gordon, Georgia, 71–75
Fort Jackson, South Carolina, 71
Fort Riley, Kansas, 120–22, 128, 129

Fritsch, Ted, 29
Fritsch, Ted, Jr., 29
Fuqua, John "Frenchy," 135, 147, 148, 154, 155, 156, 168, 179, 181, 185, 219
Furness, Steve, 199

Gerela, Roy, 156
Giacobine, Aleta, 207–08
Gifford, Frank, 202
Gilliam, Joe, 172, 177, 178, 179, 180, 185, 200, 203, 205–06
Gladieux, Bob, 37, 41, 51
Gmitter, Don, 41
Goeddeke, George, 40
Gordon, Joe, 135
Grable, Chuck, 36
Gravelle, Gordy, 179, 211
Green Bay Packers, 199
Greene, Joe, 164
Griese, Bob, 38
Griffin, Danny, 135
Gros, Earl, 56, 62, 135, 148
Grossman, Randy, 179
Guida, Bob, 171
Gulyas, Ed, 37

Haley, Dick, 54, 152, 154, 177, 178
Ham, Jack, 148, 172, 190
Hanneman, Craig, 148
Hanratty, Rosemary, 134, 164, 207
Hanratty, Terry, 38, 39, 40, 46, 54, 59, 126, 134, 155, 159, 170, 177, 181, 185, 191, 196, 200, 202–05, 207
Hansen, Butch, 20
Hardy, Kevin, 34, 51, 175
Harris, Franco, 54, 155, 156, 166, 168, 179, 181, 182, 184, 185
    Super Bowl IX (1975), 15–16, 211, 212, 214–15, 216, 217
Harshman, Dan, 37, 47, 50
Hart, Dave, 64
Hegener, Stan, 54
Heinrich, Don, 52, 53, 61
Henneghan, Curt, 38
Hesburgh, Father Theodore, 125
Hickey, Joe, 50–51, 122, 153
Hickey, Mary, 50, 122
Hilgenberg, Wally, 11, 202, 210, 215, 216
Hinsdale Associates, 144, 158
Hoak, Dick, 56, 135, 136, 148, 154–55, 165, 166, 181, 192, 217
Holmes, Ernie, 148, 164
Hornung, Paul, 56
Houston Oilers, 55, 167, 179
Howard, Ron, 193
Huarte, John, 35
Huff, Andy, 37
Humphrey, Claude, 181

Hunter, Harold, 65
Hurd, Dave, 33, 35, 51

Jankowski, Tom, 35
Jefferson, Roy, 60, 134
Jones, Charlie "Lump," 65–66

Kalina, Dave, 150
Kalsu, Bob, 129
Kansas City Chiefs, 166, 180, 181, 198
Kapp, Joe, 175
Keblisch, Dr. Peter, 129–30
Kellum, Marv, 214
Kelly, Leroy, 164
Kern, Rex, 186
Keyes, Leroy, 38–39
Kiely, Ed, 140
Kiesling, Walt, 194, 195
Kison, Bruce, 193
Kohl, Ralph, 51, 52
Kolb, Jon, 164, 165, 179, 197
Kortas, Ken, 59–60
Krause, "Mousy," 20
Krause, Paul, 217
Kuechenberg, Bob, 217
Kunz, George, 176
Kurucz, Dr. Robert, 159

Lambert, Jack, 204–05
Landolfi, Chuck, 54
Landry, Tom, 217
Laorr, Dr. Anan, 115–16
Larsen, Gary, 219
Layne, Bobby, 57, 58–59, 202
Leftridge, Dick, 58
Lewis, Dave, 167
Lewis, Frank, 54, 148, 164, 185
Liggins, Granville, 40
Lind, Mike, 56
Linehan, Ron, 155
Lison, Al, 27, 76, 82, 102, 114, 150
Logan, Jerry, 140
Lombardi, Vince, 32, 62, 126
Looney, Joe Don, 129
Lurtsema, Bob, 191, 192
Lusteg, Booth, 62–63
Lyles, Leonard, 140
Lynch, Jim, 41, 46

McCall, Don, 135
McCane, Byron, 56
McClairen, "Goose," 195
McGee, Ben, 57, 63
McKay, John, 45
McKenna, Tom, 125
Mackey, John, 175
McVea, Warren, 29
Main, Billy, 135

Malone, Art, 176
Mansfield, Ray "Ranger," 177–78, 179, 190, 191, 193–94, 197, 215, 219
Marinaro, Ed, 12, 191
Marion, Ed, 216
Marshall, Jim, 11, 192, 210, 216
Marshall, William, 116–17, 127
Martha, Paul, 56, 57. 59, 60, 64, 203
Martin, Dave, 47
Mathis, Bill, 195
Matson, Pat, 178
May, Paul, 37
Merchant, Larry, 63
Miami Dolphins, 156, 186
Michigan State vs. Notre Dame (1966), 39–44
Milie, Bob, 150
Minnesota Vikings, 11, 12, 191–92. *See also* Super Bowl IX (1975)
Minnix, Bob, 37
Moore, Ralph, 35
Mullins, Gerry, 11, 148, 172, 179, 215, 216, 217
Murphy, Tom, 80, 99, 103, 104, 105, 106–09, 112–13, 114

Namath, Joe, 191, 199
football camp (Dudley, Massachusetts), 172
National Football League (NFL), 59
college player draft, 1968, 50–54
Players Association strikes, 134–35, 173–78, 191
players who fought in Vietnam, 129
NCAA rules, 34, 49
Neff, Donald, 68–69, 70
New England Patriots, 151
New York Post, 63
Nicholas, Barbara, 124
Nineteenth Hole, The, 56–57, 59
Nitschke, Ray, 29
Noll, Chuck, 15, 117, 126, 135, 139–41, 142, 149, 150, 151, 152, 154–55, 165–66, 167–68, 203–04
and NFL players' strike, 178
"radar" theory of, 182–84
Super Bowl IX (1975), 196–98, 214
Notre Dame, 34, 48, 54, 65–66, 122–24
captaincy image at, 45–46, 57
vs. Duke (1966), 39
football recruiting at, 32–35
vs. Georgia Tech (1967), 46–47
vs. Miami of Florida (1967), 47
vs. Michigan State (1966), 39–44
vs. Navy (1967), 46
1967 football season, 45–47
vs. Purdue (1966), 38–39
vs. U.S.C. (1966), 44–45, 116

Oakland Raiders, 155–56, 166, 168, 179, 186–87, 202

O'Brien, Coley, 38, 41
Oji Military Hospital (Tokyo), 115, 118–19, 120

Page, Alan, 51, 52, 211, 216, 217, 219
Pagle, Jim, 26
Pagna, Tom, 36–37, 39, 41, 44, 46, 61, 122, 124, 172–73, 182
Parisi, Tony, 13, 70, 136, 138, 164
Parker, Buddy, 57–59
Parks, Dave, 175
Parseghian, Ara, 32, 33–34, 36–37, 38, 39, 40, 41–44, 46, 47, 49, 61, 124, 159, 197
Pascarelli, George "Yutzie," 65
Paterno, Joe, 142
Pearson, Barry, 177
Pearson, Linda, 207
Pearson, Preston, 135, 147, 148, 155, 156, 167, 168, 173, 181, 190, 191, 207, 219
Penick, Eric, 37
Pergine, John, 57
Philadelphia Eagles, 62–63
Phillips, Charles, 41
Pittsburgh, Pennsylvania, 50, 55–56, 63–66, 189–90, 200
Pittsburgh Steelers, 51, 53, 54, 58, 61, 67, 70, 187
    Alumni Weekend, 1969, 125–26, 136
    rookies, 56–59, 135, 153
    scouting reports on Bleier, 51–54
    '71 season, 148–53
    '72 season, 154–56
    '73 season, 164–68
    '74 season, 178–87
    See also Super Bowl IX (1975)
Poltl, Randy, 212
Pottios, Myron, 56

Quarterback Controversy, The Great (TGQC), 200–03
Quinn, Steve, 55

Radakovich, Dan, 179, 182, 184, 203
Rechner, Patty Bleier, 20–21, 208
Rechner, Paul, 21, 26, 208
Reger, John, 193
Regner, Tom, 34
Riecke, Lou, 159
Rizzi, John, 18–20
Rockne, Knute, 32, 50
Rogel, Fran, 195
Rokita, Robert, 53
Rookies, 56–59, 135, 153
Rooney, Arthur J., Sr., 14, 125–26, 141, 142–44, 152, 173–74, 194–95, 219
Rooney, Art, Jr., 52, 126, 138, 144, 152, 154
Rooney, Dan, 70, 138–39, 141, 147, 151, 157, 171, 182
Rowser, John, 178–79

Royal, Darrell, 49
Rozelle, Pete, 174–75
Ruple, Ernie, 57
Russell, Andy, 172, 173, 193, 202

Saigon, 79
St. Joseph School, 25–26
St. Vincent College, 56
San Diego Chargers, 62, 175
Saul, Bill, 59, 60, 71, 129, 159
Sayers, Gayle, 184
Scanella, Joe, 166
Schmidt, Joe, 62
Schoen, Tom, 37, 56, 57
Schreiter, Paul, 26, 77
Schultz, "Dutch," 27
Scolnik, Glen, 177
Scouts, football, 51–54, 144
    ratings of, 53–54
Seiple, Larry, 156
Seymour, Jim, 39, 46, 121
Seymour, John, 121, 122
Shanklin, Ron, 54, 162
Shiner, Dick, 60, 62, 140, 202
Shy, Don, 56, 61, 62
Siemon, Jeff, 214, 215, 217
Simons, John, 64
Simpson, O. J., 45, 62, 63, 139, 184, 186, 212
Skall, Russ, 32
Smith, Bubba, 40, 41
Snead, Norm, 62
Snow, Jack, 35
Southern California, University of, 44–45
Special-teams play, 166–67, 168
Stabler, Ken, 155, 202
Stallworth, John, 177, 212
Staubach, Roger, 129
Stautner, Ernie, 193
Steelers. See Pittsburgh Steelers
Stenger, Brian, 140
Stephens, John, 124
Stickles, Monty, 56
Still, Henry, 53
Stilley, Ken, 52, 53
Stills, Frank, 127
Street, James, 200
Sullivan, Pat, 200–02
Super Bowl IX (1975), 211–19
    pregame, 11–13, 15–16, 189–200, 206–10
Sutherland, Doug. 191, 192, 211, 217, 219
Swann, Lynn, 177, 178, 212
Swatland, Dick, 47

Tarasovic, George, 193
Tarkenton, Fran, 191, 199, 202, 214
Tatum, Jack, 156
Taylor, "Bones," 51, 61–62
Taylor, Dr. Arthur, 25–26

Taylor, Dr. Phil, 129, 130, 131, 133–34
Theismann, Joe, 147
Thomas, Clendon, 193
Thornhill, Charlie, 41
Timmers, Bill, 28
Timmers, Tom, 28–29
Tracy, Tom, 193
Trumpy, Bob, 178
Tulane Stadium, 11, 206
Twilley, Howard, 54

Unitas, Johnny, 194–95
Uram, Paul, 159
Urbik, Jerry, 158
U. S. Army, 122
    advanced infantry training (AIT), 74–75
    basic training, 71–73
    in the field, 83–85

Van Brocklin, Norm, 176
Van Dyke, Bruce, 155
Vietnam War, 67, 75–77, 194
    Da Nang, 113–15
    Happy Valley, 86–87, 91
    Hiep Douc, 90–111, 119–20
    landing zones, 80
    LZ Siberia, 80, 89, 90, 120
    LZ West, 79–80, 89, 90, 93, 95, 120
    Million Dollar Hill, 98–99, 108, 109, 112
    NFL players in, 129
    patrols, 82
    Que San Valley, 94
    search-and-destroy missions, 86–87
    sweeps, 82

Tin City, 87, 89, 120
    veterans, 169–70

Vikings. *See* Minnesota Vikings
Vincent, Stahle, 155
Volk, Rick, 140

Wagner, Mike, 177
Waivers, 141, 155
Walden, Bobby, 176–77
Wallace, Jackie, 212, 216
Washington, Dave, 185
Washington Redskins, 60, 126
Webster, George, 40
Webster, Mike, 177, 179, 180
Weight-lifting programs, 55, 162–63, 171–72
Weisgerber, Dickie, 25, 26, 29
Weyer, Mary, 156–57, 158
Weyer, Tom, 130, 156–57, 158
White, Dwight, 148, 199
White, Ed, 191
White, Randy, 54
Wilburn, J. R., 134
Williamson, Fred "The Hammer," 199
Wisconsin, University of, 33, 34–35
Wolski, Bill, 37
Wright, Jeff, 212

Xavier High School, 26–29

Yacknow, Jim, 35
Young, Al, 148

"Zen Football," 12
Ziegler, Ed, 37
Zimmerman, Jeff, 37, 51